Jane Fonda:
The Dramatic True Story of
America's Most Controversial Star

The little girl born to a golden Hollywood childhood.

The daughter shattered by her mother's suicide, trying to make friends with her famous father's new life.

The willing student of Roger Vadim, as he tried to make her his new Brigitte Bardot.

The smiling "girl-next-door" who posed as "Miss Army Recruiting."

The angry antiwar protestor who went to Hanoi.

The perfectionist star of movies like *Klute, They Shoot Horses, Don't They?, The China Syndrome,* and, of course, *On Golden Pond,* with her father at last.

The wife and mother working out the problems of marriage and a career.

JANE FONDA

HEROINE FOR OUR TIME

THOMAS KIERNAN

BERKLEY BOOKS, NEW YORK

This Berkley book contains the
complete text of the original edition.
It has been completely reset in a typeface
designed for easy reading, and was
printed from new film.

JANE FONDA: HEROINE
FOR OUR TIME

A Berkley Book/published by arrangement with
Delilah Communications Ltd.

PRINTING HISTORY
Delilah edition published 1982
Berkley edition/September 1983

ISBN: 0-425-06164-7

A BERKLEY BOOK® TM 757,375
Berkley Books are published by The Berkley Publishing Group,
200 Madison Avenue, New York, New York 10016.
The name "BERKLEY" and the stylized "B" with design
are trademarks belonging to Berkley Publishing Corporation.

PRINTED IN THE UNITED STATES OF AMERICA

CONTENTS

Introduction

When I published my first biography of Jane Fonda in 1973, Jane was probably the most resented, if not hated, woman in the United States. I still have in my possession letters from more than a few irate citizens who denounced me for having deigned to write about her. "Don't you realize, you [expletive deleted], that by giving that pinko slut all this free publicity you've played right into the hands of the worldwide Commie conspiracy?" went one of the milder comments received. For a while, death threats became routine. A certain amount of intimidation from other sources followed as well, for instance, a surprise visit from a pair of government agents requesting inspection of my research—a request I declined with a few spirited epithets of my own.

It is now almost ten years later. Times have changed, as, obviously, have much of the American public's attitudes toward Jane Fonda. Indeed, if opinion polls are to be believed, Jane has gone from being the nation's Public Pariah Number One to the status of one of America's most universally admired women faster than anyone in our history.

To be sure, there are still those who cannot forgive Jane her activities of the early 1970s when, seemingly out of the blue, she transformed herself from among the screen's most pleasing sex kittens into a shrill, obsessive, left-wing political

1

activist who consorted with the enemy in North Vietnam, denounced the high-flying Nixon administration as a collection of "pigs," murderers and crooks, spouted revolutionary dogma, and in countless other ways outraged traditional American sensibilities.

But by and large, Jane Fonda is back in the country's good graces again. Yet she is a different Jane Fonda than the one America first learned to love in the 1960s, then learned to hate in the 1970s. No—she is not a "new" Jane Fonda, but a different one.

Because Jane is likely to remain in the forefront of our national consciousness for many years to come, and because by her own admission she intends to continue to do everything she can to make American society different too, I have decided to write this new and updated story of her life. Who Jane Fonda is, and how and why she got to be *what* she is, are the questions I hope to enlighten the reader about in this book. It is not a book just about a movie star. Nor is it simply one about a controversial political activist. It is the story of a complex woman who appears to want dearly to become an immortal heroine in real life as well as on the screen, and who has a good chance of succeeding.

Thomas Kiernan
New York, 1982

chapter 1

"LADY JANE"

It was inevitable that Henry Fonda and his wife Frances would name their daughter, born in 1937 on the cusp of Sagittarius and Capricorn, Jane. The name "Jane" figured importantly in the families of both. Henry's middle name was Jaynes—his mother's maiden name. And Frances Seymour Fonda, a wealthy Eastern socialite whose colonial ancestors had helped to establish the state of Connecticut, claimed direct descendancy from Edward Seymour, the Duke of Somerset, in sixteenth century England. The Duke's sister, Lady Jane Seymour, was the ill-fated third wife of King Henry VIII. Indeed, it was the "Jaynes" and "Jane" connection that had ignited Henry Fonda's and Frances Seymour's interest in each other the year before in London.

In 1936 Henry Fonda, after an eight-year struggle that included a marriage to and divorce from stage and motion picture star Margaret Sullavan, was himself a rising Hollywood personality with six movies to his credit. In the spring of that year he traveled to London to star in England's first technicolor film, *Wings of the Morning*. There, at a party, he met Frances Seymour Brokaw, the vibrant young widow of former New York congressman and playboy George Brokaw, who had recently died. The story goes that, in the course of their first conversation, Frances mentioned rather haughtily that her family had founded the city of Seymour, Connecticut. Not to be outdone, Henry informed Frances that the Mohawk Valley city of Fonda, New York did not get its name from a place in Spain or Mexico, but had been founded by *his* ancestors.

"Well," Frances reportedly said, "as an actor you might be interested to know that I am directly descended from the royal family of the Duke of Somerset and Lady Jane Seymour, whom Shakespeare wrote about."

"Royalty?" said Fonda. "I am also descended from royalty." He went on to explain his noble seventeenth century Italian antecedents who had fled the persecution of the Catholic Church in Italy and settled in Holland before migrating to colonial New York in the early 1700s. Then, in a no-nonsense manner, he added, "If you and I ever have a daughter, we'll have to call her Jane."

"A daughter!" exclaimed Frances. "What makes you think we'll ever have a daughter?"

"Because you and I are going to get married someday."

Henry Fonda and Frances Seymour Brokaw were married two months later in New York. The date was September 17, 1936, and their wedding, held at Park Avenue's Christ Church, proved to be one of the highlights of the city's fall social season. Henry Fonda was thirty-one years old, his new wife three years younger. Joshua Logan, then an up-and-coming Hollywood producer-director and one of Fonda's closest friends from their summer stock days years before, flew in from California to be best man.

Frances Fonda was already the mother of a five-year-old daughter by her first marriage, and that seemed to make her want to have more children. As Joshua Logan recalled to me, "She wanted to start having kids by Hank as soon as she could. Hank was a little nervous about the idea—he wasn't sure if he was ready for children yet. He wanted to wait a few years, you see—keep the romance going. But Frances was nothing if not a determined woman. It's the primary thing I remember about her. Very organized, very aggressive, very determined, so that life went strictly according to her schedule and needs.... Within months of their wedding, Frances was pregnant."

By that time Fonda had brought Frances and her daughter Pamela Brokaw to Los Angeles, where they searched for property on which to build a home befitting his star status. They found it early in 1937, on a ridge in the steep canyon-laced hills of Brentwood, high above Sunset Boulevard—several acres of level scrubland with panoramic views of the Pacific Ocean to the west and Los Angeles to the east. Even before they were able to buy it, Frances busied herself with architects, contractors and landscape engineers, meticulously planning every aspect of the house she intended to build.

In the summer of 1937 the Fondas returned to New York so that Henry could appear in a summer stock version of *The Virginian* and then go into rehearsal for a new Broadway play scheduled to open in the fall. The play, *Blow Ye Winds*, was a failure, and shortly afterward Henry returned to Hollywood to begin filming the movie *Jezebel*, with Bette Davis. Frances Fonda remained in New York. By then she was in the advanced stages of her pregnancy and had been told by her doctors that she would have to give birth by Caesarian section. She decided to have the baby in New York rather than in Los Angeles.

So it was, then, that Henry Fonda's first child, a daughter, was born in New York's Doctors Hospital on Sunday, December 21, 1937. The date was not without its later irony. That Sunday the nation's newspapers were filled with outraged editorials about the increasing involvement of the United States, under the Roosevelt administration, in the widening military conflict in Asia.

The newborn was named Jane Seymour Fonda, in honor of her mother's historic ancestor. "Much was good-humoredly made of this by Hank and Frances," Joshua Logan said. "With all that background, it was thought that little Jane would surely grow up to be a noblewoman *and* an actress. In fact the baby's nickname instantly became 'Lady Jane.' We all called her Lady Jane for years, and even today I find it hard not to think of her in those terms."

Upon her passage into the world the infant Jane Fonda was, like most healthy babies, an amalgam of parental features. But within a few months her face began to gain definition and the dominance of Fonda genes was revealed. Her high forehead could have come from either parent. She had more of her mother's coloration than her father's, and her pale blond-red hair, which would darken into a deep russet-brown as she matured, was certainly part of the Seymour inheritance. But she was without question a Fonda. She had her father's delicate, slightly bobbed nose. She had his large, wide-set, highly expressive eyes. And she had his long, oval, deep-jawed face with its sad, taut, downturned mouth—a mouth which, whenever it broke into a smile, contradicted its own brooding implications.

Frances Fonda brought Jane to Los Angeles a month after her birth. The family settled into a rented house in the Brentwood flats while they waited for the hillside property they coveted to come up for sale. When Henry Fonda was not busy taking home movies of his baby daughter and showing them off to such friends as Jimmy Stewart, John Wayne and Clark Gable, he worked at his trade. Indeed, during the next two years he engaged in a virtual nonstop round of filmmaking as the studios struggled to keep up with the public's demand for his screen presence. In quick succession he completed ten movies. The most noteworthy were *Jesse James*, *The Young Mr. Lincoln*, and *The Grapes of Wrath*, based on the celebrated John Steinbeck novel. As a result of his performance in this, Fonda was boosted into the realm of motion picture immortality at the age of thirty-four. During this period he also made *Drums along the Mohawk*, a cinematic tale of revolutionary times in the Mohawk Valley of upstate New York, near the city that bore his name. He played a heroic pioneer settler who led a hardy group of colonial farmers in defense of their lands against the ravaging assaults of British-subsidized Indians and Tories. It was, understandably, one of Fonda's favorite roles.

While Jane's actor-father spent most of his time at the studios, her mother spent most of hers looking after Jane. Frances Fonda was intent on giving Jane the same kind of proper Anglo-Yankee upbringing she herself had had. Accordingly to a family friend, "The most important things in Frances' life were organization, self-discipline and fine manners. They were almost an obsession with her. When she and Hank married, he was lackadaisical about all three; he was a perfectionist only when it came to acting. She quickly changed that, or tried to. She was always chiding Hank whenever he didn't measure up to her view of how he should conduct himself. She'd badger him about leaving a shirt draped over a chair in the bedroom, or leaving an unwashed glass in the living room—that sort of thing. At the beginning Hank tolerated it in a good-natured way. He really went out of his way to please Frances and change his habits. But after a while it began to grate on him. No matter how hard he tried, he could never seem to satisfy. At first I think he was genuinely scared of her, as well as stunned by the changes he saw in her between the time before their marriage and the time after, especially after Jane was born. Jane's birth turned Frances into a female martinet. Everything had to be 'just so' all the time, and whenever it wasn't Frances dropped everything until it was.

"It was in this atmosphere that Jane was reared. Everything was highly organized. Discipline and order were the ruling axioms. Hank was not an outgoing, emotional man to begin with. Nor was Frances an emotional woman, at least on the surface. So everything in their life together was conducted on a cool, distant, almost starchy level.... Appearances meant everything to Frances. And whenever Jane, and later Peter, exhibited a normal childhood outburst of emotion or passion, they were quickly and soundly reprimanded for their untoward behavior. Frances was the inspiration for it all. Hank absorbed it from her and got into the habit of doing it too—probably for no other reason than to please Frances, at least mollify her."

Peter Fonda, Jane's brother, was born in February 1940, a few months after Jane's second birthday. Shortly thereafter, Frances and Henry finally acquired the property they had waited for for so long. They devoted all their free time during the following year to converting the property into the luxurious estate they had planned. When they were finished, they had a spacious home in the style of an elegant New England farmhouse, with tennis court and swimming pool, an adjoining pool house, a barn and stables, an acre of lush lawn and decorative shrubbery, another half-acre of flower and vegetable gardens, and fabulous views from everywhere.

When the family moved into the new homestead at the top of Brentwood's Tigertail Road, there was something for everyone. For Jane and Peter there was breadth and space and a fully equipped playground in which to spin out their leisure hours. For Henry there was a spanking-new tractor and other outdoor equipment with which to indulge his new hobby of home-farming. For Frances there was the tastefully decorated house for living and the nearby pool house—almost as large but more casual—for entertaining. She and Henry spent their spare time in country clothes and busied themselves with the myriad little tasks that make a perfect place even more perfect. Frances tended the flower and shrubbery beds and managed the household with the proud and prim efficiency of a museum curator. Henry passed most of his time outdoors cultivating his vegetables and adding improvements here and there to the grounds. Both Fondas enjoyed the satisfactions of detailed and pain-staking work, and they insisted that their children develop an equal appreciation for it.

By the time Jane was five she began to take exception to the nickname "Lady." She had started kindergarten classes at the Brentwood Town and Country School and found that her nickname elicited giggles and teasing from her schoolmates. To a child as sensitive and attuned to rebuff as she had become, the nickname soon provoked a sense of juvenile mortification in her.

It was a warm, open, inviting homestead that Frances and Henry Fonda had created, but aside from an occasional un-characteristic shout from Jane or Peter, it was a quiet and not very busy place during the next few years. After an initial round of parties to show it off to their friends, the Fondas reverted to a life of relative seclusion—there were not that many people in Los Angeles or in the movie business they enjoyed spending time with, Frances especially. According to Joshua Logan, one of the few regular visitors to 600 Tigertail Road, she did not feel comfortable with show business people.

"Frances was not really interested in the movies or theater. So she was always impatient when we were around, since we talked exclusively and incessantly about show business. She only enjoyed talking of children, operations, jewelry, the stock market—that sort of thing. I often wondered what she and Hank ever found to talk about, because those were subjects he had absolutely no interest in. She was highly cultivated and mature and serious about everything. We had a certain amount of cultivation, to be sure, but you would never know it, since all any of us ever did was talk shop. I'm certain Frances viewed us all with a goodly amount of disdain. She probably saw us as a bunch of children. She had little patience for us."

A further quietude descended on the Fonda estate late in 1942 when, after finishing an early wartime morale-building movie called *The Immortal Sergeant*, Henry Fonda enlisted in the Navy, leaving Frances to run the place and raise the children on her own. Except for an infrequent, brief furlough home, Fonda would be away from his family for the next three years, spending much of his time in the South Pacific. Thus, between the formative ages of five and eight, Jane saw hardly anything of her father. Her mother became the center of her universe.

And although the young Jane often resented her mother's strict behavioral demands, she formed a natural bond with her that was cohesive and highly dependent.

Frances was trying to raise Jane to be a well-behaved and proper young lady, but she was doing so in an environment that encouraged earthier interests and conduct. Her problem was compounded by the fact that Margaret Sullavan—Henry Fonda's first wife—was living nearby. Sullavan had married agent Leland Hayward at about the same time Frances married Fonda. She had had three children by Hayward in rapid succession—Brooke and Bridget, daughters, and William, a son. The Haywards had settled in Brentwood at about the same time as the Fondas. When, like Henry Fonda, Leland Hayward went off to work in the war, the two families became almost a single extended family. The Hayward children were constantly at the Fonda homestead and vice versa. Frances Fonda had always felt uncomfortable about the proximity of her husband's first wife—it was simply not the way things were done in her world. What's more, Margaret Sullavan, although always pleasant to her, was highly neurotic, a trait that in Frances' view she had transferred to her children. The Hayward children tended toward unruliness and surly rebellion. The Hayward household had never been a peaceful one, and its atmosphere of parental combat was reflected in the behavior of all the Hayward children—behavior that Jane seemed all too eager to imitate. Unsettling Frances' state of mind further was her secret fear that her husband was still secretly in love with Margaret Sullavan and for that reason had encouraged the Haywards to become neighbors.

But it would have been unseemly of Frances to give voice to her fears and dissatisfactions. So she learned to tolerate the flamboyant Haywards and their children, all the while redoubling her efforts to neutralize the ever-present Hayward children's influence on Jane, and, later, Peter.

Jane, of course, was unaware of all this. All she knew was that the wild, pretty, darkhaired Brooke Hayward and her eccentric younger sister Bridget were her best friends—indeed they could have been her own sisters. And Frances Fonda was unaware of the fact that Margaret Sullavan was secretly trying to emulate her in the way she raised Brooke, Bridget and William. The trouble was that whereas the highly disciplined approach came naturally to Frances, it didn't to Margaret—

which only served to deepen the confusion of the Hayward children and drive them into more bizarre and errant conduct.

Jane was thus caught between two distinct influences as a young girl: her mother's uncompromising rigidity about her conduct and the exotic behavioral tendencies of the Hayward children. The differences between the two left her bewildered.

Her perplexity rose when, in 1945, her father returned from the war. He was, for all practical purposes, a stranger. His "strangeness" was sharpened by the fact that he was a markedly different man from the one who had left three years before. For one thing, Henry Fonda was no longer inclined to put up with Frances' dictates about how life in the Fonda home was to be lived. Changed and matured by his experiences in the war, he became quickly disenchanted with his wife's habitual demands.

His reaction first took the form of protest, then sullen alienation. As he became estranged from Frances, so did he also from Jane and Peter, whom he saw as being hopelessly under her influence. "Hank felt like an outsider in his own house," a friend said years later.

The eight-year-old Jane understood none of this. All she perceived was that after the enthusiastic buildup for her father's return, it was nothing like it had been cracked up to be. Henry Fonda plunged back into his acting work and was able to convey to his daughter little but his sense of impatience whenever she shyly approached him with, or for, an expression of affection. As another friend of Fonda's told me, "Hank came back and found that his kids were much more like their mother than himself. He didn't know how to handle it. He was getting increasingly angry with Frances. And I think he extended his anger to Jane and Peter, since they were miniature models of her. Poor Frances, she didn't know what hit her. She didn't understand what was troubling Hank. Of course, people like her, so outwardly sure of themselves, so domineering and in-control all the time—they can never step outside themselves and see how others see them, see what it is they are doing wrong. And people like Hank—well, they can never really articulate what they want to say. They keep it all in and let the resentment fester."

Had Henry and Frances Fonda been more passionate people, their difficulties might have come to a head sooner. As it was, they sat on their differences and tried to keep their marriage going for the sake of appearances. Jane was by then in the third grade at the Brentwood School. If she had any awareness that her father was a celebrated movie star, she didn't reveal it. The Brentwood School was filled with the offspring of film and theatrical celebrities. No special notice was given to Henry Fonda's daughter.

Jane was aware of what her father did, however. Between seeing a few of his Western movies on the home projector and watching him steer his tractor intently through his huge vegetable garden, getting the soil back in shape, she formed an image of him as a rugged outdoorsman who, in his remote, adult way, shared her growing fantasies about cowboys and Indians, horses and cows, buffalo herds and lynch parties.

With her father home, Jane began to neglect her dolls and other feminine interests for the life of a tomboy. Except for a special social occasion, her usual mode of dress around the house was a cowboy hat and boots, blue jeans and a flannel cowboy shirt. Peter followed suit, and much of their after-school time was spent with Jane leading him and a few of the neighborhood kids on forays to distant corners of the property. They made imaginary raids on Indian villages, defended their own forts from marauding Redskins, mounted mock cavalry charges on horses borrowed from their playground carousel, rounded up wandering doggies and saved damsels in distress from the clutches of Black Bart villains—just as they had read about in books and seen in the movies.

It was a happy time for Jane because she had a talent for acting out the various roles, and she would take the lead to get things going. Often, though, she would become bossy when her playmates failed to respond immediately to her enthusiasms—a trait obviously picked up from her mother. "It pleased her to have other kids following her, even if most of the time it was only her little brother," Brooke Hayward recalled. "The more response she received, the more inventive she became." Jane liked the sense of authority the games produced in her and could go on at them for hours, bitterly resenting the peal of the old school bell in the cupola that was the signal that it was time to abandon the games and report to the house for an adult-inspired activity—usually lunch or dinner.

When her father was at home, puttering around the gardens or refinishing an old piece of furniture in his shop, she trailed after him like a duckling, shyly but incessantly asking questions about this or that, imitating his distinctive amble, and more often than not getting in the way. To Henry Fonda, his agricultural and carpenterial pursuits were in his words, "a form of therapy." He would set himself a task and then plunge into it with a concentration and dedication that brooked no interruptions. Consequently he often grew testy at the persistence of Jane's curiosity and sent her scurrying with a curt dismissal.

Jane had finally got people to drop the nickname Lady Jane, more as a result of her boyish interests and energy than through any verbal persuasion. She had definitely graduated from the "little lady" role she had been molded in by her mother earlier. She was tall for her eight years. The silky champagne hair of her infancy had darkened to a burnish, and she began to grow pudgy, losing the doll-like quality she had possessed as a four and five-year-old.

Henry Fonda's first acting assignment after his return from the war was the starring role in *My Darling Clementine*, in which he played the legendary Wyatt Earp, marshal of Tombstone, in search of the killer Clantons. When the picture was released in 1946, he scored heavily with the critics; they generally agreed that his version of the much-portrayed Earp was the definitive characterization. Before the war, Fonda had established himself as one of America's foremost Western actors. His natural drawl, at once hesitant and authoritative, his slightly stooped, wary stance, his loping gait and his uniquely authentic face, strong but not blatantly heroic—all contributed to his credibility. When these traits were coupled with his actor's sense, which was restrained and unmannered—almost indifferent (although he was anything but indifferent about his craft)—audiences were galvanized. Fonda was certainly not a magnetic man in real life, at least not in the sense of a high-energy screen Lothario. But through the chemistry of his diffidence and honesty, he had become a magnetic actor.

He had also proved that he could reverse the coin of the character with which he was most generally identified to show another side. He could play contemporary comedy with a droll credibility, yet give his characters in serious dramas an engaging accessibility. His face was American bedrock in the minds of millions of moviegoers, and the magic of his attraction was the security that his face, and the style associated with it, provided. Audiences believed in Henry Fonda and were never forced to endure a "performance."

My Darling Clementine was the first movie Fonda had made with John Ford as director since *Grapes of Wrath*, and it was the first for director and star together in an area in which both had had individual successes, the Western. During the month or so before the start of filming, Fonda was required to grow a beard. This was much to the consternation of Jane, who suddenly detected an air of extra menace in her father. Only long, patient explanations by Frances finally persuaded Jane that her father had not turned into an ogre. The explanations also served to impress on Jane just exactly what it was her father did for a living. She was a bit disappointed to learn that he was not a real cowboy, only a play one. But inasmuch as he was in his own way doing essentially what she liked to do, her admiration and respect for him deepened. Fortunately the beard came off shortly after filming began.

At nine, Jane Fonda continued to be absorbed by her tomboy fantasies. Occasionally her mother dressed her up and sent her off to children's parties in Beverly Hills and Bel Air, but she hated these functions and spent most of her time hovering shyly and uncomfortably on the fringes of the festivities. When reports of her timidity filtered back to her mother and father, they reacted with the anger and frustration anxious parents often feel about children who seem to resist fitting in.

Parental pride is an easily bruised quality. Although both Henry and Frances themselves were basically shy and private people, when required they were accomplished in the exercise of social intercourse. They were determined, therefore, that their children grow up practiced in all the social graces and be able to hold their own in a roomful of their peers.

Jane resented her parents' insistence on thrusting her into crowded rooms of babbling children. The sense of inadequacy that had been brewing in her made it virtually impossible for her to react in any but the most antisocial way, and her relative isolation during the previous few years put her at a further disadvantage. It was time, her mother decided, to change all this. The trauma and agony of being forced to participate in upper-class childhood society was, nevertheless, a necessary price to be paid for a proper education. Besides, her inexplicable fears and resulting behavior were an unflattering reflection on them.

When Jane reacted with displeasure, sometimes even tantrums, about being sent on these training forays to other children's homes, her parents' embarrassment prevented their understanding of her childish anxieties. Her recalcitrance constituted an injury to their pride, a slap in the face of their expectations that their children be perfect junior editions of themselves. Henry and Frances hoped that Jane's timidity was just a stage she was going through, the result of her hypersensitive nature.

For Jane, the parties and other functions she was sent to were a juvenile form of hell. She could not understand her parents' insistence on her attendance when she had made it so clear that she wanted no part of them. Pressed for explanations, she could only shrug and make vague excuses that would be dismissed before she got halfway through them. She hated her own inarticulateness about the problem; it only made her feel more inadequate. And she hated her parents' failure to read between the lines of her reticence, their unwillingness to understand and assuage her fears in a way that was meaningful to her. But she remained basically an obedient child, even though her parents' wishes at times occasioned the unendurable shame caused by childhood insecurities. Though she grew numb each time with the almost diabolical shame that childhood insecurities often provoke, she grudgingly obeyed their wishes.

Early in 1947, Henry Fonda made the last film he owed Twentieth Century-Fox on his contract there. Afterward, he resolved to reinvigorate his career by going back to his real love, the theater. His restlessness had reached the point that even he now realized that his usually foul disposition at home was partly his own doing. He was growing bored with his hobby-farming diversions and was becoming less and less communicative with his family. He ached for something that would give him the kind of satisfaction that, in the past, he only seemed to get from the stage. As a result, Jane Fonda, not yet ten, would go through the first important change in her life.

chapter 2

FROM WEST TO EAST

During the spring of 1947, Fonda received word from Joshua Logan in New York that Logan and a little-known writer named Thomas Heggen had written a play based on Navy life in the South Pacific during the war. Logan was certain the title role would be perfect for Fonda's postwar return to Broadway. Fonda flew to New York that summer and Logan read him the work, which they called *Mister Roberts*. Fonda was highly impressed and agreed to do it. He returned to Brentwood, made one last Western for John Ford—*Fort Apache*—and then returned to New York.

Mister Roberts opened on Broadway in February 1948. It was an instant smash hit, with Fonda earning the kind of reviews most actors never dare dream of. On opening night the audience did not merely give the play a standing ovation; they shouted themselves hoarse. The curtain kept going up as the actors took bow after bow. The audience wouldn't leave. Finally Fonda was forced to make a curtain speech. "This is all Tom and Josh wrote for us," he said. "If you want, we can start all over again." As critic John Chapman reported in the next day's *Daily News*, "I hung around a while, hoping they would."

Mister Roberts represented a reunion of old friends now embarked on an exciting and profitable new venture. Leland

Hayward, who had moved his family from California to rural Connecticut after the war, was the play's producer. Logan, in addition to being its coauthor, also directed it. Fonda was the star and was now faced with the happy prospect of a long run. Within days orders were coming in for seats that would not be available for at least two years. Frances Fonda decided that there was only one alternative to the prospect of a two-year separation from her husband. That was to move the family East.

Frances reached her decision out of her usual pragmatism but also out of a growing sense of desperation. Leland Hayward and Margaret Sullavan had announced their intention to divorce. Frances feared that her husband might be thinking in similar terms. She was intent on saving their marriage despite signs on Fonda's part that he was no longer interested. His success in *Mister Roberts* had given him a new sense of self-esteem, but in working toward it he had further distanced himself, emotionally as well as physically, from Frances and the children.

In midsummer of 1948, Frances, Jane and Peter crossed the country and settled into a spacious house near Frances' parents' home in Greenwich, Connecticut. Jane was decidedly unhappy about the move. Tigertail Road had been her home and it had not occurred to her that she would ever need another. After the freedom and casualness of the Brentwood estate, Greenwich seemed like a luxurious prison. She was no longer permitted to run around in her Western garb, and she found herself chastised more and more often by her mother for her unintended breaches of the strange new Eastern etiquette. Frances, anxious that Jane learn the sophisticated customs of upper-class Greenwich, forced her to dress up when visitors came by. And when fall arrived, she was enrolled in the exclusive Greenwich Academy, where most of the students—teachers too—spoke as though their jaws were wired together. Jane was mystified.

The only relief she got during those first few months was when the Hayward children suddenly appeared on the scene. Margaret Sullavan, recently divorced from Leland Hayward, had decided to follow Frances Fonda's example and settle in Greenwich.* Although it was a relief to Jane to have the Hay-

*In her 1977 memoir about her family, *Haywire*, Brooke Hayward wrote in detail about her mother Margaret Sullavan's compulsive, almost manic, behavioral demands on her children after they had moved to Connecticut. Brooke

wards nearby once again, her mother got little pleasure from
it.

Jane soon found out that at least in one way, Easterners
were not as sophisticated as Southern Californians. Like that
of her school in Brentwood, the Greenwich Academy's student
population consisted mostly of children of well-to-do and socially prominent parents. Unlike Brentwood, the school was
not accustomed to having in its student body the children of
Broadway-Hollywood celebrities. With the Fonda name a
household word throughout the country, Jane suddenly found
herself the object of the kind of deferential treatment and attention she had never before experienced. It was not so much
that her schoolmates treated her differently; it was the adults
who did so—teachers, school administrators, the parents of
the other children. At first she was too preoccupied with her
own insecurities, and was barely aware of it. It did not take
long, though, before she began to notice a certain deferentiality
in the way her teachers approached her and the covert glances
of parents arriving to pick up their children. The parents' attitudes eventually percolated down to their children, and before
long Jane was treated as a celebrity by them as well.

Her mother was aware of the likelihood of this happening.
Although there was something about it that secretly pleased
her, Frances tried to impress upon Jane the importance of not
letting it affect her. This, of course, only made Jane more
aware of her special place in the world in which she was now
living.

Jane, on no account of her own, suddenly found herself the
most popular member of the sixth grade at Greenwich Academy. It was a happy change of events, for her quick acceptance
enabled her in small measure to overcome her painful shyness
and move more easily into the society of eleven-year-olds. But
as is often the case with insecure preadolescent children who
suddenly find themselves in the limelight, her enthusiasm for
her new role frequently overboiled. She became rambunctious
around the classroom and often led her eager-to-follow classmates in conspiracies of misbehavior that resulted in more

failed to mention that much of the inspiration for Margaret Sullavan's demands
came, unconsciously, from Frances Fonda. Sullavan sought more than ever to
emulate Frances' style of childrearing. "If only I had been Jane and Peter's
mother," Sullavan once said, "and Frances had been the mother of my kids.
Everything would have been all right."

trouble for them than her. A classmate once recalled, "There was this shed on the school grounds where we all used to go to listen to Jane tell her dirty traveling salesman stories."

Whether the stories were ones she had picked up by eavesdropping on her father and his cronies is uncertain, but soon complaints were made about Jane by a number of parents. They had been delighted at first to have their children associate with the famous Henry Fonda's daughter. But their vicarious pleasure was eventually disrupted by what they considered to be the insidious effects young Jane and her classmate Brooke Hayward were having on their youngsters. Word of their displeasure eventually reached Frances, who reacted with her usual stern reprimands. Jane thereupon reacted by getting herself thrown out of the Girl Scouts, along with Brooke Hayward, for unbecoming conduct.

After a year in Connecticut, the whole point of the Fonda family's move from Brentwood began to appear moot. Henry Fonda spent less and less time in Greenwich, even on weekends. When Frances learned that he was having a secret romance in New York with Susan Blanchard, the twenty-one-year-old stepdaughter of composer Oscar Hammerstein, her mood went from unhappy to distraught. With their father seldom around, yet unaware of the growing breach between him and their mother, Jane and Peter nagged their mother for a return to Brentwood before the beginning of the school year. It was not to be. Frances Fonda would not face living at Tigertail Road without her husband, and she was convinced that by staying close and persevering, she could get him back.

In September 1949 Jane entered the seventh grade at Greenwich. Approaching her twelfth birthday, she began to change physically, having shot up sharply in height over the summer and lost some of her chubbiness. Though not happy with what she still considered to be her enforced stay in Greenwich, she managed to console herself with her few friends and her daily round of activities—school, horseback riding, pet-raising and so forth. She had discarded most of her cowboy-and-Indian fantasies and replaced them with more genteel, albeit still boyish, Eastern ambitions. At riding school on Saturdays she often had a chance to watch a group of local hunt club members gather on horseback in their colorful costumes and set off behind a pack of yelping dogs in pursuit of foxes. This sight gave birth to an ambition to one day embark on a career as a master of fox hounds. She would also watch with fascination the way the local veterinarians handled returning horses or hounds that had injured themselves in the hunt. She admired the combination of authority and compassion they exercised in their approach to the animals, and she resolved to become a veterinarian when she grew up. She nurtured these dreams, but kept them to herself.

By the winter of 1949 Jane's mother, though bravely trying to keep up the appearance of a happy and fulfilled woman, had become privately consumed by depression. Thus, Jane's only regular adult family contact was with her grandmother, who was at the house with increasing frequency. In a sixty-three-year-old Sophie Seymour's sense of balance and her still-vigorous enthusiasm for the marvels of childhood, Jane finally found someone who loved and accepted her on her own terms.

Just before her twelfth birthday, Jane's father quietly explained to her that he and her mother had decided to divorce. It was only half true: it was he who had made the decision and announced it to Frances Fonda a few weeks before. Henry Fonda was intent on marrying the adoring Susan Blanchard as soon as he could disentangle himself from Frances.

Jane's first reaction was to consult with Brooke Hayward. Brooke later said, "I explained the delicious intricacies of shuttling between divorced parents and painted a rosy picture of the good times Jane could expect to have with her father on her visits to see him in New York." Divorced fathers, Jane learned, tended to go overboard in their generosity, and besides, they tended to give up being disciplinarians during their brief visitation periods with their children—at least Leland Hayward had done so.

Whatever sense of reassurance Jane had received from Brooke was soon shattered by the events that followed. Shortly after Henry Fonda moved his belongings out of the house in Greenwich, Frances Fonda fell into a depression so profound that she had to be placed in a private mental hospital in the Hudson River town of Beacon, New York, called Craig House. It was true that when, during the next couple of months, Jane visited her father in New York, he was different from the remote, diffident man she had known. He took her to museums, restaurants and movies, and otherwise lavished attention and gifts on her. But when she went back to Greenwich she would find her grandmother, who had moved into the house to take care of her and Peter in their mother's absence, full of gloom and worry. Despite her cheery announcements to her grandchildren that Frances was expected home soon from the hospital, Sophie Seymour could not hide her own deep anxiety about her daughter.

And yet, after being at Craig House for almost two months, Frances Fonda seemed to be making progress in her struggle to recover from what had been officially diagnosed as "severe psychoneurosis with depression." She had recovered fairly quickly from her initial debility during the first month of her hospitalization, and had impressed her psychiatrist, Dr. Courtney Bennett, with her recognition of her difficulties and her efforts through therapy and medication to overcome them. Only Sophie Seymour knew that Frances had bitterly vowed never to live to see her husband divorce her. Divorce was not an acceptable state of affairs in the Seymour family. "It meant failure," a friend of the family once said, "and Seymours never failed at anything."

By the first week of April 1950, with the soothing scent of spring creeping up the Hudson Valley, Frances had begun to talk to her doctor about returning home. Doctor Bennett agreed that she was coming along nicely and that perhaps by May she would be ready to go back to her family.

But at 6:30 A.M. of the morning of April 14, a night nurse at Craig House, Amy Grey, entered Frances' room with a wake-up glass of orange juice. She was surprised to find the bed empty, "but I assumed that Mrs. Fonda had risen by herself." She placed the juice on the night table and crossed the room to knock on the bathroom door, which was closed. She noticed a piece of paper lying on the carpet near the door and paused to pick it up. It was a note, addressed to her and written in Frances Fonda's fine, graceful script. "Mrs. Grey," it read, "do not go into the bathroom, but call Dr. Bennett."

Amy Grey gazed at the bathroom door for a moment in alarm. Then she left to find Dr. Bennett. Bennett arrived a few minutes later and found Frances sprawled unconscious in a pool of blood on the bathroom floor, her throat slashed. Bennett felt a flutter of pulse in Frances' wrist and worked frantically with towels to staunch the flow of blood from the deep wound in Frances' neck. But before any other lifesaving measures could be taken, Frances Fonda was dead.

Another note lay on top of the toilet seat. In it Frances

apologized to the doctor and to her parents. "This is the best way out," it ended.

When Henry Fonda was notified by his grief-stricken mother-in-law later that morning, he turned to stone, according to Joshua Logan. Sophie Seymour ordered her daughter's body taken immediately to a mortuary in Hartsdale, New York, near Greenwich. That afternoon a private funeral service was held. Frances was cremated, and her ashes were buried in the Seymour family plot in a Hartsdale cemetery. Fonda was at the service but was in such a state of shock that he barely heard a word that was said. Jane and Peter, still in the dark, were kept at home.

Shortly after her mother's death, the news was broken to Jane. Her father, the Seymours and the Haywards agreed that Jane was not old enough to handle the concept of suicide, especially when it related to her own mother. They decided on a ploy. Although the true story had been featured in the local papers, they told Jane her mother had died of a heart attack. They cautioned all who knew the truth to cooperate in keeping it from Jane and Peter; all newspaper and magazine subscriptions to the house were canceled. Jane, although stunned, appeared to take the news calmly. With the doting encouragement of her grandmother, she managed gradually to turn her attention back to her school and extracurricular activities.

With Frances gone, the house was quickly sold and a new one, also in Greenwich, acquired. Mr. and Mrs. Seymour moved in with Jane and Peter and became, in effect, their foster parents. Their presence during the next year was a calming influence on Jane. Eugene Ford Seymour was eighty years old but still lively and alert. Sophie Seymour looked after him with wry humor and no-nonsense compassion, and she took the same approach to Jane and Peter.

Jane, as she started the eighth grade at Greenwich Academy in the fall of 1950, was losing more of her preteen awkwardness and blossoming into a pretty but still slightly pudgy adolescent. She grew faithful to her books, had a tight circle of friends and, except for an occasional sad reverie about her mother, was quite happy with her grandparents. The Seymours bore no visible ill will toward her father and did everything they could to encourage Jane's devotion to him. Fonda visited the children frequently during the following months and kept close tabs on their progress. For a while he kept a rein on his perfectionism when he was around them, but he found it easier to be more sanguine about Jane than Peter, then ten years old. Unlike Jane, Peter was unable to accept his mother's death; his behavior became atrocious.

The plan to continue to keep the truth about her mother's suicide from Jane did not succeed for long. The following fall, according to Brooke Hayward, after she and Jane had begun the eighth grade at Greenwich Academy, they were leafing through a fan magazine together one day during an art class. The magazine had a story about the suicide of Henry Fonda's wife. Brooke had been warned beforehand never to mention the truth to Jane, and when she saw the article's headline she tried urgently to flip the page. But she was too late—Jane had spied it.

"Jane turned it back and silently read the truth," Hayward related in the book she wrote about herself and her family. "Afterward she did not say a word about it to me, nor did I dare bring it up."*

*Brooke Hayward, *Haywire*, Random House, New York, 1977.

chapter 3

THE TROJAN WOMAN

Jane told no one that she had learned the truth about her mother's death. But she could not put it out of her mind. During the next few months she agonized over it, plunging periodically into deep reflective moods in her attempts to understand why her mother had done what she did. In view of the fact that Frances had been so strict and demanding of Jane as a child, Jane began to believe that somehow she was responsible for her mother's suicide, that her errant behavior in the previous years had so disappointed Frances that she had killed herself as a way of inflicting some sort of punishment on Jane.

Jane's remorse had the effect of sharply altering her behavior: she became solemn, almost mirthless in school and at home. It also had the effect of producing a constant desire to please her father, who still traveled to Greenwich one or two Sundays a month to visit her. She began to live in mortal fear that if she failed to please him, he too would find reason to abandon her permanently. She resolved to do everything she could to curry her father's favor. By then, to Jane, approval represented love.

As Jane's thirteenth birthday approached in December 1950, her father introduced her to Susan Blanchard. He told Jane that he and Susan planned to marry and expressed his hope that Jane and Peter would come to feel as much affection for her as he did. Jane accepted the news without any rancor and shyly sized up her stepmother-to-be. Susan, only ten years older, had a delicate, refined beauty that beguiled Jane.

Jane's hair had finally settled into its permanent natural color—brown tinged with hints of russet and blond, depending on the light. She was still taller than most girls her age, but with her distinctive Fonda features she believed herself to be homely and clumsy. Susan Blanchard left her filled with pre-adolescent awe and a dream of one day becoming as beautiful herself. Rather than resenting Susan, Jane developed a crush on her and was thrilled when Susan seemed to take a genuine interest in her.

Henry Fonda and Susan Blanchard were married on December 28, 1950, while his children were on their school vacations. The newlyweds journeyed to St. John in the Virgin Islands on New Year's Day for what they thought would be a two-week honeymoon. Their stay was interrupted soon after they arrived, however, by an urgent message from Greenwich. Peter had shot himself.

Whereas Jane had found a way to function in the wake of Frances Fonda's death, Peter still hadn't. His already fractious conduct had turned bizarre and irrational after his mother's burial, and he had become a chronic problem to his father and grandparents.

As Peter later told it, he may have been trying to commit suicide. "I was visiting the R. H. Kress estate in Westchester. I'm not sure if I was really trying to kill myself or not, but I do recall that after I shot myself, I didn't want to die—and I came very close to dying. Jane tells me the doctor came out of the operating room and said I was dead, that my heart had stopped beating. My sister is prone to dramatize, as I am. He may have said things were looking tense, but regardless of what the doctor said, that's how she took it. She thought it was all over for me. Anyway, I was conscious after I shot myself [with a .22-caliber pistol]. I was also very scared, and I got the chauffeur to drive me to the hospital in Ossining."

The bullet pierced his liver. "It took the doctors a while to understand it was a gunshot wound; there wasn't a lot of blood. I was beginning to get a little dopey, but I remember that they didn't know what to do. There was just one doctor around who knew how to operate on bullet wounds, and they finally got him on the phone. He had been the Sing Sing prison surgeon for years, and Ossining Hospital at that time was right next to Sing Sing. Anyway, the man saved my life. I was in intensive care for four weeks."

With the help of the Coast Guard, Henry Fonda was rushed to his frightened son's bedside. The trip was an agony for him. First his wife and now his son—would there be no lid on the price he would have to pay for his newfound happiness and freedom? He was profoundly angry at Peter but resolved to make more of an effort to get involved with his children. As for Peter, "I guess my father's remoteness from me had something to do with that incident. But now I see that the life of an actor is a very strange thing, and I can see how it interferes with raising children. But my father's nature is, or was, incommunicative."

Jane was taken aback by her brother's brush with death but was discouraged from talking or even thinking about it. Once Peter recovered, their grandparents forbade the children from dwelling on it, just as they prohibited discussion of all unpleasant events. Life returned to normal.

With the approach of fall, arrangements were made for Jane to enter the Emma Willard School for Girls in Troy, New York. Emma Willard was an expensive private boarding and day school whose principal function was to prepare its students, mostly the daughters of wealthy and socially prominent families throughout the East, for entrance into such colleges as Wellesley, Smith and Vassar—in those days still exclusively women's schools. Yet Willard was not simply a "finishing school"; it had a rigorous program of instruction and a wide-ranging classical curriculum.

At first Jane rebelled against the idea of being sent to boarding school—it meant another major upheaval in her life. But her father and grandmother, having conferred, were adamant. Sophie Seymour was getting too old to serve as both Jane's and Peter's daily overseer. Besides, she believed strongly that her two grandchildren's behavioral problems were solely the result of their continued daily exposure to the troubled Hayward children. Only by distancing them from the Haywards would Jane and Peter have a chance to blossom on their own, she decided.

Sophie had managed to convince Jane's father of this, and

he agreed to impose his will. Jane finally acquiesced when it became clear that she could not dissuade him. Her acquiescence was hastened by the sympathetic urgings of Susan Blanchard Fonda, whom Jane's father deputized to convince Jane of the wisdom of going away to school. By then Jane had begun to hero-worship her father's new wife. Susan promised Jane exciting times in New York with herself and her father during school holidays.

Jane later said about her time at Emma Willard, "It was ghastly—all girls, and that's unhealthy." But when Jane was fourteen and in her sophomore year, the company of boys, by her own admission, was the last thing she sought. She still had strong feelings of inferiority about herself, and at that point in her life boys only sharpened them. On the surface, according to most who knew her, she was a placid student during her first two years at Willard. At the same time she seemed driven by a desire to please. In the words of one of her teachers, "Jane was industrious in her schoolwork and ambitious in tackling special campus assignments, but for the most part she kept to herself. She was slow to approach a classmate, start a friendship, or ask a favor. She was generally more respected than liked. She hovered on the fringes of things, happy when included in some activity but unwilling to assert herself without being invited."

By the time Jane was ready to start her junior year, though, she had begun to make tentative efforts to step out of her self-contained world. She was aided to a great extent by Susan Fonda, who was not yet far enough removed from her own adolescence to be insensitive to Jane's situation. Susan went to great lengths to be a friend to Jane once she had settled into being Henry Fonda's wife. Jane responded like a hungry infant to the bottle.

Shortly after his marriage to Susan, Henry Fonda purchased a town house on East Seventy-fourth Street, a few steps from Lexington Avenue in Manhattan's upper East Side. He had decided to remain in New York and continue working in the theater, and the new house was to be his permanent headquarters. He and Susan had the house refurbished, including bedrooms for Jane and Peter so that the children could spend their school vacations there, and moved in during the fall of 1951. The train trip from Troy to New York City took only three hours, so Jane was able to spend an occasional holiday weekend and her school vacations visiting her father and stepmother.

At fifteen Jane was still taller than most of her schoolmates. Although she still felt self-conscious about her "awful" looks, she was gradually growing into a handsome girl. Her short hair, coupled with her long, prominent Fonda jaw and slightly pug nose, gave her an appearance that seemed somewhere between "cute" and pugnacious. Within another year the rest of her facial features would catch up to her already fully developed jaw and her cheeks would begin to shed their noticeable pudginess. But now, living in a world in which looks meant everything, she was thoroughly and constantly dissatisfied with herself.

Whenever she came to New York to stay at her father's house, she found the mood much more relaxed than when her father had been living with her mother. For one thing, Fonda had found a new hobby to fill the gap left by his retirement from outdoor living: painting. It was an activity that was much more demanding of his penchant for painstaking craftsmanship, and he pursued it for long, solitary hours. He had part of the attic of the new house converted into a studio. Jane would often spend an entire weekend on Seventy-fourth Street without seeing her father, except to say hello and goodbye.

Fonda was, at least for a while, happily married and engaged in another successful Broadway play—*Point of No Return*. In Susan he had found a young woman who was bright and energetic, as well as beautiful and genuinely interested in his work. She knew and understood the theater and was happy to circulate in the world of celebrated performers, directors, producers and writers. In the bargain, she related well to his children and took much of the burden of their upbringing off him.

Jane not only discovered in her youthful stepmother an effective mediator between herself and her father, but also an increasingly sympathetic and helpful friend. Susan introduced Jane to the glories and mysteries of New York City. She took Jane along on her rounds of hairdressers, department stores, specialty shops, luncheons and movies, and included her in as many other grown-up activities as she could squeeze into a weekend or vacation. Jane soon began to return to Emma Willard from her stays in New York with the ambition of one day becoming as sophisticated and charming and beautiful as Susan.

"It was wonderful," Jane has said about her relationship with her stepmother. "I remember Susan—twenty-five and a ravishing beauty—at a Parent's Day at school. I was so proud of her I almost flipped."

Jane's attachment to her father's third wife may have represented the happiest time of her young life. Susan built up Jane's confidence in herself, and their easy relationship quickly became the envy of Jane's schoolmates. When she returned from her trips to New York with stories of the fantastic times she had had and the "incredible" people she had met, disguising her enthusiasm behind a casual, almost bored, narrative, Jane's stock at school soared. Whereas before she had kept pretty much to herself, more out of timidity than out of the snobbery her classmates thought her manner represented, she now found herself invited to become a member of the student inner circle at Willard. The innermost circle of girls called themselves caustically "The Trojan Women," after the ancient Greek tragedy by Euripides and because they all felt isolated from the mainstream of life in Troy, New York. Jane soon became a Trojan Woman.

It was not long before Jane started thinking of Susan Fonda as more than just a stepmother. As Susan once recalled, "After a while, Peter asked me if he could call me Mother, and Jane said she was going to call me Mother, too. The Seymour side of the family got very angry."

Jane started her junior year at Willard, in the fall of 1953, in a much more improved state of mind than when she had first enrolled. The time had come to start thinking of college. Like many of her schoolmates, Jane's thoughts were on Vassar. A pair of new ambitions also started to form as she pondered her future. One had to do with ballet, the other with art.

The dream of becoming a ballerina was a common fancy among girls her age, and Jane began to approach her daily ballet class with single-minded devotion. She enjoyed the discipline, the hard work, and the feelings of grace and coordination the classes gave her. The satisfactions were great, and occasionally she got a taste of the power of performing that made them even greater. She understood that to pursue a career in ballet demanded an almost superhuman dedication. At that point in her life she was eager for something to which she could

dedicate herself. She ignored her teachers' gentle discouragements that she was too tall to become a really first-rate ballerina
and pursued her classes with heated determination.

The other ambition was slower to establish itself, but later
it became even more powerful. It flowed primarily from her
father. Henry Fonda had by then thoroughly immersed himself
in painting—it was no longer a form of recreation for him,
but a serious avocation. Fonda was serious enough about it to
recommend art to Jane as a worthy course of study. She too
had a talent for it. Both Frances and Henry had tried to give
their children an early appreciation of painting, starting back
in their Brentwood days, and it was the one form of personal
expression that Henry encouraged in Jane throughout her adolescence. Although father and daughter had increasing difficulty relating to each other in most other ways, she responded
to his encouragement.

The faculty at Emma Willard had been after Jane for some
time to take part in the Campus Players' dramatic productions.
She had resisted because she felt, being Henry Fonda's daughter
and living in the shadow of his fame as an actor—no matter
how advantageous that shadow sometimes was—that she would
be judged on the stage according to standards different from
those applied to her schoolmates. On the few occasions she
had tried to talk to her father about acting, he had clammed
up or glossed over it, suggesting painting and the study of art
as a more worthwhile and potentially fruitful pursuit. So art it
was, at least for a while.

At sixteen, Jane discovered boys during a summer spent
partly in California and partly in Greenwich. Suddenly she
hated the isolation of Emma Willard and begged her father to
enroll her in one of the many private girls' schools in New
York City. But Fonda refused. He had finished *Point of No
Return* and was about to embark, in the fall of 1953, on a
cross-country tour of the *Caine Mutiny Court-Martial* prior to
bringing that new play into New York. In addition, he and
Susan planned to adopt a baby and were waiting for arrangements to be completed. They would not have any time for Jane
if she were to live in New York.

Jane swallowed her disappointment and continued at Willard. Once she accepted her father's decision, she expanded
her activities at school. She pressed on with her ballet and art

studies, tolerated her academic courses and set out to engage in a few extracurricular activities. She finally gave in to requests that she join the Campus Players and auditioned for a play. Since Willard was an all-girls school, female students were required to play the male parts in student productions. Jane was a bit abashed, therefore, when she was given a male role for her stage debut. It was the title role in Christopher Fry's *The Boy With a Cart*, a staple of the school-and-college dramatics circuit.

The play called for threadbare costumes and lots of makeup, so it wasn't difficult for Jane, with her short hair, to disguise herself as a boy. Anne Wellington, former headmistress of Emma Willard, recalls that Jane acquitted herself well as the Boy in the Fry play. "She was nervous and self-conscious but had a definite presence and showed obvious talent."

Her next stage outing was in her senior year, when she won the role of Lydia Languish in Sheridan's farce *The Rivals*, another costume production. Again she did well, according to Miss Wellington. "In fact, her performance was memorable."

Jane was immensely pleased at the reception she received and was doubly excited to learn that she was able to hold the audience's attention, even make it laugh. She conveyed her excitement to her father, who had experienced similar feelings thirty years before. He stoically acknowledged her enthusiasm but remained aloof to any suggestion of an acting career. Jane's enthusiasm waned.

It was not long, though, before it revived. In the spring of 1955, as Jane approached her graduation from Willard, she received a phone call from her Aunt Harriet—her father's sister—in Omaha. Harriet, whose married name was Peacock, had followed her brother into the Omaha Community Playhouse back in the late twenties and had remained active in it for three decades. She was a member of the fund-raising committee and was planning to ask her brother to return to Omaha for a week during the early summer to do some benefit performances. Having heard about Jane's interest in acting at school, she thought it would be amusing to include her in the week's festivities.

Along with several of her classmates, Jane had been accepted at Vassar. She was looking forward to starting there in the fall, but her plans for the summer were vague. Her aunt's phone call was a godsend. Harriet Peacock asked her if she would like to be in the Playhouse's benefit production of *The Country Girl* with her father. "It was a small part," Harriet later said, "but I thought it would lend a nostalgic family quality to the production, and the people of Omaha would be thrilled to see Hank's daughter on stage with him." Jane leaped at the idea but was cautioned by her aunt not to whisper a word to her father yet, since she hadn't discussed it with him.

When Harriet did raise the subject with her brother, he was nettled. He agreed to do the benefit, but he wasn't sure it would be good for Jane to have him around for what would amount to her stage debut. Harriet told him that she had already talked to Jane and that she was eager to do it. Henry demurred further. He suggested that it might be better for Jane to be cast in another play without him. Harriet countered with the argument that having all three Fondas involved in the production would be good publicity. Since the point of the benefit week was to raise funds for the theater, the more publicity it received the better. Her idea was to have Henry play the male lead in *The Country Girl* with Dorothy McGuire, the well-known actress who had also gotten her start at the Playhouse, in the title role. Jane would have a small part, and Peter could be included in a backstage capacity.

Fonda finally agreed, but on the condition that Jane not simply be given the part but be required to earn it. Harriet thereupon called Jane back at Emma Willard and auditioned her over the phone. With Fonda's condition satisfied, plans were set for the production.

When Jane graduated from Emma Willard in June, her face still had a hint of the pudgy, boyish pugnacity of her childhood, but her figure had thinned out considerably and she had developed a modest bosom. She was well-mannered in the style of the prototypical Willard girl and, with the exception of a few irritating teenage affectations, well thought of. Her vocabulary was liberally laced with Eastern schoolgirl superlatives like "marvelous," "fantastic," and "adore," and her voice, usually calm and modulated, carried faint overtones of London. She was still shy and often haunted by feelings of inferiority, but her education had taught her how to mask her insecurities under a veneer of schoolgirl sophistication.

Soon after graduation she was on her way to Omaha with

her father and brother. "On the plane to Omaha," her father recalled much later, "something about the way Jane was listening to me—as one adult listens to another—got me to talking about myself and the rough time I'd had getting started in the theater. I'd never talked to her just that way.

"At rehearsals I was determined not to pull professional rank on Jane, but now and then she'd look at me for help, and I couldn't not make suggestions. She soaked up direction like a blotter.

"In one scene, Jane had to enter crying. That isn't easy—walking on at the height of an emotional breakdown. I didn't want to watch. I didn't think she would be able to handle it. I was sure she'd just end up looking phony-dramatic. But I was last off the stage before her entrance and first on afterward. Well, Jane came on wailing and wet-eyed, as though she'd just heard that Vassar was not going to admit her that fall. I couldn't believe it. I couldn't believe she was acting. I thought all her anxieties had broken through the Fonda facade and tumbling out. But the minute she cleared the stage her face relaxed, she looked at me and said, 'How'd I do?' She didn't understand that she'd done what many professionals couldn't do in a lifetime."

chapter 4

VASSAR

Nineteen fifty-five was a signal year in the lives of all three Fondas, although the signals were increasingly discordant for each. For Henry Fonda, it was the year he reached his zenith as a film star with his screen portrayal of Mister Roberts. It was also the year his personal life began to disintegrate again after a modestly contented period of marriage. For Jane, it was the year that marked the start of her unsteady passage from restrained, restless schoolgirl to anxious, searching young woman. And for Peter, by then a blade-thin, volatile fifteen-year-old, it was the year the momentum of his emotional dislocation shifted into high gear. The personal troubles that haunted each of the Fondas caused such friction that by the end of the year the emotional climate of the family had grown thick with unexpressed rage.

The troubles had their immediate genesis the year before when Henry Fonda, making the movie version of *Mr. Roberts*, fell into a bitter feud with his old friend and director of the picture, John Ford, about how the movie should be made. Fonda eventually prevailed, but in doing so he alienated not only Ford but a number of other pals, including Leland Hayward and, for a time, Joshua Logan. When the film was released in 1955, Fonda was again acclaimed for his portrayal of Roberts.

He got little pleasure from the glowing notices, however. Unhappy with the movie and perceiving himself as the victim of a conspiracy of Hollywood betrayal, Fonda was alternately despondent and a dynamo of seething, unrelieved anger. Fearful of speaking out against his colleagues lest he hamper the public's reception of the movie, he turned his ire on his family. The first to feel the brunt of it was Susan. At first she blamed his disagreeableness on the fact that he was approaching fifty and was depressed about aging. But he eventually grew so hostile that she began to have doubts about their future together.

Jane's graduation from Emma Willard and the successful week she spent at the Omaha Playhouse with her father constituted the only pleasant interlude in an otherwise troubled period. During her last few months at Willard she had overcome some of her timidity about boys and had begun to accept an occasional date, although the dating ritual was severely circumscribed by the school's stringent rules and curfews as well as by its inaccessibility. Most of her dates were with young men from the nearby Rensselaer Polytechnic Institute, but they were more in the nature of field exercises in the protocols of a young lady's expanding social experience than realistic male-female relationships. And although Jane had overcome some of her shyness, her sense of inadequacy in the presence of boys was still powerful. Her easy banter within the society of her female schoolmates became an uneasy reticence once she stepped off the school grounds in the company of a boy. She was concerned more than ever with her weight, her complexion, her looks and what she felt was her dubious attractiveness to members of the opposite sex. Her anxieties were compounded by her certainty that their interest in her was due only to her name.

This was just one facet of her existence that she found irksome. Her relationship with her stepmother, which had been a happy and salutary one during the previous three years and had helped Jane through the trials of adolescence, was threatened by the sharp discontent she now witnessed between Susan and her father. Jane saw her father withdrawing moodily as he had done the year before her mother died. Jane's loyalty to Susan was suddenly thrust into conflict with her visceral love of her father. As she sensed the threat of an imminent breakup, she felt powerless, frustrated and increasingly unhappy.

Henry and Susan had adopted a baby girl in November of

1953 and named her Amy. Much of the life in the Fonda household during the following two years had revolved about the child. Jane, although away at school much of the time, became the kind of surrogate sister to Amy that her own step-sister, Pamela Brokaw, had not been to her; during Jane's youth, Pamela had spent most of her time in boarding school. Having lived through the breakdown of one marriage at an age when she really hadn't understood what was going on, Jane was highly sensitive to the breakdown of this one.

In the best Fonda tradition, all intimations of trouble were kept hidden. Susan Fonda made great sacrifices to keep the marriage together, but by midsummer of 1955 Jane could see exactly what was going on. Her growing sense of the imper-manence of things in her family, coupled with the contradic-tions she began to divine on her own in her father's character—especially the perfection he demanded of others but seemed more and more to lack in himself—deepened her anxiety.

Then there was her brother. Peter had managed to get through the Fay School, a boys' secondary school in Southborough, Massachusetts, the year before. He was now enrolled at West-minster, another boarding school for boys in Connecticut. Al-though she did not see much of Peter, Jane felt an increasingly protective tie to him, the more so now that he had become the prime object of their father's impatience and disdain. Jane's graduation and her brief fling at acting in Omaha had caused Henry Fonda to modify his strict expectations of her. Indeed, Jane could almost palpably feel the change in his attitude toward her; suddenly he was treating her on occasion as a grown-up. As he did so, though, his despair over his unruly son intensified. When they were all together, Jane often found herself forced into the role of mediator, trying to excuse Peter's often manic behavior to an uncomprehending father, trying to explain their father's angry seethings to her self-destructive brother.

When the film version of *Mister Roberts* catapulted Henry Fonda back to screen stardom, he was given his pick of movie offers. Despite the loftiness of his intentions, the one he chose succeeded only in compounding his unhappiness and intensi-fying the ten ions and frustrations within the family. Fonda agreed to r the role of Pierre in Dino De Laurentiis' epic productio Tolstoy's *War and Peace*. The picture was to be shot i around Rome, beginning late in the summer of 195 ided to show Jane and Peter the Italian capital for a few weeks before they had to return to their respective schools in September. Consequently, shortly after finishing their stints at the Omaha Playhouse, they flew to Italy and settled in for the rest of the summer at a small rented estate on the outskirts of Rome.

In much the same way Jane discovered how her mother had died, so did Peter. Sitting in a barber's chair in a hotel in Rome, he later said, he picked up a movie magazine and read about his mother "slashing her throat in an insane asylum." When he went to his father for an explanation, he received a curt evasion. And when he learned that his sister had long known about it, the last barrier between himself and his anxieties about his mother crumbled. He brooded around Rome, unable to take comfort from anyone. Left to his own devices, he began to drink wine by the quart and wander through the humid city in a drunken daze. Jane, in the meantime, did little in Rome, she later reported, "except eat figs and get fat and watch Gina Lollobrigida, a neighbor, through binoculars."

In September Jane returned to the United States to begin her freshman year at Vassar College. Despite her brief stage experience in Omaha, she still had no ambition to pursue an acting career. She was intent instead on making art her major field of study, partly because she knew it would please her father. More important for the moment, though, was the task of conquering the academic and social intricacies of Vassar's highly competitive world.

Jane's transition to college was made easier by the fact that her old friend Brooke Hayward was also enrolled. They had seen little of each other during the previous four years and had a lot of catching up to do. Brooke had graduated from the elite Madeira School in Virginia and spent the summer traveling on her own through Europe. She appeared to Jane not only more beautiful but more worldly and sophisticated than herself. Yet Jane's family difficulties seemed to pale into insignificance compared to Brooke's. Both Bridget and Billy Hayward suffered from chronic mental problems and were in and out of institutions, and their mother Margaret Sullavan was being treated by psychiatrists after a severe breakdown of her own.

Physically and spiritually, Vassar was the Emma Willard School twenty times magnified. The college was nestled in a large, parklike setting on the outskirts of Poughkeepsie, New York. It was a few miles north of Beacon, where Jane's mother had taken her life, but far closer to New York City than Troy. The Vassar campus was enclosed by an eight-foot high wrought-iron fence and was a pleasant mix of Georgian and neo-Gothic architecture set amid expansive lawns, fine old trees and winding drives and paths. In 1955 it was the sort of school to which young women of privilege and intelligence were sent to complete their formal education, acquire a sophisticated cultural veneer and prepare for "marriage, motherhood and menopause," in the words of one of its more sardonic graduates.

It is doubtful that many of the girls who started at Vassar in 1955 were thinking about the menopause component of that axiom, and motherhood was probably considered only in terms of avoiding embarrassing pregnancies. But marriage was surely in the forefront of the minds and emotions of most of the girls who were installed in Vassar's sylvan setting. Indeed, from most parents' point-of-view, this was the only justification for spending upwards of $10,000 to send their daughters to Vassar over a period of four years: to provide their offspring the exposure to the most favorable conditions for making a desirable marriage. A good education was certainly desirable, but Vassar's strong point was the proximity of its students to young men of proper social and financial standing from such colleges as Yale, Amherst and Wesleyan. "Everyone was in such a hurry to get married," Jane said later. "If you didn't have a ring on your finger by your junior year, forget it."

Having grown up in an environment in which social achievement and standing were no trivial matters, and using her still-youthful stepmother as a model for her own dreams, Jane was no different in her expectations than most of her classmates. Yet there was another side to the coin. She had grown up in the company of show people. She had a famous father and had already appeared with him on stage. She could drop the names of celebrities she knew with the same ease and familiarity that other girls used when talking about the high school boyfriends they had left behind. She had actually dined at Clark Gable's, had rough-housed with Jimmy Stewart, had been patted on the head by John Wayne, had been pecked on the cheek by Bette Davis. To a residence hall full of seventeen-year-old girls, many of whom nurtured secret fantasies of film stardom for themselves, or at least wondered about what it would be like, Jane quickly became an object of admiration and envy.

She had by then learned to feel at ease in the company of

girls. But Jane was still, in those beginning months of her first year at Vassar, more quiet and introspective than outgoing. Aside from Brooke Hayward—superficially a more beautiful, talented and interesting girl who had already decided to become an actress—she made few close friends. At first she applied herself diligently to her studies; French, music and art history were her favorites. The responsibility of making good, a constant ingredient of the lectures she had been receiving from her father, still weighed heavily on her.

It became obvious to Jane during the winter of her freshman year that the marriage between her father, who was still in Rome, and Susan, who was in New York with two-year-old Amy, was over. Stories had begun to surface in the gossip columns to the effect that Henry Fonda had succumbed to his own reputedly aristocratic Italian heritage by romancing a beautiful Venetian noblewoman. When the stories got back to Jane, she was hurt—first because Susan was suffering; second, because her father had not kept her informed about what was going on. Jane was old enough to realize that her father, in his failure to include her in the latest secrets of his personal life, was trying to be discreet. But she was now inclined to attribute his incommunicativeness to plain dishonesty, especially in the light of past experiences. She grew bitter about the pattern of dissembling she felt he had established between them.

In many ways Jane was still emotionally immature. The emotional traumas she had suffered between her eleventh and seventeenth years because of the loss of her mother and the erratic behavior of her father remained largely unresolved. The results were increasing attacks of anxiety about everything under the sun—herself and her own place in the world, her father, her brother, her stepmother and, most of all, the seeming impermanence of things—attacks she had been trained to repress. For someone brought up to worship the virtues of order and perfection, the constant breakdown of these virtues within her own family left her with a shaky, perhaps even neurotic, confidence in herself and her world.

As Jane passed her eighteenth birthday during Christmas vacation in December 1955, she was able to look back on a year in which her world had changed markedly. The physical differences between the high school senior at Emma Willard and the college freshman at Vassar were becoming considerable. She had reached her full of height of five feet seven and a half inches and was nearly fully developed. Her Omaha acting stint had given her increased self-awareness and even a touch of self-confidence. Through a program of stringent dieting, she had lost the residue of baby fat she had carried through Emma Willard and was delighted to find herself reshaped into a slim, lithe, coltish young woman. It was an appearance she had to work hard to maintain, however, since she enjoyed eating and the Vassar cuisine, though it was a notch above ordinary institutional food, was heavy in starches. Like many other girls at the college, Jane became caught up in obsessive worries about her figure. She began to engage in the routine of eating a full meal, then hastily retreating to the bathroom to throw it up before it had a chance to do its deadly work on her system.

The rules and restrictions on the girls at Vassar were much less confining than at Emma Willard. Weekends especially were freer, and the girls were allowed to leave the campus as long as the proper permissions were granted. Jane responded to her new freedom with gusto. With her father still in Italy, she spent as many weekends in New York as she could, usually staying at the house with Susan and Amy. When she found that young men were increasingly attracted to her, she began a steady round of weekend dating. This was not the remote, awkward ritual of the year before; it was the painful and confusing rite almost every shy first-year college girl went through.

At first, Jane was like almost everyone else at Vassar—her social life was motivated primarily by a desire to conform to and compete in a world of ambitious, sophisticated young women on the make. But because of who she was, she quickly learned that the competition factor did not really apply to her. She was singled out as someone special and was besieged with the attentions of young men who came down for weekends from Yale and other elite colleges of the Northeast. As far as conforming was concerned—well, she soon grew bored with that imperative. She rapidly learned to set her own fast pace, and it was not long before she drew ahead of most of her classmates in the dating-and-romance race.

Not that a long-standing romance was her goal. Quantity and variety, rather than singularity and permanence, were the things she sought in her contacts with the opposite sex. If Jane entered Vassar a good deal less sophisticated and practiced than most of her classmates, she rapidly altered the balance. Once she discovered the excitement and sweet satisfactions to be had from an intensive social life, she pursued it determinedly. Her schoolwork suffered accordingly.

When Henry Fonda returned to New York in the spring of 1956, his still-dark mood was not lightened by what he discovered. He was disturbed by reports of Jane's less than dedicated approach to her studies at Vassar, but since she appeared to be getting by, he kept his criticisms to a minimum. Peter's problems at Westminster were another matter altogether, though. The youngest Fonda seemed to attract trouble the way honey attracts a bear, and nothing his father did or said to him seemed to have any effect.

Fonda resolved to try to make something positive out of the coming summer. He arranged to take a house on Cape Cod so that he and the children could have some time together, and when Jane expressed an interest in having another go at acting, he used his influence to get her a summer apprentice's job at the very place he had started when he came East in the summer of 1928—the Dennis Playhouse.

By the spring of her freshman year Jane was of two minds about acting. She had enjoyed her previous summer's stage venture in Omaha and had especially appreciated the brief camaraderie she had achieved with her father. Although she loved the excitement of being onstage in front of an audience, of giving a performance, she still had no confidence that she had real talent. And as Henry Fonda's daughter, she could not bear the idea of making a fool of herself. And yet Brooke Hayward seemed destined for an acting career. Brooke and Jane had gone from being close friends to being friendly rivals in their first year at Vassar. If Brooke was so intent on an acting career, Jane felt that perhaps she herself should give it more thought.

Her father had recognized her gift for acting when she had perfomed with him in Omaha, but he refused to acknowledge it to her. If he was mildly amused at her sudden if tentative interest in the theater, he was not a man who dreamed of seeing his children follow in his footsteps. Indeed, since he had experienced so many hardships as a young actor, his instincts were to discourage Jane whenever she talked about it, however vaguely.

Jane had taken his discouragements seriously. There was so much that was unspoken between them that she was never certain whether he disapproved because he believed that she was without talent, or whether his negativism was merely protective. Whichever, she was now able to talk a little about the theater and acting, and it pleased her that she finally had a common ground on which she could relate to her father, however tentatively. Even though he usually dismissed her enthusiastic perceptions as the naive ramblings of a neophyte, or changed the subject altogether, she was discouraged but not deterred. And as more and more people at college wondered why she was not pursuing acting, she decided that a few months in summer stock would settle the question in her mind once and for all.

Since he was living nearby, Henry Fonda saw Jane act in one of the Dennis Playhouse's apprentice productions and gained a greater appreciation of the gift he had perceived in Omaha the year before. Nevertheless, he continued to maintain his silence in the face of Jane's growing enthusiasm. She played the part of a maid in a Restoration comedy. "When she came on," Henry Fonda told an interviewer years later, "the audience reacted in an almost physical, audible way—a straightening up and intake of breath. What a position to be in, trying to remind yourself that you were her father! If you were any other SOB you'd say, 'Get that girl into the theater,' and you'd use a ship to get her there. But of course I never let her know that."

Later that summer, Fonda accepted an invitation from the Dennis Company to play the lead in a play called *The Male Animal* for a week, with Jane as the ingenue. The production was a great success. Although Jane was noticed primarily because she was on the same stage as her father, the three weeks of rehearsals and performances were the happiest times "I had ever spent with him."

Yet by the end of the summer she was more confused than ever. She had hoped for some positive indication from her father about whether her growing interest in acting was justified. He conceded that she could probably get somewhere as an actress. But he indicated through his lack of enthusiasm that such a career was still not what he had in mind for her. Whether he wanted the life of a young society matron for Jane, or was simply trying to shield her from the torment he had seen so many other young performers go through in their struggle to succeed, remained unclear. Whatever the reason, his reticence left Jane with more questions about herself, and fewer answers, than she'd had at the beginning of the summer.

She returned to her sophomore year at Vassar that fall feeling more muddled than ever about her future. She had gotten to love acting but at the same time was afraid of it. "The college put on a Lorca play," she once recalled, "and I played the lead, a young Spanish girl who stood in a window and sang songs and cuckolded her husband. I knew almost nothing about the motivations of the character I played. By then I was conscious enough to look for things in the character, but I didn't know how. There was nothing behind the emotions I showed. I didn't know how to show that the emotions came from something and that the words had meaning. I really hadn't decided to become an actress at that point."

On the one hand, she wanted to. On the other, she didn't. "What I really wanted was to get out of Vassar."

chapter 5

POUGHKEEPSIE
TO PARIS

Part of Jane's desire to leave Vassar stemmed from the final breakup of her father's marriage to Susan. But it was also driven by a still-deeper dissatisfaction with herself. As she once told an interviewer, "I was brought up where people didn't express what they really felt. You hid everything. You hid your fears and your sorrows and your pains and your joys and your physical desires. Consequently I was a zombie, living somebody else's image, and I didn't know who I was."

Jane's identity crisis manifested itself in an almost complete abandonment of her studies after she had been back at Vassar for a few weeks, and in a plunge into a life of steady dating and drinking. Even Brooke Hayward, much more experienced than Jane in social and sexual matters, was surprised. Jane quickly got "a reputation for being easy," she said. "It was almost a joke."

Jane herself once confessed that she became totally irresponsible during her second year at Vassar. "When I discovered that boys liked me, I went wild. I was out all the time. I never studied."

One "boy" who knew her then concurs. "Jane suddenly turned into a sex pistol," he recalls. "I liked her a lot at first. But then I found out that I wasn't the only one she was sharing her body with. I dropped out of her scene. It was as though

43

she was in a race to see how many guys she could bring under her spell. There was something frantic about it, about her. She wasn't smooth at all, or very subtle about it. I guess it was her way of trying to grow up."

Or get thrown out of Vassar. The school was hard put to contain her. She became a "sophisticated delinquent," in the words of another witness to the time, hurtling toward a confrontation with the college authorities. When the confrontation came, they would not fulfill her wish to be expelled. Instead they informed Jane's father, in California for several months of moviemaking. Henry Fonda read her the riot act over the telephone. She begged him to let her drop out of Vassar. He said no.

Jane thereupon plunged into a torrid love affair with a student from Yale. Vassar did not permit its students to marry while still in school. Jane saw this as a way to get out of college, and after a few weeks she began to press her Yale boyfriend to marry her—immediately! "He had the good sense to decline," she reflected several years later. Her crusade to get out of college remained thwarted.

Early in 1957, Jane's father announced that he was going to marry Baroness Afdera Franchetti, the beautiful noblewoman he had met in Italy when he was filming *War and Peace*. The wedding took place in Fonda's New York townhouse on March 10, and both Peter and Jane came down from their schools to be present.

Afdera Franchetti was twenty-four years old when she married Henry Fonda. Many of his friends remarked with wry, almost sad humor on his growing penchant for women much younger than himself. His own children, both now in the flower of their respective rebellions, were not above wisecracks themselves, although they made sure to make them out of their father's hearing. At the wedding, Jane and Peter made a private bet that when the time came for their father to take his next wife, she would be younger than Jane, and the one after that would be younger than Peter. They had a hilarious time speculating on the age of his ninth or tenth wife, regaling several other guests with stories of their father feeding her from a bottle and instead of making love to her, diapering her in the bedroom.

Their jokes were literally laced with bitterness. Neither Jane nor Peter liked Afdera. She had replaced Susan, who had been more of a mother to them than their own mother, and they felt

uncomfortable in her presence. Afdera was flamboyant, fey
and suffused with an aura of languid Mediterranean decadence
that was completely alien to their sensibilities. Moreover, her
English was tiresomely inadequate for decent communication.
Jane distrusted the way she insinuated herself into the Fonda
household and hated the way their father let her take charge
of things. "He was a puppy at Afdera's feet," and the contrast
between the way he treated her and the way he treated Jane
and Peter sharpened the edge of their resentment.

The two Fonda offspring went back to their schools unhap-
pier and more anxiety-ridden than ever. Jane continued her
efforts to get thrown out of Vassar during the spring. Unprepared for an examination, she filled her blue book with draw-
ings and handed it in. The college refused to flunk her or punish
her and insisted that she take a makeup exam instead. Restricted
to the campus, she started sneaking out. One weekend the
authorities discovered that she was absent when she shouldn't
have been. Believing that she had finally succeeded in her
efforts, she returned to face the desired music. "But the pro-
fessor said he understood that my father had just married for
the fourth time and that I was emotionally upset. I wasn't,
really. I'd just gone away with a boy for the weekend."

Peter Fonda was even more avid in his self-destructiveness.
He says today that when he went home for the wedding, he
tried to talk to his father about the difficulties he was having
at the Westminster School. He got no sympathy from Henry
Fonda, only a curt lecture on the responsibilities of being a
Fonda.

Peter returned to school and started swallowing phenobar-
bitals to calm himself down. After a couple of fistfights with
teachers, he was threatened with expulsion. Peter called Jane
at Vassar—their father had left on his wedding trip to Europe—
and pleaded for help. Jane borrowed a car and drove to West-
minster the next day. She found Peter hiding in some bushes
in a drug-induced daze, talking to himself. With her father in
Europe, Jane called their Aunt Harriet in Nebraska. Harriet
told her to put Peter on a train to Omaha, that she and her
husband would look after him until their father returned.

It was the second time Henry Fonda had been interrupted
on a wedding trip by Peter's antics. He flew from France to
Omaha in a state of high dudgeon. He and Harriet decided that
Peter should remain in Omaha with her and her husband. They

would see that he got psychiatric help and would look after his schooling. Reluctantly Peter accepted the decision, but things would get worse for him before they got better.

Henry Fonda returned to New York to find more trouble awaiting him. Jane told him that she was going crazy at Vassar and had to get out at all costs. She still wasn't sure what she wanted to do with her life, she conceded, but she was sure that she was wasting it in Poughkeepsie and would never be happy in college. Recalling his own frustrations as a college youth, and suddenly afraid that Jane might go the way of her mother, Fonda dropped his former inflexibility and asked her what she wanted to do. Seizing the opening, Jane asked him to finance her for a year in Paris, where she would pursue her art studies and also learn French. He was amenable to the idea, if only reluctantly so. After all, many college girls took a year off from school to study in Europe. And since Jane seemed genuinely interested in something he thought worthwhile and had encouraged her about, why not?

Jane was relieved by her father's agreement. But there were conditions. First, she would have to finish out the spring semester at Vassar, and in the process salvage her grades. Second, she had to give up her frenetic social life.

Jane did both. Then, early in June 1957, she took her last train ride from Poughkeepsie to New York. A few weeks later, she flew to Paris.

Although Jane had convinced her father that her ambition to become a painter might be real and that a year of study would give fruitful support to that ambition, her argument was little more than a pretext to get away from school, from home, from her problems. "I went to Paris to be a painter," she said, "but I lived there for six months and never opened my paints. I was nineteen, an age when you know you are not happy but you don't know why, and you think a geographical change will change your life."

Jane's living arrangements in Paris had been made for her before she left New York. When she arrived in late June, she moved into a dark, elegant apartment in the fashionable Sixteenth Arrondissement. The apartment belonged to an ancient countess who boarded young American girls. It was in a somber building on the Avenue d'Iena, halfway between the Arc de Triomphe and the Trocadero and almost directly across the Seine from the Eiffel Tower. The location couldn't have been more pleasant for an impressionable American girl tasting for the first time the sophisticated pleasures of Paris. Jane soon learned to hate it. "It was an apartment with everything covered in plastic," she said, "where everything smelled, where young ladies were not supposed to talk at the table and where I was absolutely miserable."

When she started her art studies at the Académie Grande Chaumière, she found the instruction, which was in French, mostly idiomatic and much too rapid for her tenuous grasp of the language. However sincere she might have been in her desire to study art, she was out of her element in the classrooms and studios of the school. She found life much more interesting outside, in the busy, vibrant streets of the Latin Quarter. Her concentration thus diverted, she quickly lost all interest in her studies and began to spend most of her time trying to learn the language in the crowded bistros and zinc bars of the Left Bank.

Among the leading lights of Paris' cultural life at the time was a group of hyper imaginative young men and women, many of them Americans, involved in putting out a literary quarterly called the *Paris Review*. Its editor was George Plimpton, a talented essayist and scion of an old, wealthy New York family who, several years later, would become celebrated in America as a humorous reporter of Walter Mitty-type adventures. Jane met Plimpton. Through him and his band of powerful intellectual cronies, she gained instant entrance into Paris' Bohemian smart set—a mélange of expatriate poets, artists, writers and rich young hangers-on.

Jane, just short of her twentieth birthday, joined the group with gratitude and a desire to please. Much of her time was spent hanging around the office of the *Paris Review*, bantering, flirting and running errands. She found the company easy, the talk fast, risqué and amusing, the social life wicked and exciting. The level of sophistication was far above her own, but she was clever and observant. Soon she was able to keep up with the rapid, esoteric chatter that swirled around her. She was even quicker at becoming adept at the nightly partying and bistro crawling.

Artists, literary people, filmmakers—these were the people who made up Jane's circle of acquaintances in Paris during the fall and winter of 1957. She met not only Americans but Frenchmen as well, and many took to pursuing her with barely concealed lust. The cafés and ateliers of the Left Bank became her home, and she spent increasingly less time in the musty confines of her apartment on Avenue d'Iena. One night, at a gathering at Maxim's, she met the French film director Roger Vadim, a man whose notoriety as a sexual libertine preceded him wherever he went. Vadim had been the "discoverer" and first husband of Brigitte Bardot, and probably more than anyone else in Europe was responsible for the emergence and public acceptance of the erotic feature film. The night he and Jane met he was with his second wife, Annette Stroyberg, also a film star. A tall, slender man with a long, melancholy face, Vadim looked at the daughter of the celebrated Henry Fonda first in cold appraisal, then with mounting interest. Jane, feverishly self-conscious under his gaze and aware of his reputation as a blatant womanizer, bristled, then tried to ignore him. Vadim, who among other things was known to have a knack for prescience, filed her away in his memory.

Once past her twentieth birthday, Jane's "year" in Paris abruptly came to an end. Word had gotten back to her father that she had abandoned all pretense of studying art and was running with Paris' profligate crowd. Fonda heard rumors of sexual promiscuity and other forms of malfeasance on Jane's part and exploded with rage. He ordered her back to New York.

Chastised yet resentful, Jane settled uneasily into her father's house on Seventy-fourth Street early in 1958. As if to show him that her intentions remained good, she enrolled at the New York Art Students League to resume her painting studies. She also signed up at the Mannes School of Music, which was next door to her father's house, for piano training, and at Berlitz to study French and Italian. To underline her seriousness, she worked during the spring in the New York office of *Paris Review*, traveling about Manhattan to solicit ads from publishers and bookstores.

A friend who worked for a fashion magazine asked Jane to model some clothes when the magazine needed someone to pose free for a picture layout. One of the editors saw the pictures. Impressed both by Jane's name and by the way she photographed, she expressed an interest in using her in a larger way. Although Jane still did not think of herself as outstandingly attractive, she liked the idea of being a model and decided to pursue it. She also met an ambitious young actor named James Franciscus, with whom she started a romance.

By late spring Jane had proved to herself that she was capable of doing hard work and sticking to it, even though it was without any long-term purpose. Her immediate purpose was to please her father, to atone for her wasted time at Vassar and in Paris. But if she was looking for words of praise or approval from her father, she still seldom got them. After all, she was simply doing what she was supposed to be doing, and Henry Fonda could never see the point of bestowing praise on someone merely because he or she did their job. When Jane came home with an animated tale of what she had accomplished that day, her father would acknowledge it with a distracted grunt and turn to other things. So, although Jane was almost obsessively busy that spring, her grip on her future remained flaccid.

"It was frustrating," she recalled in later years. "I wanted to jump in and start playing concertos instead of studying scales. I wanted to paint masterpieces, but painting became steadily less enjoyable and more difficult to do. I thought people who looked at what I painted expected something of me that I couldn't live up to. As soon as I finished a canvas, I'd be hypercritical of it. Underneath everything, I still thought about becoming an actress. That was what I wanted to do more than anything else, so I spent a lot of time figuring out reasons why I shouldn't. It was selfish and egotistical, it gave no enjoyment, I wasn't pretty enough, and so on. The truth is, I was just afraid to try."

chapter 6

THE STRASBERG CONNECTION

In 1958, Lee Strasberg, a short, diffident man who might have been mistaken for an aging waiter at Lindy's Restaurant, was the talk of the film and theater world. A more unprepossessing "star" could not have been imagined. But then, he was not a star in the conventional sense. Indeed, he was not even at that time an actor, nor, for that matter, a director or producer. Some called him a teacher, but such an appellation was inadequate to describe what he did. Others resorted to words like "guru," but this implied the possession of mystical powers and exaggerated what he did. Still others used the term "high priest," and if one can imagine a rundown former Greek Orthodox church on the seedy West Side of Manhattan as the modern equivalent of the ancient Temple, then the phrase came close to applying. Not that what Strasberg did had anything to do with religion. Yet his single-minded devotion to a unique dramatic philosophy was imbued with such religious zeal that it attracted hundreds of fanatical and famous disciples. His temple was called the Actors Studio.

By the mid-1950s the Actors Studio was not just a place where stage and movie stars were conceived and born; it was a place to which long-established stars and soon-to-be stars made pilgrimages in order to learn the magic formulas of the "Method," as Strasberg's acting theories were simplistically dubbed by the press. It was the dream of almost every actor and actress to be admitted. Thanks to the press, the public imagined the Studio to be a school, a place where one went to take "acting lessons." This was not the case at all. Lessons, strictly speaking, were not given. The atmosphere was more like that of a seminar, with Strasberg doing most, if not all, the talking. His "students"—celebrated and unknown alike—hung on every word. "Sessions," as they were called, were held twice a week in the converted West Side church; the rest of the members' time was spent rehearsing scenes or exercises which they would eventually present to Strasberg's critical eye.

Since the Studio was a members-only establishment and membership was limited to those elite few who could pass Strasberg's high audition standards, and since thousands of actors and actresses were eager to partake of the Stanislavskian system, Strasberg hit on the idea of giving private classes. No sooner had he announced this than he was besieged by hundreds of eager acolytes willing to pay $35 a month to enroll. Strasberg was soon giving three two-hour classes a day in the small theater of the Dramatic Workshop, a combination acting school and repertory theater situated next to the cavernous Capitol movie theater on Broadway.

Strasberg's wife, Paula, a former actress, became the general factotum of the great man's private classes. Although Lee had become the high priest, many thought Paula Strasberg the power behind the throne. Her style was a perfect complement to her husband's seemingly sour, phlegmatic disposition. A tiny, stout, gregarious woman, she became den mother to dozens of striving, often starving actors and actresses, well-known and obscure, who passed through the Strasberg classes.

The Strasbergs were also noted as the parents of Susan Strasberg, an engagingly fragile young actress who had, at an early age, made an auspicious Broadway debut with her creation of the title role in *The Diary of Anne Frank*. During the spring of 1958, while Henry Fonda was appearing nightly in a hit Broadway play called *Two for the Seesaw*, he spent his days making a movie in which Susan Strasberg was his co-star. The film, called *Stage Struck*, was a remake of an earlier Katharine Hepburn movie about a young actress seeking Broadway fame. It was being made primarily as a vehicle for Susan Strasberg's motion-picture debut in a leading role. Normally Fonda would not have become involved in such a venture,

especially in view of the fact that he had been asked to play
second-fiddle to a teenager. But he was bored with *Two for
the Seesaw*. He agreed to make the movie primarily as a favor
to its director, Sidney Lumet (who had directed him in *12 Angry
men*), and also because it gave him the opportunity to film in
New York. As a result, a series of events was set in motion
that would profoundly affect, of all people, Jane Fonda.

Jane got to know Susan Strasberg as a result of her father's
role in *Stage Struck*. Although Henry Fonda had no time for
Lee Strasberg, the Actors Studio or the theory of Method acting, he liked Susan Strasberg and spoke well of her to Jane.
Jane visited the set and the two struck up a friendship. Susan
introduced Jane to several of her friends, most of whom were
young performers studying with her father. Although Jane found
these busy, animated young actors and actresses fascinating,
their discipline and single-mindedness made her uneasy. "I
didn't like what I saw the acting profession do to people who
went into the theater," she said shortly after, perhaps a bit
defensively. "All the young actresses I've met are obsessed
with the theater. They think and talk only about one thing.
Nothing else matters to them. It's terribly unhealthy to sacrifice
everything—family, children—for a goal like that. I hope I
never get that way. I don't believe in concentrating your life
in terms of one profession, no matter what it is."

That summer Henry Fonda took time off from *Two for the
Seesaw* to make another movie, this one in Hollywood. He
rented a house in the exclusive Malibu Beach Colony and
brought Jane and Peter out to join him and Afdera. Also staying
at Malibu for the summer were Lee and Paula Strasberg, attending to their friend and student Marilyn Monroe, and their
children, Susan and John. Their house was just down the beach
from the Fondas'.

Jane resumed her friendship with Susan Strasberg, and they
spent many days together on the beach or at each other's houses.
Jane met many among the constant stream of show business
visitors to the Strasberg abode, which Paula Strasberg ran almost like an open house. The highly animated conversations,
which seemed to go on around the clock, were all about the
theater and movies, actors, actresses and directors, theory and
gossip. Jane listened, mostly. She admired the raucous Jewish
warmth of the Strasberg household, which was in stark contrast
to the studied, formal casualness of her own. She began to

envy, too, the powerful sense of commitment everyone displayed toward the business.

One night she went to a party and encountered longtime Hollywood director Mervyn Leroy, who was there with his children, Warner and Linda, both about Jane's age. Their conversation turned to the question of why Jane hadn't done any acting since the summer at Cape Cod. Jane replied diffidently that she didn't think she was up to being the kind of actress she would have to be as the daughter of Henry Fonda, to be anything less than perfect would be an embarrassment. Leroy scoffed and asked her if she wouldn't like to play Jimmy Stewart's daughter in *The FBI Story*, which he was directing. He was serious. Jane, suddenly presented with the possibility of an acting job, didn't know what to say. All she knew was that the thought of it scared her.

Later she tried to talk to her father about it, but he was enigmatic. "If you're going to be an actress, you don't want it to be as Jimmy's Stewart's daughter in *The FBI Story*," was his answer. The implication was that he didn't approve of the idea of Jane getting an acting part through the influence of high-placed friends.

She mentioned it the next day to Susan Strasberg and some of her chums on the beach. One of them was a young man named Martin Fried, a directorial protégé of Lee Strasberg's who had been staying at the house. Fried wondered aloud why Jane hadn't got into acting long before; she was obviously attractive and projected a natural vibrancy and vitality that might take her a long way. Jane responded by reciting her misgivings about being Henry Fonda's daughter. The issue became the focus of the discussions and conversations among the young people over the next few days. Personal magnetism, physical grace, singular good looks, intelligence, distinctive and attractive mannerisms—Jane had all these qualities in abundance, it was decided. Even if her name hadn't been Fonda, she possessed enough in the way of personal qualities to be a candidate for success. The real question was: Did she have the obsessive need to act, the inner fire, the drive and ambition—not to mention the talent—to succeed?

The only way for Jane to find out would be to try. And there was no better way of trying than under the tutelage of Lee Strasberg.

Susan Strasberg talked to her parents about Jane. Paula

Strasberg called Jane over to the house and questioned her. The questions were incisively personal and cut through the shield of Jane's wariness. Then she talked to her husband, who agreed to give Jane an interview and retired with her to a quiet corner of the house.

When Strasberg talked to someone he didn't know well, he gave the impression of talking past the person. His voice, with its strong trace of Middle Europe, was so flat and expressionless as to give the impression of disdain. As he talked, his face unconsciously assumed an expression of distaste. To someone who didn't know him well, he appeared unfriendly and impatient, even hostile. If that someone happened to be shy, fearful—insecure, the experience could be unnerving.

As Jane answered Strasberg's probing queries about herself, she found herself opening up. He was gruff, almost surly—not unlike her father—but his questions and comments had a sympathetic quality that her father's had never had. "He talked to me as if he were interested in me," she said later, "not because I was Henry Fonda's daughter. He could sense that I wanted to act but was afraid to."

"The only reason I took her," Strasberg has remarked, "was her eyes. There was such panic in her eyes." Part of Jane's panic may have been due to her fear of being inspected by this man of spectacular reputation whose judgment had been sought by stars of the magnitude of Marlon Brando and Marilyn Monroe. When Strasberg consented to have her in his classes starting that fall in New York, without the usual long wait for a vacancy, Jane, for one of the few times in her life, felt a real sense of accomplishment and self-esteem.

She had survived the first test—the spotlight of Strasberg's cold but sympathetically perceptive judgment. The dogmatic seriousness and dedication she detected in him when he talked about "the work" filled her with a sense of sober anticipation. What this mysterious "work" consisted of, exactly, she wasn't altogether sure. But although she had often listened to her father ridicule the Method, she sensed that it was important and that something significant might come from her exposure to it. Within Jane's being the wheels of purpose, however vaguely felt, slowly began to revolve.

Jane Fonda's arrival that fall in New York was to be an event. Rumors of her coming had circulated for weeks, and even the most celebrity-jaded class members were aquiver with anticipation. For Jane was the daughter of Henry Fonda, by then a legend, indeed an institution, in the American entertainment industry. Henry Fonda not only enjoyed worldwide fame, he possessed the kind of high-powered respectability and influence that everyone in Strasberg's classes—famous and unknown alike—craved for themselves. Simply by being his daughter, Jane Fonda was perceived as being imbued with the same qualities. Everyone was curious to see what she would be like. Somehow, having her in the classes would be the next best thing to having Henry Fonda there.

But there was more to it than that. The sense of anticipation that flowed from the rumors that Jane would be joining the classes was animated as much by envy and resentment as it was by awe over the Fonda name. Up to then, few if any children of movie stars had followed successfully in their parent's footsteps. Jane's prospective arrival was heightened by the fact that Henry Fonda had publicly blasted Lee Strasberg and the Method as "useless garbage." Strasberg's students were nothing if not rabidly loyal to their teacher. If she came, Jane Fonda would be coming from the enemy camp. The feeling was: Who did this Jane Fonda, with nothing more than her name and her privileged background to recommend her, think she was enrolling in Strasberg's classes?! Many of the students had been struggling in obscurity for years, and those who had made it had lived through their own long spans of impoverished darkness. Not a few secretly hoped that if and when Jane arrived, she would prove abjectly inept as an actress.

chapter 7

A STUDENT
ONCE MORE

Arrive Jane did. At the time I was working at the Dramatic Workshop and I recall the day vividly. I had a tiny office off the cramped lobby that led to the auditorium where Lee Strasberg held his classes. The lobby was as usual noisily swarming with actors and actresses awaiting the start of the afternoon's session. Suddenly, a hush fell. Unaccustomed to such an abrupt change in the decibel level, I glanced out of the office to see all eyes focused on the lobby's narrow entrance. There stood an attractive but visibly nervous young woman dressed in an elegant beige silk-tweed suit and matching four-inch high heels. She was, I guessed correctly, Jane Fonda.

With Jane was Susan Strasberg and Martin Fried. "My God," I thought, "why didn't Suzy clue Jane Fonda in on how to dress?" The standard garb of the female students in those days was something black, bohemian and vaguely gypsy-looking. Jane looked like she had just stepped out of a Bergdorf Goodman catalogue. Only Marilyn Monroe came to Strasberg's classes dressed to the nines, and she got away with it because she was—well, Marilyn Monroe.

Jane didn't have to be introduced; the rumors of her coming had been confirmed, and her face, which bore the indelible Fonda trademark, was immediately recognized. Jane was an instant celebrity, if only because of her name. The jealousy quotient, always high in Strasberg's classes, became unspokenly feverish.

As Saul Colin, the managing director at the Dramatic Workshop, recalled it years later, "She was like a frightened deer hiding behind this forthright Fonda manner. She was tall and well dressed and made up like one of those society girls I always see coming out of the shops on Fifth Avenue. She spoke in rapid bursts, with the strong quivering tone of voice American girls think make them appear well-bred. She had a lot of phoniness . . . but the way her eyes locked onto mine, as if trying to reach for a life ring before drowning, made me sympathetic. I could feel the intensity behind her snobbish manner . . . and the anguish. The poor girl really felt quite out of place. But she had something. . . ."

Another who recalled meeting Jane that first day—one of Strasberg's veteran students—said, "Jane came in with Susan Strasberg just before the class began. Lee ignored her, but everybody else immediately knew who she was. You could feel the tension that always preceded a class swell up like an overblown balloon. I mean, she was Henry Fonda's daughter and all that, and everyone was dying of curiosity. I was amazed to see how much like her father she looked—the resemblance was uncanny. That's all we talked about after class, how much like her father . . . I came out, and there she was talking to someone. She smiled at me, and I could see she was a bit nervous and apprehensive. I was surprised at how tall she was. She was dressed very chicly, wearing sort of a pinkish suit and high heels, with her hair up. But she looked as though she didn't know what to do with herself. Which was funny, because if she felt awkward, we felt even more so. There was something about her that right away said class. If anything, I think a lot of us felt a little less sure of ourselves in her presence. You know how you're always measuring yourself against other people? Well, there she was, feeling insecure, when it was us who were feeling even more insecure. I think the way her presence made us feel—her name and the kind of glossy aura she projected—was a source of a lot of the resentment on our parts there at the beginning. Oh, we pretended to be friendly, but I know almost everyone in the class was dying to see her make a fool of herself."

Jane would later say about her exposure to Strasberg that "Lee Strasberg changed my life." About her start in the classes, she said, "I was awfully frightened. I didn't know what to expect. For the first month or so I thought it was all pretty ridiculous. But then something happened and I became thoroughly involved in it."

What happened was that, in great fear and trepidation, Jane performed her first "exercise" in front of Strasberg and the class. It took her much more than a month to summon up the courage. Her initial feelings that the classes were "all pretty ridiculous" were nothing more than her instinct for self-protection at work, masked as Fonda superiority.

Performance of an "exercise" was required of every new Strasberg student. It was the student's initiation rite into the mysteries of the Method. Until one performed an exercise, thereby exposing oneself to the critical scrutiny of Strasberg and the other students, one was not accepted by the others as a bona fide member of the class. An exercise consisted of anything the student wished to do, within a specified framework, and was carried out in two basic parts. The first was usually a physical action—jumping up and down alone on the stage and chanting the words to a favorite song, for instance. This part of the exercise was designed to expose the level of personal inhibition under which the beginning student labored, and to see how he or she dealt with it. The second part consisted of a "sense memory" or "private moment," in which the student acted out in pantomime some event from his or her life that had a particularly emotional meaning. Designed to test the student's ability to define and express emotion, it was considered a measure of his or her imagination, daring and talent.

A new student approached the day of the first exercise with dread, for it was truly a different and frightening experience. No matter how dense and deceptive a mask of self-assurance one wore in everyday life, the exercise stripped it away and exposed one's private insecurities and inhibitions for all to see. It was a moment of truth for the untested actor, and it was not unusual for the more timid among Strasberg's students, fearing exposure and ridicule, to put the performance of their first exercise off for months—indeed, there were those who never got up the courage to do it at all. They attended classes faithfully, but remained rooted to their seats, content to receive their pleasure vicariously as they watched other more hardy souls expose themselves.

At first the twenty-one-year-old Jane remained superficially calm and superior as she observed others go through their agonies. Her father's criticisms of Strasberg's methods were fresh in her mind, and she took refuge in them as a balm for her inner fears. Yet she envied those who had the courage to proceed in the face of their fears, then get caught up in the enthusiasm of having done so; she saw how it filled them with confidence, even cockiness. Even more, she envied the attention they received from Strasberg. It became clear to her that this was the only way to get the great man's attention—to expose herself and run the risks.

As she sat inactive through the early classes, Jane began to get the hang of things. She gradually learned that Strasberg was not to be feared. To her surprise, he did not react to the new students' often inept exercise performances with the expected ridicule. Rather, he gently criticized and offered fatherly suggestions about how they could improve. It was the presence of the older students, many of them accomplished and highly acclaimed actors, and the thoughts she imagined they would harbor if she took the stage—possibly breaking out into sarcastic laughter (it had happened with others)—that held Jane back. "I didn't believe in myself," she said. "I couldn't stand the thought of exposing myself, of being attacked and torn to pieces."

But she was also anxious to receive an indication from Strasberg of whether she had anything besides her name upon which to attempt to build an acting career. And she grew intent on proving something to her father, who treated the stories she brought home about the classes and Strasberg's methods with testy condescension. So, with the encouragement and guidance of the few friends she'd made, she finally set a date for her first exercise and busied herself with its preparation. As the day approached, she grew more nervous and fearful than ever and even considered calling in sick. But her courage prevailed. When the appointed hour came, feverish with terror, she took the stage.

"You see so many exercises, I forget what it was she did," said Delos Smith, a longtime member of Strasberg's classes. "I do remember that the class was particularly crowded that day. A lot of people from the other classes had heard about it and were there to see Jane fall on her face. But she didn't. In fact, she was marvelous. You could actually see a radical change go through her. The first impression she gave was her nervousness, but everybody is nervous the first time—I did exercises for six years and was as nervous the last time as I was the first. Then you could see her start to relax and get caught up in it. Pretty soon she was letting it all hang out. Everybody was impressed. Not only with the actor's talent she showed, but with her guts."

That first performance revealed a lot about Jane Fonda. It revealed her desperation and panic, of course. But more important, it revealed an instinctive gift—the ability to move around on a stage, to block out distracting external stimuli and zero in on her own space and time. Although the exercise was rough-edged and overblown, marred at the start with the anxious amateur's self-consciousness and tendency to rush, it contained very definite intimations of talent. Most remarkable of all, her presence and magnetism dominated the small stage; even with other students on it, all eyes were drawn to her.

Strasberg made no departure from his usual dry and clinical tone when he began to analyze Jane's effort for the rest of the class. But his voice grew more lively as he went along, the way it always did whenever he perceived that something unusual had occurred. His critique was at first a letdown for Jane. It was only after the class, when everyone flocked to her and congratulated her, "accepting" her into the group, that she felt she might have shown something. And when Delos Smith, one of Strasberg's closest observers, added that Strasberg had been more ebullient than usual, and explained what that meant, her spirit soared.

"My life changed radically within twenty-four hours," she has said of the experience. "It was just a night-and-day difference. Before, I'd been scared and extremely self-conscious—I was one person. After that exercise I was somebody else. From then on, I worked harder than anybody else. I was more ragged than anybody else. I was the rattiest, wannest, most straggle-haired. . . ."

Jane was hooked. She plunged almost obsessively into the life of Strasberg student and striving actress. "I've never seen anyone involve herself so much," Brooke Hayward, also taking the classes by then, said. "She worked at it seven days a week."

"It was like a light bulb going on," according to Jane. "I was a different person. I went to bed and woke up loving what I was doing."

Her enthusiasm didn't merely grow; it exploded. "Now, I

know that nothing that happened to me before last fall really counts," she said a year later. "It's a fantastic feeling when you've finally found out where you're going. You're happier. You're more productive. You're nicer. Whether I'll make it is something else again, but at least I'm finally channeled." But if she was pleased with the hard ambition she had finally discovered, she remained disappointed in her higher hope—that of achieving her father's approval and respect.

Henry Fonda had already made it clear to Jane that he didn't believe in acting schools. And his feelings about the theories of the Method, which Jane started to expound as though she had been the first to uncover them, were by then well-known. He was glad in his paternal way that Jane had at last discovered an abiding interest, and although he occasionally indulged her enthusiasm for talk about acting, he would quickly become bored with her evangelism, shutting her off with an indifferent shrug. And when he was in one of his darker moods he would barely respond to her at all. As Jane began to find herself, the pain she felt as a result of her father's continuing indifference grew more profound.

"I used to come home from Lee's classes so full of what I was doing," Jane recalled to a reporter, "and my father would say, 'Shut up. I don't want to hear about it.' There was one time, for example, where I had just done a marvelous scene in class. And it was like I was on fifty Benzedrines. I bumped into my father and got into a taxicab with him. I was panting with excitement. I wanted to tell him about it. And I could see his curtain come down. He smiled, but I just didn't get through."

When questioned about this a few years later during an interview for the *Saturday Evening Post*, Henry Fonda, tears welling in his eyes, said, "Well, I don't understand this. Maybe I'm—maybe I do things that I'm not aware of that mean something to other people. I don't know what she means by a curtain coming down. It may be that I'm trying to hide my own emotions, and to her it's a curtain coming down. Now, I'll relate this story, because it began long before Jane started studying to be an actress. She was with a young beau of hers who was just getting started in the theater, and he and I were talking about using an emotion, having to feel an emotion on the stage. I told him about the process I go through, likening it to a seaplane taking off. There's a section on the underside of the seaplane called a step. When the plane starts its takeoff, it is very slow in the water, very sluggish, but as it picks up speed, it gets up on that step and starts to skim across the water before lifting off. I used to feel that if I could get myself going, I could get up on that step and nothing could stop me. Then all I had to do was hold back, hold the controls down, because then I was going, I was soaring. Anyway, about a year later I found myself in a cab with Jane going downtown, and Jane said, 'Do you remember the story that you told about soaring?' And she said, 'Now I know what you mean. It happened to me today.' Well, I can get emotional right now remembering Jane tell it, and probably the curtain came down to hide that emotion. Because for my daughter to be telling me about it—she knew what it was like! Well, I wasn't going to let her see me go on like this."

The interviewer, Alfred Aronowitz, asked, "Why not? Don't you understand she wants to get to you?"

"Well, gosh," Fonda replied, "she does get to me."

"I know," Aronowitz said, "but she wants to know she's getting to you. She's such a demonstrative person."

"Well," Fonda said, "I'm not."

Whether it was due to professional impatience or a basic personality defect, Fonda's continuing indifference to Jane's striving was like acid sprayed on the seeds of her self-discovery. She still did not give up hope of someday winning her father's esteem and respect. But her increasing self-confidence, most of which she now derived from Strasberg, gave her the will and determination to set her own course, independent of her father's reactions to her. It would be an exaggeration to suggest that Strasberg became, at least for a while, a surrogate for Jane's father. Yet his influence did become the dominating one in her life for the next year. Obtaining his approval became her first priority.

"You see," Jane said to another interviewer at the time, "with Lee nothing more was demanded of me than what I felt innermost. Lee Strasberg, someone who was not related to me, was saying, 'You are sensitive, you are good, you are worth something.' No one had ever told me that before. He was the only person I'd ever known who was interested in me without having to be. Lee somehow imparts dignity and gives you confidence in yourself."

After her return from Malibu and before starting her classes with Strasberg, Jane had moved out of her father's house.

Earlier in the summer a fellow student she had known at Vassar, Susan Stein, had come down to New York with the intention of obtaining an apartment. Susan was the daughter of Jules Stein, the wealthy founder of the Music Corporation of America. Known in the entertainment world as MCA, it was one of the largest talent and booking agencies in show business, with agents on both coasts representing many of the biggest stars in motion pictures, theater and television, including Jane's father. Susan suggested to Jane that they share an apartment. Jane broached the subject with her father and got his permission to move with Susan and a third roommate into a small duplex in a converted townhouse on East Seventy-sixth Street, just two blocks from her father's house. In her mind, the move was another important step in the process of gaining her independence.

Another large talent agency of the day was an organization called Famous Artists. Working there at the time was a young agent named Ray Powers. Powers represented the young actor Jody McRae, the son of Joel McRae. Jody McRae's girlfriend at the time was Jenny Lee, the third person Jane had moved in with.

Powers said, "One day Jody McRae asked me to see Jenny's roommate, Jane. At first I didn't realize the Jane he was talking about was Jane Fonda. I said I'd see her, and we set up an appointment. When Jane came into the office, she had just started taking Lee Strasberg's classes. After realizing who she was, I said, God, she could be something great and I would give her a guarantee that she would be a movie star. At first she was doubtful, but I kept calling her and meeting with her and saying, 'You really can do it, you know.' She kept going to Strasberg's classes that fall, and gradually, between the stuff she was getting from him and my constant encouragements, she began to believe that maybe she really could do something. As a result, I became her first agent. She could easily have gone with MCA—after all, it was owned by Susan Stein's father, and it was her own father's agency. But I found out right away that her father didn't take her acting very seriously— he thought it was just another lark. And he wasn't helping or encouraging her in any way. And she was bulldog-determined that if she was going to make it at all, it was going to be without his help."

Powers said that after Jane began to think seriously about

an acting career, he had to devise a new image for her. "She was known around New York as a sort of fashionable debutante, and I had to get her to stop having her picture taken at balls and other society functions. Nobody in the entertainment business would take her seriously, being a debutante, so I got her to stop wearing all that makeup and those smart clothes and persuaded her to start wearing the uniform of the serious young actresses of the day, which was the black leotard outfit—you know, the bohemian look. Well, she did, and we had pictures taken of her, looking very stark and kind of dedicated, and sent them around to all the movie studios. And that's how it really started."

At twenty-one Jane was taller than most of her contemporaries. Her thick, dark-gold hair fell to her shoulders when she didn't wear it up in a knot or have it coiffed into the beehive hairdo so popular in 1958. Through constant dieting she had reduced her weight to about 120 pounds. Her upper cheeks had lost the fullness of her teenage years, and when her hair was up, her face had a ballerina's gaunt expression. Her steep, broad, rounded forehead was like a smooth palisade above her wide-set eyes. The rest of her face was elongated, angling sharply from her prominent cheeks to her long jaw, its length accentuated by the pouty triangular shape of her mouth. Her teeth were large for her mouth, especially the upper ones; when she smiled, which she did with a suddenness that was unexpected from so stern a mouth, her slightly convex teeth jumped out in a flash of brilliant white.

Jane's long graceful neck climbed out of a supple, well-shaped body. Her breasts were high and compact, and her wide-shouldered, high-waisted torso curved to well-rounded hips. Her legs were shapely but had a dancer's thickness, especially in the calves. Her feet were large, as were her hands, but she possessed long, slender, graceful fingers that belied the curious chunkiness of her upper arms. She was at once a fragile and sturdy beauty and had a look that was considerably different from what one usually saw in the fashion magazines at the time. It was a decidedly girlish look, appealingly scrubbed and unexotic, and her long serious face in repose gave her an added touch of vulnerability and innocence.

As Jane began to see the real possibility of an acting career opening up, she grew less and less interested in the idea of "marriage and having babies," a notion Powers says she was still clinging to when he first met her. According to Jane, after going through several abortive relationships during the previous three years, "I was terrified of being vulnerable. I had never been able to sustain a relationship. I'd always gone through the first stages, the passion, the expectation, and then become disappointed. I vowed I wouldn't get married unless someone gave me a good reason to."

Although he had accepted her animated metamorphosis, Henry Fonda still considered Jane's acting studies as little more than an experiment, and he did not expect her interest in this one to survive any longer than her other enthusiasms had. Her unalloyed energy and her growing impatience to make a mark as an actress, although she had not yet acted in anything, continued to dismay him. Still distrusting anything that came easy or cheap, and trying to protect his daughter from what he was sure was her naiveté, he lectured her about the years it would take to learn her craft and the special critical demands that would be made of her because of her name. The latter was something she was already well aware of. As for the former, she had little use for her father's cautionary advice in the face of the encouragement she was receiving from Strasberg and others.

It's likely, moreover, that Henry Fonda's indifference to Jane's stories of Strasberg's wisdom and genius convinced her that her father, was, in certain respects, out of touch with things. And as far as intellectual and emotional nourishment were concerned, Jane was getting much more from Strasberg than from him. Strasberg had become a positive, encouraging force in her life. He had opened her up to all the possibilities that lay before her, whereas her father remained dour and dyspeptic about them.

As Brooke Hayward was to say about the Jane Fonda of early 1959, "Acting gave her the kind of applause she never got as a human being. I've never seen ambition as naked as Jane's."

chapter 8

THE MACHINERY
OF STARDOM

Henry Fonda's admonition to his daughter about the long struggle she would face quickly turned hollow when, early in 1959, his old friend Joshua Logan learned that Jane was studying with Lee Strasberg.

Logan, though not a public champion of the Method, had spent time in Moscow with Stanislavski and considered the theory worthwhile. Moreover he knew the Strasberg family, having directed Susan in the film version of *Picnic* and Marilyn Monroe in *Bus Stop*; he was particularly fond of Monroe and believed that she had gained invaluably from her allegiance to Lee Strasberg. Finally, Logan was a showman with finely tuned instincts for what attracted the public. He believed the public would be singularly attracted to the daughter of Henry Fonda after he saw how she had blossomed physically upon her return from Paris. He had encouraged her to take up acting, promising to showcase her quickly in a movie or play, and had been surprised at the vehemence with which she declined any interest in an acting career. Thus he was doubly surprised, a year later, to discover in a gossip column that she was studying acting with Strasberg. His showman's instincts began to churn.

Logan had recently acquired the film rights to a popular novel called *Parrish* and had gotten Warner Brothers to finance it with him as producer and director. *Parrish* was a sentimental love story about a young boy and girl. Logan had already signed the little-known New York stage actor Warren Beatty for the boy's part, hoping to use the picture to launch Beatty on the road to movie stardom. With the same idea in mind he was searching for a young unknown actress to play opposite to Beatty in the girl's role. When he heard about Jane being in Strasberg's classes, he knew he had to search no further. As he told me, "I immediately saw the marvelous possibilities. To introduce the brother of Shirley McLaine and the daughter of Hank Fonda together in their first movie would give the picture a wonderful publicity touch!"

Logan located Jane and offered her the part, contingent on a screen test. By that time she was fully committed to becoming an actress. Despite her father's misgivings about Jane's jumping in over her head in her first acting job—misgivings which Logan had to do much to allay—she accepted the offer.

In her screen test, which she made with Beatty in New York, Jane came across well. With no experience before a camera, she used the tips Logan gave her—mainly to relax and not to "act"—to good effect and passed the test to Warner Brother's satisfaction. Logan, even more pleased than Warners by the way Jane performed, immediately signed her to a seven-year personal contract which called for her to star in one movie a year. Ray Powers, who by then was Jane's official agent at the Famous Artists agency, told me that the contract called for her to receive $10,000 a year.

Fonda history was repeating itself, although this Fonda was one-up on her father. "I could barely contain my enthusiasm after seeing her test," Logan said. "I tested Brooke Hayward the same day. She and Jane were friendly rivals and I thought it was only fair of me to do so, especially since Brooke was my actual goddaughter and Jane was only my informal one. But Jane surely stole the show. I knew immediately that she was destined for stardom."

Jane's date with stardom had to wait a while, as in fact did Warren Beatty's. To ensure the picture's box office appeal, Logan decided established stars like Vivien Leigh and Clark Gable should play the two leading roles. When he couldn't get them, and then when script problems arose, he decided to abandon *Parrish* and concentrate on something else. Armed with Logan's promise that he would quickly find something else for her to star in, and propelled by her growing ambition to graduate from the Workshop and be accepted into the Actors Studio, Jane worked more intensively than ever in Strasberg's classes.

Meanwhile, her modeling activities were rapidly expanding. She was sent by Powers to see Eileen Ford, the owner of the leading model agency in New York, and was enlisted promptly in the Ford stable. "She was something," Miss Ford recalled. "She was terribly insecure about her looks and the impact she had on people. She was astonished to learn that people would be interested in using her, and paying her as well."

Within a short time Jane's modeling work raced ahead of her acting opportunities. With the help of Eileen Ford's aggressive marketing tactics Jane began to appear in fashion spreads for major magazines, and it was not long before she made a few covers. "I used to hang around newsstands watching the people who bought the magazines," she once said. "I thought I looked pretty, but not really beautiful." Her visibility on the newsstands turned her into a celebrity in her own right in New York. Jane was no longer being perceived solely as the daughter of Henry Fonda.

In April, true to his promise, Logan acquired the film rights to another property—a play called *Tall Story* which had been running on Broadway through the winter. It had been adapted by the well-known playwriting team of Howard Lindsay and Russell Crouse from an earlier novel by Howard Nemerov, about college basketball and gambling scandals, entitled *The Homecoming Game*. The leading roles were those of a college basketball star mixed up in a bribe attempt and his cheerleader-girlfriend. Again Logan wanted to use Warren Beatty, but he says that the executives at Warner Brothers were by that time against casting two unknowns in the leads. Forced to decide between Jane and Beatty, he chose Jane. For the male lead he opted for Anthony Perkins.

Logan sent Jane to see the play the night before it was due to close, without telling her he had her in mind for it. She sat next to Tony Perkins, the young, lanky film and stage actor who, a few years before, had costarred with her father in a Western called *The Tin Star*. "I knew Josh had already cast Tony in the movie version of *Tall Story*," Jane said. "But I didn't realize he had me in mind. I must confess I hated the play, and I thought the girl's part was too small. The next day Josh sent me the script for the movie, and wow! What an astoundingly large part for the girl. I loved the script. I couldn't believe I was going to have such a large part."

If Jane's critical faculties seemed limited by excessive concern about the size of her part, she was responding no differently from the way any other actor or actress typically does. And like most, once she knew the part was hers, she grew overly anxious about it. It had been one thing to dream of attaining stardom—the dreams bore no responsibilities and no exposure to public criticism. But now she was confronted with the prospect of actually exposing herself to the public, and she grew uneasy. She started to lose sleep, waking up at night with unpleasant dreams—mostly reprises of her childhood dreams of rejection and persecution. She also suffered from a severe case of boils, a chronic condition that had a habit of surfacing whenever she was under stress. She later said, "I knew some people in the movie busine. s would be nice to me because my name was Fonda. But I wanted to make it on my own merits. There's loads of difference between growing up in a theatrical family where someone else is doing the great things, and doing something yourself. After I signed the contract, I began to have doubts about myself."

Jane's doubts were intensified by an experience she had in June. Filming of *Tall Story* was not to start in Hollywood until September, so Ray Powers arranged for her to play the ingenue lead in a two-week stock revival of *The Moon Is Blue* at a theater in suburban New Jersey. Hurriedly prepared, inadequately rehearsed and indifferently directed, the production provided Jane with her first real professional acting job. Without her father's presence to divert the spotlight from her, she was on her own. She learned rapidly that she knew a good deal less about acting than she thought. A number of her acquaintances came to see her and were understandably liberal in their praise and congratulations, but she felt she hadn't been good. Ray Powers said, "When you come right down to it, she was miscast. She had none of the right qualities for the virginal girl she played, but we wanted to get her some exposure in front of audiences before she started *Tall Story*."

Jane tried to use the acting techniques she had learned from Strasberg, but somehow nothing worked. She could not conquer her nervousness and relax in the role. "I flopped around the stage in control of nothing," she admitted shortly afterward. "Control is what I'm after. Control is the whole kookie secret."

The experience was a sobering one. In perparing for *The Moon is Blue*, she worked diligently on the "acting problem" the part presented. But she became so embroiled in the theoretical dimensions of the character—trying to solve such questions as motivation and intention—that she never got a firm grip on it.

It was a salutary experience, nevertheless, for instead of feeling defeated by what she considered to be her failed debut, Jane resolved to improve and to refine her understanding of what it took to be an actress. Moreover, it gave her an appreciation she hadn't had before of her father's obsessive perfectionism about his craft. She may not have been ready to follow her father's advice about working gradually toward a career. But she understood his notions about "babying up to a part" as opposed to trying to swallow it whole, then flamboyantly spitting it out and calling the result a performance. And she would thenceforth be disinclined to proselytize her father in the wonders of the Method. "It's supposed to be terribly difficult being yourself onstage," she told a reporter after her Fort Lee debut. "But now that I know how hard it is, I admire my father enormously."

Not that she had lost faith in the Method. On the contrary, she began to understand more clearly what it was and how it could help liberate her from the prison of her still bottled-up emotions. And when she heard Strasberg say one day to his students that her father was more of a Method actor than most self-styled Method actors, except that he was a natural one, her faith was given a boost.

According to Powers, Logan was planning an intensive publicity campaign for Jane in connection with *Tall Story*. She was to leave for Hollywood in July for wardrobe fittings and preproduction publicity. Shortly before departing, she met with Logan and Tony Perkins in Logan's New York apartment to discuss the script. Perkins recalled, "There was a photographer there, and he wanted publicity pictures of us necking on the couch, sort of a preview of a scene in the movie. Jane turned pale. It was her first encounter with one of the absurdities of this business, and it was as if she said to herself, 'My God, is this what being an actress means?' You could see her take a deep breath and say to herself, 'Well, I guess it is, so OK, let's get it over with.'"

In launching Jane as his new star, Logan had to make sure

that she was able to handle the publicity-related activities that would be an integral part of her rise. So he sat her down and outlined his plans and expectations, coaching Jane on how she should act and what she should say in the many interviews she would soon be giving in Hollywood. Since, in *Tall Story*, she would be playing a wholesome all-American girl spiced with a dash of wanton sensuality, he tutored her on how to promote that image to interviewers and photographers. Of course she should have no difficulty, he confidently assured her, since those were precisely her most striking qualities.

Logan's enthusiasm about Jane's prospects encouraged Henry Fonda. Logan was absolutely certain that she would have a successful debut in movies and would quickly become a star. Fonda had every reason to respect Logan's judgment, and his friend's optimism lifted some of the burden of his skepticism about Jane's chances. He even began to show some interest in her work. Jane was surprised, on the eve of her departure for Hollywood, to find her father more expansive and talkative than he had ever been about acting and the movie industry. He urged her to ignore the whispers of nepotism that would inevitably surface in the press when the publicity campaign started and her association with Logan became better known. He also advised her to trust Logan and follow his dictates as a director. "But," he cautioned, "don't allow yourself to feel pushed."

"I wondered what he meant by that for a while," Jane later said. "Then I recalled. When you're in front of a camera, you automatically feel you have to do things because the film is turning. He was saying not to be intimidated by the camera, not to be forced into doing things that are unnatural, which is the mistake every novice film performer makes."

Fortified by Logan's and her father's encouragement, yet still uncertain about her ability and fearful of the consequences of public failure, Jane prepared to leave for Hollywood. As departure day approached, her tension grew even more intense than it was the day she had done her first Strasberg exercise. The day before she left, "I raced around Manhattan like mad, then ended up in tears at home. I worried about falling flat on my face and having everyone ask, 'What's all the talk about?'"

On the day Jane was born in 1937, newspapers told of American military involvement in the Far East and editorialists wondered in print about its implications in view of the Roosevelt administration's promise to keep the United States aloof from the gathering war clouds in the Orient. When Jane left for Hollywood twenty-two years later for the birth of her acting career, America's newspapers were speculating on a similar question. Two United States "military advisers" had just been killed in a terrorist attack at the Bien-hoa military base in South Vietnam, becoming the first Americans to die in a war the American people were scarcely aware of. Jane, preoccupied with her anxieties, took no notice of the stories.

chapter 9

FROM STUDENT TO STAR

Upon arriving in Hollywood, the first order of business for Jane was not moviemaking but publicity. She met with representatives of Warner Brothers to create an official studio biography. The two-page document began: "Jane Fonda is a blonde, beautiful and talented answer to Hollywood's search for new personalities. Joshua Logan is so confident in Jane's ability and popular appeal..." Studio biographies are devised primarily for use by the press. Jane insisted that no mention be made of her mother's suicide and that the fact that she was Henry Fonda's daughter be soft-pedaled. But the press, as subsequent events would prove, was less interested in Jane as a "new personality" than in the fact that she was, indeed, Henry Fonda's daughter.

Shortly after her arrival, Warner Brothers gave a large cocktail party in Jane's honor so that Joshua Logan could introduce her formally to the press and to some of Hollywood's leading luminaries. The next day some of the local newspaper accounts hinted caustically that Jane's publicity debut had been a disaster and drew the inevitable comparisons with her father, who had been there.

"The stories about my being nervous were true," Jane conceded later. "It had never happened to me before. Usually I'm not nervous, because I don't know what's going to happen.

But that day I'd been through wardrobe fittings and walked into a roomful of men and couldn't even see one female. Everyone was looking at me and I just got this tremendous feeling of cynical indifference from everyone. I burst into tears. Then I saw my stepmother [Afdera]. I went over to her, and she gave me a sedative, which relaxed me. Most of my fear at the press party was because the value of such a gathering depends a lot on what you have to sell. If you're Marilyn Monroe, a press party is great. Her strap can break or she can just stand there, and they all know her. But who cares if my strap breaks? The only thing you have to sell is personality, and I felt they were thinking, 'What's all this fuss about plain Jane.'"

Cajoled and prodded by Logan and Warners, Jane gamely kept her nose to the publicity wheel. Her next tasks were the obligatory interviews with the leading movie columnists— Louella Parsons and Hedda Hopper.

Louella Parsons, whose column appeared in hundreds of newspapers throughout the country, was the doyenne of the Hollywood gossips. So important was she considered that studio publicists cultivated her like a rich spinster aunt with a terminal disease. She didn't go to her subjects; they came to her. Jane was driven to her home by a Warner's publicity man who carefully coached her in the car about how to act with "Lolly." It struck Jane as being a bit distasteful and dishonest, but she went along with it.

"I shall never forget the way she looked when she breezed into my house from the beach where she had spent the day trying to get a suntan," Louella Parsons wrote a few days later. "She was wearing a white blouse and yellow skirt, with her hair wrapped in a tight turban, which she called her 'babushka.' In her hand she carried a bright blue balloon which she said she found on the curb outside my home—the color effect was most becoming." The publicity man had done his job well.

"Jane is a pretty edition of Hank," Parsons continued. "She appreciates that Henry Fonda is her father and that she received her first chance...because her name is Fonda. She has the same soft brown eyes [sic], light brown hair, and her profile is amazingly like that of her father."

Jane was learning to her dismay that she was not going to be judged on her own merits, and that even so astute an observer as Louella Parsons was reputed to be was no guarantee of accurate reportage.

The inevitable questions about Jane's love life and her feelings about marriage were asked. "When I marry," Jane replied, "I want it to be for all time. I have grown up with divorce, and I want to feel sure before I marry."

The rest of the column painted Jane as a wholesome, normal American girl who "loved swimming, tennis and painting," who "looked about 14 but is quite a mature young lady," and who tried to put to rest the rumor that she didn't get along with her stepmother Afdera by saying, "She improves with acquaintance."

The syndicated column, which appeared nationally on September 13, 1959, was Jane's introduction to the huge community of movie fans who hung on Louella Parson's every word. "Quite a girl, my old friend Hank Fonda's daughter," Parsons concluded. "Beautiful, talented and charming. I invited her to come to see me again soon." The seal of approval was stamped and official.

Jane's next stop was Hedda Hopper, Louella Parsons' bitter rival and Hollywood's second most influential syndicated gossip. After her, the rest of the Hollywood press corps was given its shots at Jane. She quickly grew bored with the sameness of the questions and dissatisfied with the image that began to form, yet she dutifully continued to play her role as the grateful and cooperative newcomer, taking special pains to seem at once sophisticated and starry-eyed.

Meanwhile, there was a movie to make. Filming on *Tall Story* started in late summer. "I found it all very strange. I felt alone, surrounded by lights and unfriendly faces. I didn't question Josh, though. I'd known him all my life, and I thought that if he believed I could do it, I could. But the role itself didn't mean very much. I just came to the set whenever I was called."

Henry Fonda visited the *Tall Story* set one day and watched his daughter play a love scene with Tony Perkins. He was a bit nonplussed to see how casually Jane produced the warm-blooded passion the scene called for, but was delighted at the ease with which she seemed to have picked up movie acting. Although he didn't mention it to her directly, he proudly told a reporter, "Jane has made more progress in one year than I have in thirty." High praise indeed, if a shade hyperbolic. What was important to Jane was that she had finally gotten a favorable public response out of her father.

It turned out not to be much comfort, however. Nor were Logan's gentle encouragements. The further Jane got into the filming, the more at sea she felt. Midway through the thirty-five-day shooting schedule, "I was in a total panic. I constantly felt like I was falling off a cliff. And there was this camera that was like my enemy. I hated it. I was always trying to hide from it, and I hated the way I looked on the screen when I saw the rushes."

It was a normal reaction for a newcomer to movie acting. So were her feelings about the tediousness of filmmaking. "Everybody told me how much time there would be when there was nothing to do, but it's the sort of thing you don't really believe until you're involved in it. Once I spent an entire day waiting to be called for a shot, and a newspaperman who turned up on the set wrote that I was bored. I wasn't bored." She couldn't have been, for she was in a continual state of terror.

"Tony Perkins was wonderful. In many ways I learned so much from him. He was a total professional. Take the lights, for instance. You're always working with those enormous lights in your eyes. Some people keep squinting. I went to Tony and said, 'What do you do?' And he said, 'You do it, just do it. You forget about the lights.' And that did it. I just forgot about them." So much for Method acting.

Indeed, whatever notions Jane had brought with her to Hollywood about using the theories and techniques she had learned in her Strasberg classes soon dissolved. She had too many other things to concentrate on. "It was much more complicated than I'd imagined. I always thought that you go on and pretend the camera isn't there when you shoot a scene. But that's not so, I soon learned. You have to play to the camera when you act. You relate to it in a certain way, with consciousness of the lights and all sorts of technical matters. You learn such fascinating things—like the fact that the audience's eyes tend to go to the right side of the screen, so you try to get over to the right side of the set. That's a subtle form of scene-stealing. Or you might play a scene in which you are face to face with someone. Then you do it again for close-ups and different angles. You still have to get the same intensity of emotions each time, the same sincerity, even though you are acting in those second shots all by yourself. When it was my turn to cue Tony for his close-ups with me off camera, I would read my lines and really put feeling into them. But when he cued me, he just read his lines and I couldn't work up the proper reactions. When I realized that, I told him I'd make a deal with him. If he would read my cues properly instead of just in a dead voice, I'd do the same with his. Otherwise, I would just throw them away."

Although he endorsed the Method for stage acting, Logan had little use for it when making movies and would have none of it from Jane. He wanted her simply to be as he saw her—a pretty, lively, excitable version of her father. He wanted her to relax, say her lines, hit her marks and find her key lights; he and the editors would take care of the rest in the cutting room. He knew that in Jane he had a novice actress of great seriousness and little confidence. But somehow her interior panic dominated her persona before the camera and disguised her insecurity, imparting an aura of energy and vitality. He recognized this early in the shooting and used it to Jane's advantage. It gave her character quite a different shading from the one he had planned. But by and large, he realized, it was better. He knew from reviewing the dailies that she had all the requisites of stardom and that the picture, no matter how inexperienced she appeared at times, would launch her successfully.

Jane wasn't so certain, despite Logan's assurances. And as shooting continued, she grew even less sure. Not only did she remain intimidated by the cameras and the lights, but she was convinced that the crew, many of whom were veterans who had worked with her father, were treating her like a child and laughing behind her back. Perhaps it was unjustified paranoia on her part, a compound of her fear of being measured against her father and her still deeply felt horror of being exposed to ridicule. But it deepened as the shooting progressed.

It did not take her long to realize the picture was not going to be good. An air of defeatism pervaded the set long before the filming was completed. With the help of her highly developed sense of guilt she became certain that it was her fault. But it wasn't. The blame fell on Logan's shoulders, and it was partially due to the fact that he miscast Tony Perkins in the lead role. Perkins, for all his melancholy screen appeal, was simply not athletic enough to be believable as a collegiate basketball star. Upon release of the movie six months later, Perkins' ungainly cavortings in the basketball scenes would give the film a laughable transparency that overshadowed whatever good points it had—which, with its weak story, were few enough. In spite of his skill as an actor, he was plainly miscast, and the blame had to rest ultimately with Logan.

The screenwise crew had perceived Perkins' limitations immediately and concluded that Logan either didn't know what he was doing or else was simply using the film as a vehicle to launch his "discovery," Jane Fonda. They were glad for the work and were not inclined to let Logan know of their feelings. They let their cynicism bounce off the actors instead.

Logan later said of the picture: "It was not one of my prouder moments as a screen director. I should have known better than to get involved in *Tall Story*. I did it more out of a sense of obligation to Warner Brothers than anything else. Nevertheless, I'll always remember it with a bit of fondness for what it represented—Jane's debut. I'll tell you this. With the exception of Marilyn Monroe, I have never worked with a more talented actress than Jane Fonda."

By the time filming was completed, Jane was emotionally exhausted and distraught. She misunderstood the crew's frequent *sotto voce* cracks. She was sure they had been directed at her out of contempt for her incompetence, when the fact was that they had been meant for the production itself. She felt herself a thorough failure. She loathed Hollywood and the whole filmmaking process. Like a wounded animal, she fled back to New York and the sanctuary of Lee Strasberg.

Shortly after her return, *Look* magazine came out with a two-page feature on Jane and her experiences in Hollywood. It was her first major national exposure, and it was only a matter of days before she found herself being recognized in the streets of New York and even hounded for autographs. The dividends of the Logan-Warner Brothers' publicity campaign were beginning to pay off. Within months she would be on the cover of *Life* and would be the subject of feature stories in most of the other major magazines. Superficially, she remained unaffected by the star buildup. There was no sudden imperiousness or throwing of tantrums; because of her exposure to her father's stardom through the years, she was fairly levelheaded about her own rise to fame. Deep within, however, the buildup increased her anxiety—she had visions of it all exploding into ridicule once *Tall Story* hit the screens.

Jane swallowed her apprehension and tried to resume her life as an independent young actress and model in New York. Although she now had no desire to marry, she had discovered since her return from Paris that she possessed a powerful need for a steady man in her life. Two of her serious attachments in the previous year and a half had been to aspiring actors. Her romance with James Franciscus had ended on a bored note, followed by an unexciting relationship with Sandy Whitelaw, a socialite interested in the theater. Most of her other relationships had been with actors too. By the fall of 1959, she seemed genuinely upset about her inability to sustain a relationship.

Jane blamed it on the men she had been with. "Actors are so boring," she said at the time. "It's very important for a young actress to have men around her. So many actresses tend to forget they're women, and most actors are so self-centered they don't have the time to remind them."

One of her former boyfriends saw it another way. "Jane was so insecure and hungry for love that she tried to swallow you whole. She was a tremendously sweet and lovable girl, very intense when she was in love, but very demanding too. She took much more than she was able to give. Oh, she was generous with her time and money and all that, but it was as if she used these as substitutes for real emotion. There was something deep inside her that she kept to herself and wouldn't yield, would give to no one."

Another old friend says, "I hate to sound Freudian, but my guess is that Jane was looking for a father—someone strong and secure and domineering whom she could follow. My strongest memory of her is that she was a girl who always needed to be told what to do. She had a tough time making decisions, even the tiniest decisions. But all she got were guys who were as insecure as she was, who couldn't make decisions, and she would eventually become infuriated by them and drop them. She needed badly to be led."

With her life by then uncompromisingly dedicated to an acting career, Jane was limited in her choice of men. But although she professed little admiration for actors, she continued to involve herself with them. "I spend most of my free time mothering some of the boys in my classes," she said to a newspaper interviewer.

"I'm probably the biggest little mother in all New York. Almost every one of them has some kind of problem. They need someone to listen to their troubles." Despite the trace of sarcasm in Jane's words, one of the young actors was about to become the central love of her life.

chapter 10

TIMMY
EVERETT

Timothy Everett, the son of itinerant blue-collar parents, was born in the upper Midwest and grew up in North Carolina. With a love and talent for the theater which he nurtured throughout high school, he came to New York when he was eighteen to break into show business. He was an engaging young man who could do everything—sing, dance and act—and it was not long before he had a topflight agent and a featured role in an important long-running Broadway play, *The Dark at the Top of the Stairs* by William Inge. He followed this initial success with a starring role in a second play, *The Cold Wind and the Warm*, and then was signed to an exclusive motion-picture contract by Otto Preminger. His first job with Preminger was to be a featured role in the film version of *Exodus*.

During his first three years in New York, Timmy Everett had achieved a great deal and was on the threshold of a splendid career. A slight, fair-haired young man of medium height and soft Southern voice, he was not the type to be noticed immediately in a roomful of people. But he had an energy and electricity that practically jumped out of his body and made anyone nearby quickly aware of his presence. His face was attractively boyish, and his sleeve-worn vulnerability could melt the heart of even the most jaded women. He had only one problem. To get his part in *The Dark at the Top of the Stairs*,

80

he had submitted to the homosexual advances of the play's author, William Inge, and had served as one of the much older Inge's steady lovers for several months. Afterwards, he became extremely insecure about himself and his sexual identity. In the world of witty, gregarious, preening New York show people, he became as high-strung as a racehorse.

Like many young actors in New York, Everett spent almost every cent he earned on lessons of one kind or another. He studied singing. He was forever in dance studios. And he was a member of Strasberg's classes.

"I knew Jane from class, but just to say hello to," he recalled to me in a series of interviews for this book. "During the summer of 1959 I was in Hollywood and went out to visit Tony Perkins, who was a friend of mine, while he was making *Tall Story* at Warner Brothers. Tony introduced me to Jane there, and I was surprised that she remembered me because she used to look right through me in class. Back in New York that fall, I went to a Thanksgiving party one night, and she was there with someone else—one of her boyfriends. I had been admiring her from a distance all that time, but I'd always thought she was, well, too good for me. I would have liked to have done a scene with her for Lee, but I'd always been afraid to ask her. At the party, I got a little high and worked up the courage to ask her about doing a scene. She said she'd love to."

Jane and Everett decided to do a scene from *Adventures in the Skin Trade* by Dylan Thomas. He was living in the cramped railroad flat his parents rented on the lower West Side of New York. There was no room to rehearse there, so he had to go up to Jane's apartment on Seventy-sixth Street.

"It was a beautiful place, the most fantastic apartment I'd seen in New York, with an upstairs and a downstairs. We'd been rehearsing the scene all week. I'd come, we'd rehearse, talk a little, then I'd leave. Well, this one night, after we finished rehearsing, Jane asked me if I'd like to stay for a drink. I said sure, so she made me a drink, then turned on some music. We talked a while, the lights were low, then all of a sudden we were looking at each other in this strange way. I just got consumed by this wave of tenderness and desire, and so did she. We ran upstairs to the bedroom, tore our clothes off and stayed in bed for three days."

Everett told me that the three days—undoubtedly an exaggeration of the actual time—cured him of his anxiety about

his true sexual orientation at least for a while. It was the beginning of a vibrant but turbulent love affair that spanned almost
two years and had lasting effects on both of them. They lived
together on and off for the next year and a half until pleasure
turned to pain and, for Everett, pain to suicidal despair. "It
was just fantastic at the beginning," he remembered. "We were
so much in love, and she taught me so much about the right
way to live. That Christmas she showered me with expensive
presents—I mean, I wasn't used to that kind of lavishness. I
hardly had a thing to my name, I didn't know how to act in
company, my clothes were threadbare, I had no sense of style
or anything. She taught me a lot. I taught her, too. I taught
her something about emotions, I think—you know how emotional a person I am—and I taught her about lovemaking and
how to show love."

In December, just before Jane's twenty-second birthday,
Joshua Logan came to her with a new proposition. He was
going to direct a play for Broadway, a complex psychological
drama about what happens to a well-bred young girl who's
raped by a hoodlum and then accused of inviting his attack.
The play was by Daniel Taradash and was called *There Was
a Little Girl*. Logan wanted Jane to play the lead—it was the
perfect chance for her to make a splash on Broadway just when
Tall Story was due to be released.

Henry Fonda was back in New York and had opened in a
new play himself, and Jane met with him to discuss whether
she should take the part in *There Was a Little Girl*. According
to Jane, "My father thought the play and the part weren't right
for me. It was about rape and I was to play the girl who was
raped. I think he wanted to protect me from what he thought
would be a disaster. But I thought, 'Who am I to turn down
such a part—the leading role in a Broadway play?' It was a
great opportunity. I knew that every young actress in New
York would have given her eyeteeth for the part, and after I
read for it, Josh and the producers wanted me. Three days
before I accepted the part, my father called me and begged me
to turn it down. But I didn't."

According to Ray Powers, Henry Fonda was incensed that
Logan wanted to cast Jane as a girl who is raped. He was
further angered over the question of money. "Jane really had
mixed feelings about doing the play," Powers says. "She was

getting a lot of pressure from her father over the rape thing, and in addition Logan was only going to pay her something like a hundred and fifty dollars a week, an incredibly low salary for a starring role on Broadway. Jane was sure the only reason Logan wanted her was because he could get away with paying her so little. First she wanted to do the play, then she didn't, and it went on that way for a while. Logan started reading other actresses but kept coming back to Jane. Finally, Jane decided to take the part. The whole thing was sort of messy over the business of money, and Jane became a little disillusioned with Logan."

Logan assembled the cast and rehearsals got under way in January of 1960. "I loved the rehearsals," Jane said. "I loved working with a group, and I began to see for the first time that when a group works together with real love, art happens. I savored every morsel. It was like belonging to a family. I was doing exactly what I wanted to be doing. I enjoyed making myself fit the part, making myself frail as a woman, and vulnerable and weak. I had always thought of myself as strong and independent, a self-sufficient type, the way I was brought up. Now I began to have some idea of what there was to life and what I had been missing. I loved the routine of acting in a play every night. I had had so little responsibility in my life that I loved having demands made on me—to be someplace at a definite hour, with something definite to do. I began to feel a connection with myself. I felt accepted."

Logan took the company to Boston for a brief out-of-town tryout. Everett went along to be with Jane and recalled that on opening night she received a standing ovation. "I've never seen anyone so happy. She was really good in the part. The play had its weaknesses, so did the part for that matter, but she brought more to it than was there. And the beauty of it was that it was instinctual. You could just see it coming out of her once the curtain went up."

"Doing that play was a big turning point for Jane," Everett claimed, "much more so than *Tall Story*. It was the first really important acting job she'd ever had, and the whole play revolved around her. Even though the play didn't run, she learned what it was to be an actress, what her emotional problems were all about. And she really learned that she had emotional problems. Up until that time Jane the person and Jane the actress

were two separate people. When she did the play, the two
became one and stayed that way afterward. That's when she
really started to change."

The experience was an epiphany for Jane. She received
excellent reviews in Boston, and one of the reviewers even
failed to mention her father. "The Boston critics said I was
fragile, when I'm really strong as an ox. They said I was coltish,
febrile, virginal, translucent—me! I realized I had created
something that moved an audience. From there on I wanted to
do nothing else in life but become the greatest stage actress
there ever was."

More important than her notices was the fact that playing
the part forced her to crack the vault of years of suppressed
emotion. "Now that I was determined to be a successful actress,
I had to find out how to bring out all the emotions I had learned
to inhibit. It's difficult. I used to be so polite about acting
during that first year I was studying. Whenever I read for a
part, I'd tell the director that so-and-so was much more suited
for it than me. You didn't catch me doing that anymore. I
learned that there were fifty girls just as good and maybe better
waiting to take my place. I stopped worrying about whether I
was being asked to read because I was Henry Fonda's daughter.
I began to get more confident and aggressive."

She enjoyed the way acting brought her out of herself, but
it also created further difficulties. "I began to see that the
problems of Jane Fonda the person were the same as those of
Jane Fonda the actress. Acting, when you're serious about it,
is tough. It hurts. It has to hurt, otherwise, you're not acting.
All you've got to draw upon is yourself. If you're shallow, if
you've got no emotional depth, you're not going to act very
well, especially in a part that is highly emotional. It will come
out all surface and without truth. The serious actor tries to get
at the truth of a character. To do that you have to really reach
into yourself. I was not used to reaching into myself, and when
I did with this part, I was at first surprised to find that there
was something there, then astonished to learn how thoroughly
well-hidden it had been."

Jane had a lot of prodding from Logan during rehearsals.
At one point she later remembered him saying, "I don't think
you can do it, Jane. You're going to fall behind your old man.
When the curtain goes up, there'll be a ghost of your father
sitting in the chair."

"I got so mad," Jane said. "I knew he was using every trick he could to make me do my best, but I hated some of them." She also felt the first conscious stirrings of being in competition with her father.

The play had its New York opening on February 29, 1960, at the Cort Theater. It was Jane's debut on Broadway, and she could not have hoped for a happier beginning. Although the play was roundly blasted by the New York critics as a trite, cliché-ridden melodrama, Jane's personal notices were glowing. Brooks Atkinson, the authority of authorities, wrote in the next day's *New York Times*: "Although Miss Fonda looks a great deal like her father, her acting style is her own. As the wretched heroine of an unsavory melodrama, she gives an alert, many-sided performance that is professionally mature and suggests that she has found a career that suits her." John McClain, another critic, hailed her performance as a "personal triumph," calling her "a resplendent young woman with exceptional style and assurance. Jane Fonda has a fine future but not, regrettably, in this play."

At the customary postpremiere party at Sardi's, everyone stood and cheered Jane when she entered. The play would run for only sixteen performances, but despite its failure, it served to launch Jane as a genuine stage star and galvanized her intent to excel as an actress.

She worked like mad, according to Everett. "She did scenes with me, with others and by herself. I had already sort of made it on Broadway, and now that she had it was beautiful. We were really happy together, and we shared everything. The only rough part was when we went over to her father's house. Here I was, sort of a starry-eyed young novice having to talk with Henry Fonda. I was just twenty-two at the time. I was shy and nervous and uncomfortable in that plush house. I felt out of place, but Jane really went out of her way to make me feel at home. But I just couldn't communicate well with her father. He didn't talk much, and he sort of remained aloof from everything. We used to sit down to dinner with him and Afdera, and sometimes other people, everybody all dressed up and these servants and everything sort of hushed and somber. Jane would run her hands up and down my thigh under the table, and I would have to kill myself to keep from bursting out laughing.

"I wasn't sure at the time whether Jane's father liked me or not, and that made me even more nervous. He never said much

to me, but I remember one night when I thought he was going
to strangle me. It was at a party—it was during *There Was a
Little Girl*, when Joshua Logan was leaving to go to the Coast
or something—and Henry Fonda was there. Jane gave a little
sentimental speech about Logan. Then all of a sudden she burst
into tears and went on in this very dramatic, theatrical way. I
mean it was all genuine emotion and everything. Well, later
on her father came rushing up to me with this evil look on his
face. He grabbed my neck in a headlock and said something
like, 'What have you done to her to make her act this way!'
You see, Jane never showed her emotions in public before,
and when he saw her do it, he really got upset. I think he
blamed me because he saw how gushy I was, and he figured
she got it from me.''

Henry Fonda was deeply disturbed by Jane's relationship
with Everett. In the beginning Fonda remained stoic, but as
time went on and he saw how possessive Jane was becoming
about the young actor, his dismay became vocal. His disapproval caught Jane just at a time when it would have the worst
effect on her pride and self-image. She had become filled with
the power of her potential as an actress. She was dependent
on Everett. And she was involved in the process of trying to
work her way through the tortuous maze of emotional self-
discovery. For the first time in her life she felt a burning
compulsion to defy her father—she decided that she was not
going to live under the thumb of his influence forever. But she
required assistance.

Ray Powers claimed that Timmy Everett had begun to act
as a sort of manager of Jane's life and career. He thought her
principal attraction to Everett stemmed from the fact that he
was such a powerful performer himself—"uninhibited, daring
and quicksilverlike. Jane felt a desperate need for psychological
reinforcement as an actress, so unsure of herself she was still."
Everett, with his experience and authority, provided it. Everett
had begun to view himself not only as a performer, but also
as a teacher and coach. Jane responded eagerly to his authority.
Everett thus became, for a while at least, her unofficial mentor,
as well as her lover. His increasing influence in Jane's life not
only disturbed her father, but also Logan, Powers, and others
involved in her career. Nevertheless, she resisted all efforts to
disconnect their relationship.

Commenting later on Jane's alleged dependence on him,

Everett said: "It's true that she began to look to me for guidance, but I think that was because I was the only one giving her positive input. Everyone else Jane was close to was finding reasons why she shouldn't do this or that. I was total positive reinforcement to her, so it was me she ultimately clung to.

"But there was something else, which I only learned later. It was this little trick Jane had, and I think it's really a key to understanding what makes her tick, even today. You see, she had this really profound need to get her direction, her sense of herself and of what to do at any given moment, from someone else, and it had to be a man. Now, if what she chose to do turned out to be successful, she would take credit for it her-self—she had made the right decision. But if it turned out not to be successful, then she would excuse it by saying that she'd put her trust in someone and he had misguided her—so it was not her fault. She did this with Logan on the play, and later she did it with me."

"Just after *There Was a Little Girl*," Everett recalled, "Jane and I started to see psychiatrists. She'd been talking about it all winter, and we also began to see that we had problems between each other. The main problem was with her, though. I mean, she was growing confused about herself and her emotions. She wanted to be able to feel more, and she knew she couldn't until she was able to get rid of some of the inhibitions against feeling that had been instilled in her all her life. Don't get me wrong, it's not that she was a mummy or anything like that, but she had difficulty getting in touch with the really deep feelings she knew she had buried.

"For instance, one of the things that really had her puzzled was why she didn't feel more about her mother and the fact that she killed herself and why she killed herself. I remember her telling me that when she first found out about her mother, she just laughed and then tried to shut it out. She realized this was not a normal reaction, that it was a kind of symptom of emotional dishonesty. That's it, she was bent on learning how to become emotionally honest. This became the most important thing for her. I think she felt a little ashamed that she still wasn't able to stand up to her father when she disagreed with him, that she took refuge in other men to get around facing up to him. She felt she couldn't be emotionally honest with him. When she tried to talk to him about the way she felt, he would turn off and leave her stranded.

"I talked about emotions a lot with her, and she could see that in my own way I was very honest emotionally—I mean, I may have been insecure, but I didn't try to hide it like Jane did. I let it all hang out and damn the consequences. I'm really the one who put the idea of seeing a psychiatrist in her mind, and pretty soon she was more insistent that we do it than I was. But we did it together. She went to her doctor and I went to mine. Then we'd talk about our sessions afterwards."

The Strasberg approach to acting was extremely sympathetic to psychoanalytic theory. His techniques of dramatic analysis were centered in his perceptions of what was hidden in his students' personalities and characters. He endeavored to break down the wall in each student between the actor and the person and to make them one. When he delivered a critique of an actor, his language was studded with psychiatric jargon about intention, motivation and the unconscious. His classes bore a more than passing resemblance to the group therapy and psychodrama sessions that were popular in those days, and it was not unusual for the more affluent among his students to undergo psychoanalysis once they had been introduced to the pseudoanalysis of the Method.

The language of the Method was a highly particularized and metaphorical one, which added to its mystique. If an actor was serious about the Method, he quickly learned to speak the language. Jane's reasons for starting psychoanalysis reflected her familiarity with the language. "An actor's violin is his body, inside and outside, and when you play and it's flat you say, 'Well, I better find out why it's flat. And what do I do to tune it up?' I was brought up in a very restricted kind of way—you know, one doesn't raise one's voice, one never says what one feels. If someone said something I didn't like, I would never challenge it.

"Now this is a great impediment, because to be a good actress you have to go out onstage and, to use cliché, hang out your dirty laundry, your clean laundry or whatever. In other words, you've got to be free to show whatever it is that has to be shown, you can't hold things back. I've discovered that the problems of Jane Fonda the actress are exactly the same problems of Jane Fonda the human being. I know that the better I can become as a human being, the more fulfilled I will become as a person and the better I will become as an actress."

On another occasion she said the reason she went into analysis was that "I figure this 'know thyself' business is very important for an actress. Daddy's been married four times, and I don't think its had any bad effects on me, but analysis might show that it has. And that would be useful to know, wouldn't it?"

Tall Story was released in the spring of 1960 while Jane was still basking in the reviews of *There Was a Little Girl*. The picture was universally vilified, and although Jane was not roasted the way she had feared, she was not given particularly good marks either. The most encouraging review came from Howard Thompson in the *New York Times*, who called the movie, "A frantic attempt at sophistication and a steady barrage of jazzy wisecracks about campus sex. . . . The gangly Mr. Perkins jounces around convincingly enough, but near Miss Fonda he generally gapes and freezes, and who can blame him? The pretty newcomer shows charm and promise in her film debut."

Most of the other reviews were content to draw comparisons between Jane and her father. The most charitable was *Time* magazine's comment: "Nothing could save this picture . . . not even a second-generation Fonda with a smile like her father's and legs like a chorus girl." Jane was distressed by the reception, but she quickly put it out of mind. She was convinced that she was a stage actress. "Everything is best for me when I'm on stage. That's when I come alive."

She and Everett spent the rest of the spring in a furious round of acting studios, dancing lessons, sessions with their analysts and trips out of town. "We used to take my father's old car," Everett said, "and leave town every chance we could. We took weekend trips out to Long Island, up to the Catskills, down to Atlantic City—we were really having a good time. I was staying with Jane most of the time at her apartment, but sometimes when Susan Stein was having company, we'd go down and stay at my parents' place. There wouldn't really be any room there, so we'd sleep on the couch in the living room. My parents would walk in and out in the morning, and Jane would pop out of bed and give them a big hug. She really liked them, and they liked her. One thing about Jane—she always had this respect for, I don't know, ordinary people, people who had to work, who had tough lives. . . . She always had this thing about the underdog, which was something I really liked about her. She didn't feel self-important, and she had none of the silly affectations a lot of young theater people had."

At the end of the season Jane was given the New York Drama Critics Award as the most promising new actress of the year for her performance in *There Was a Little Girl*. "It gave her a big lift," Everett said. "But by then she was so involved with other things that she couldn't stop to enjoy it. She had a play to do in summer stock at the Westport Playhouse. I had to go to St. Louis to play the lead in a summer production of *The Adventures of Tom Sawyer*, so we were apart for a while. But then she flew out to see me, and we had a great time together. As soon as we got back to New York, she had to start rehearsals for another play."

The new play was Arthur Laurents' *Invitation to a March*, a comedy about conventionality versus nonconformity. "As soon as I read for it, I knew I had to have the part," Jane said. "The part of Norma Brown was the story of me—a conventional girl, a sleeping beauty who is awakened to love by the kiss of a boy."

Timmy Everett was considered for the role of the boy, but it was decided that he and Jane were too intimate in their private lives. The role went to another actor. The production, which had a cast that included Eileen Hackett, Celeste Holm and Madeleine Sherwood, opened in New York on October 29, 1960. The reviews were decidedly better than those for *There Was a Little Girl*, and the play ran for three and a half months. Jane's personal notices were even more glowing than the play's. Whitney Bolton called her "the handsomest, smoothest and most delectable ingenue on Broadway," while George Oppenheimer of *Newsday* said she had a "glow that almost dims the moonlight. Here is surely the loveliest and most gifted of all our new young actresses." And Kenneth Tynan, in the *New Yorker*, waxed rhapsodic: "Jane Fonda can quiver like a tuning fork, and her neurotic outbursts are as shocking as the wanton, piecemeal destruction of a priceless harpsichord. What is more, she has extraordinary physical resources."

"That was Jane," Timmy Everett told me. "That was her way of foisting the blame off on other people. Actually, when I come to think about it, her father was much the same way."

Recalling the play Jane said, "I enjoyed the opportunity of working with two fine actresses," referring to Eileen Hackett and Madeleine Sherwood. "I had so little experience and knew so little about the technique of how to sustain a performance. I learned that they were able to sustain their performances whether the audience was or wasn't responding and laughing at the expected times. They could play to a full house or to a small house. At first I used to wonder at the way they did it, and then I found I was able to do it once in a while myself. In the beginning, when I first went out onstage, I always felt like apologizing to the audience. I suppose I felt unworthy to appear before it. If I sensed resentment on the part of anybody in the audience, I'd start to fade out. For a long time I felt I had to know who was in the audience. Sometimes I'd go up to the balcony to look at the faces and guess how they were going to respond to me. If I saw mean faces, I'd feel terrible."

Timmy Everett remembered the months Jane spent in *Invitation to a March* as a crucial transitional period in their relationship. "Things were beginning to happen with Jane that I don't think she even expected. She was really into her analysis, and she was beginning to dredge up a lot of emotion. Sometimes it was almost too much for her, but she kept at it with the determination of an addict looking for a fix. Oh, we were still in love, still hanging out—in fact, that Christmas was the greatest Christmas I ever had.

"Jane was always worried about my appearance and my shabby clothes. I think a lot of the flak she was getting from her family and friends about me had to do with the way I dressed. She was always buying me an expensive shirt or sweater so I'd look better. That Christmas she went out and bought me an eight-hundred-dollar cashmere overcoat. My God, that was the most expensive present I had ever had in my life. It was a beautiful coat; in fact, I still have it.

"We had Christmas dinner at her father's house, and it was fabulous."

Those were the good memories Everett had. A less pleasant one was the fact that he and Jane had begun to quarrel. "It was early in 1961 when it started, I guess toward the end of *Invitation to a March*. Jane was unhappy in the play. She liked going to the theater, but she didn't feel comfortable in the part and was generally feeling depressed. Also her analysis was getting her down—she was in a hurry to get it all out, but it was coming slowly and she was feeling frustrated.

"I was feeling pretty frustrated myself. I was supposed to have played one of the lead roles in *Exodus*, but Preminger dropped me at the last minute in favor of Sal Mineo. Out of that atmosphere we began to argue. Pretty soon we were fighting like cats and dogs. She was demanding a lot of me emotionally, and of course I had my own emotional problems. I wasn't able to give her what she needed all the time, when she needed it, and she'd get furious with me and I'd get furious with her. We were awfully young and immature in many ways. It was an unhappy spring. I could feel her start to draw away from me, and that killed me because I was still desperately in love with her. I still think to this day we might have worked it out with a little time, but I don't know. She had a lot of pressure on her, both inside and out, and so did I. But we really were in love with each other, even then when it was really bad. If we'd been able to love ourselves the way we loved each other, we might have stuck it out. But then Voutsinas came into the picture, and, well, that was that."

chapter 11

THE VOUTSINAS
FACTOR

Andreas Voutsinas was an aspiring director who was considerably older than Jane. A Greek national brought up in Ethiopia and educated in London, he had managed during the midfifties to ingratiate himself into New York's theatrical community from the home base of his cold-water flat on West Forty-sixth Street in Manhattan. Although he worked irregularly in the theater, he was a constant if mysterious fixture in Lee Strasberg's private classes and had achieved a certain notoriety as the sometimes escort and personal acting coach of several well-known actresses, among them Anne Bancroft. He was flamboyant and worldly, spoke several languages and affected an air of weary European decadence. He dressed in the Strasberg style—dark shirts, ties, jackets—and accented his proletarian garb with berets and cigarette holders. A student of directing, he occasionally landed an acting job and invariably was cast in roles that were heavily suggestive of homosexuality and sinister villainy.

"Voutsinas saw himself as the European version of Strasberg," a member of the Actors Studio recalls. "He considered himself Lee's principal protégé, although Lee didn't, and he was out to have the same influence on people Lee had. A lot of people thought he was a laugh. There was something basically silly in the way he went about it. He was so transparent about manipulating his way around that you couldn't really dislike him for it. He obviously had some attraction though, because look who he was associated with. These were serious relationships too, I mean, Annie Bancroft swore by him for a while."

During 1960, while Jane and Timmy Everett were at the height of their stormy love affair, Jane was offered the female lead in *No Concern of Mine*, an experimental Actors Studio project that was to be presented during the summer at the Westport Playhouse. Voutsinas was the director.

"I was still so in love," Everett told me, "that I didn't notice anything happening at first. I went up to Westport to spend some time with Jane. We'd be lying around with no clothes on, and Voutsinas would walk in and take off his clothes. I had a pretty good body then—Jane used to say how much she loved my body—and Voutsinas had a really ugly body. Jane and I used to joke about him. But he was really getting into Jane. I mean, he was directing her in some really deep hypnotic way, and the way he talked to her about herself began to make an impression on her. Later that summer, when she came to see me in St. Louis, she was much more enthusiastic about him. She was talking about how he had brought out a lot of sensitivity in her that she didn't realize she had."

Jane had decided that she was ready to make her bid to get into the Actors Studio. She had been to the Studio on several occasions as an invited observer and was convinced that the work she was doing in Strasberg's private classes was child's play compared to what she could accomplish in the Studio. Besides, admission to the Studio was the greatest symbol of achievement for any young New York actor—proof that one was truly among the elite of the theatrical world. Getting admitted became her overriding ambition. Yet she remained terrified of the audition process.

Voutsinas persuaded Jane to do a scene under his direction from *No Concern of Mine* for her audition. She performed before the Studio's governing board of Cheryl Crawford, Elia Kazan and Strasberg. Despite her nervousness and the rough edges she revealed, they accepted Jane. Elia Kazan said at the time, "I always thought of her as an interesting theater personality, but not until now did I realize she could be a major talent." This was high praise indeed, much more vital to Jane than anything the theater reviewers had said about her thus far.

She felt indebted to Voutsinas for having orchestrated what she thought was her greatest success—admission to the Actors Studio.

For some time Jane had been receiving weekly paychecks in accordance with the terms of her contract with Joshua Logan. Her contract was for $10,000 a year. Added to that was the money she was still making as a model, plus money she received from the trust fund her mother had left her. In the period of a year she had become financially independent. With the extra funds she had accumulated, and as a gesture of her independence, she announced that she was going to start paying her father back for supporting her after she had dropped out of Vassar. With the rest of her savings, she purchased a cooperative apartment of her own on West Fifty-fifth Street, just off Fifth Avenue, and proceeded to decorate it with expensive antiques and paintings. "I'm twenty-two and I'm spoiled," she explained to the press. "I never had to know what a dollar is about. The only way to learn is to do it myself. It gives me a good feeling to pay my own way."

Peter Basch, a well-known photographer of actresses who had been hired to do publicity photography for *There Was a Little Girl*, got to know Jane well. Just after she moved into her new apartment, Basch asked her to collaborate on a photo essay he had been commissioned to do for *Cavalier* magazine. The theme of the feature was to be Jane Fonda playing different well-known movie roles as a variety of famous directors might see her. The photos would be valuable publicity exposure for Jane, and she consented. One of the roles they agreed to photograph was from the film *Les Liaisons Dangereuses*, directed by Roger Vadim, a picture that was causing a loud controversy at the time because of its nude scenes. The scene called for Basch to photograph Jane partially nude. Basch recalled that Jane was pleased with the way the photos turned out and gave her clearance for them to be used in *Cavalier*.

"But," he said, "her father heard about it and had a fit. Next thing I knew, *Cavalier* called and told me that one of Henry Fonda's press agents was trying to persuade them not to print the pictures. I consulted with Jane and she was very angry at her father. She told me to go ahead, I told *Cavalier* it was all right, and the pictures appeared. But I understand Jane had quite a flap with her father over it."

As Jane grew more concerned about money, she realized

that her contract with Logan was constricting her financially. Like all such personal-service contracts, it contained a clause that allowed Logan to "lend" her to other producers for whatever salaries they were willing to pay for her services. With Jane becoming more of a name, her worth was escalating. Her earnings would be paid to Logan, however, not to her, and she would continue to receive the modest weekly stipend her contract called for. If Logan were paying her $10,000 a year and her services on a future project called for her to receive $100,000, Logan was able to pocket the difference.

In addition, Logan's autonomy over her career enabled him to lend her out to whomever he wished. Although she remained grateful to Logan for having launched her, by early 1961 her faith in his judgment, as a result of *Tall Story* and *There Was a Little Girl* had diminished sharply. Logan was generally well regarded as a producer-director, but many at the Actors Studio considered him out of touch with what was really vital in films and the theater of the sixties.

Among the harshest of Logan's critics was Andreas Voutsinas. His judgment of Logan did not escape Jane; she had cast her future with the Studio and was increasingly embarrassed to be associated with him. In March, her discomfort was sharpened when Logan lent her to another high-powered producer, Charles Feldman, for the motion picture version of Nelson Algren's popular novel, *A Walk on the Wild Side*.

Jane was ambivalent about it. With memories of *Tall Story* still fresh in her mind, she was reluctant to do another picture. Moreover, Voutsinas urged her not to do it, claiming that she was allowing herself to become Logan's chattel. Jane had no choice, however, short of engaging in a legal battle with Logan.

Everett said that by the time she began to make *A Walk on the Wild Side*, "Jane and I were having lots of trouble. Voutsinas had really gotten a hold over her, almost against her will. She would keep telling me, 'Don't let him get in control of me. I don't want him around me.' Then she would turn around and praise him and acknowledge her need of him because he was really teaching her how to express herself and work on all the different aspects of her emotional nature.

"I think Jane's main fascination with Andreas had to do with the fact that he brought out the meanness of her personality. He showed her a completely different side of herself. She was sick of being the goody-goody girl—it nauseated her that people only saw her in one way. Andreas was showing her—or she thought he was—how to express all the hidden rage she had, how to be mean and ugly without feeling guilty about it. She liked what that did for her. It gave her a completely new dimension. Once she learned to handle it as though it were a natural part of herself, instead of some kind of abnormality to be kept buried, it gave her a sense of power and confidence she'd never had before.

"Jane used to be paranoiac about herself. She was always worried about what other people were thinking or saying behind her back. People who are like that are people who are afraid of being found out, and they go to all kinds of lengths to keep from revealing themselves. But Jane knew that as an actress she couldn't continue to keep herself hidden. That was the great problem during our relationship, and once she started psychoanalysis and began to dig things out, she wanted more and more of it. Then she wanted to get it all out at once, the good and the bad, and Voutsinas helped by constantly getting her to act out everything she had been instinctively trying to hide.

"That's when Jane really began to change. She enjoyed the ability to be herself without feeling guilty about the impressions she made. It gave her a kind of internal toughness and security she'd never had before. We started to have terrible fights. Of course, I was just as much to blame as she was because I didn't really understand what was going on. She used to say our relationship had become like a roller coaster—you know, the incredible highs and the depressing lows—and it was. But all the time she was gaining more security, while I was losing whatever I had, which wasn't much to begin with. After Voutsinas got his grip on her, I started to become paranoid about what they were saying about me behind my back. I felt terribly threatened by Voutsinas and desperate about the prospect of losing Jane. I started doing lots of stupid things."

Jane arranged for Voutsinas to work with her as her personal coach during the filming of *A Walk on the Wild Side*. As such, he became her constant attendant—some said Svengali—and more or less took over the management of her career during the next two years. He orchestrated her development both as a personality and as an actress, much to the grief of many of her coworkers, friends and family, and was instrumental in shaping the image of the new, outspoken Jane Fonda that developed during her second movie venture in Hollywood.

Jane and Voutsinas arrived in Hollywood in April 1961 to start *A Walk on the Wild Side*. Although based on the Algren novel, the script was a loose interpretation that exploited the more lurid aspects of the book. It turned out to be a tawdry melodrama filled with unbelievable characters who were, for the most part, portrayed by unbelievable, miscast actors. Not the least of them was Jane in the role of a petulant prostitute. Jane saw the role as a chance to deflate her image as the sugary all-American girl and prove that she could play characters carved from the seamy underside of life. To underscore the new image, which the intense Voutsinas was helping her to sculpt, she started to sound off in the press.

"Two years ago Jane Fonda was a terrified youngster facing movie cameras for the first time," Hedda Hopper wrote during the filming of *A Walk on the Wild Side*. "This time it's another story. . . . She came in to see me a tall, glossily groomed young woman in an olive green suede tailored suit, hair brushed severely away from her face and coiled in a knot at the back of her head. It was soignée and very different from the shoulder-length bob and ingenue appeal of the Jane of two years ago. . . . At 23 she isn't thinking of matrimony; in fact she rocked me back on my heels with her outspoken ideas about marriage. 'I think marriage is going to go out, become obsolete,' she said. 'I don't think it's natural for two people to swear to be together for the rest of their lives. Why should people feel guilty when they stop loving each other?'"

The interview appeared throughout the country on July 9, 1961, under the headline JANE FONDA THINKS MARRIAGE OBSOLETE. Hedda Hopper's breathless reaction to what she called Jane's "radical views" may have been disingenuous, but the column provided fresh fodder for the Hollywood publicity mill. Attributed to her in follow-up interviews were such statements as: "If you're going to get married, it should be done properly. You must be able to make compromises and sacrifices, and I'm not ready to do that. I couldn't maintain such a relationship. I don't think I'll ever be able to do it and it doesn't bother me too much." And: "I enjoy my independence and the moment anyone tries to restrict me, I resent it and run the other way. Some people have a need to feel needed, but I don't." And: "Hollywood's wonderful. They pay you for making love."

To call Jane's ideas "radical views" in 1961 was certainly an overstatement, but enough readers were incensed by them to write thousands of protesting letters to Hedda Hopper and other columnists. They dutifully reported on the controversy. Of course the moguls at Columbia Pictures, where *A Walk on the Wild Side* was being filmed, were delighted, as were Jane and Voutsinas.

Jane's new outspokenness extended itself to her work as she put herself more and more in the hands of Voutsinas. Peter Basch was on the set of *A Walk on the Wild Side* to take still photographs. "There was a great deal of tension," he remembers. "Jane was adamant about playing her part according to Voutsinas' interpretation, and this caused a fair amount of trouble between her and the director, Edward Dmytryk. She was very defensive about Andreas. Just about everybody connected with the picture resented having him around all the time. I liked Andreas, and I think he probably did some good things for Jane, but I think he was also using her to his own ends. He was very imperious and didn't seem at all bothered by the resentment he provoked. But it bothered Jane, even though she tried to hide it."

A member of the crew of *A Walk on the Wild Side* recalls that Jane "was delightful to work with in every respect but one. She was warm and considerate, but she insisted on having this creep Voutsinas around all the time. I don't know what their real relationship was—I find it hard to believe that there was anything sexual between them, even though there was a lot of hugging and kissing. He was supposed to be her coach, and there was always a lot of whispering back and forth between takes and so on. I didn't get it. Voutsinas was a sort of preening little guy all filled up with his own self-importance, and he had a distinctly effeminate manner about him."

Hollywood columnist Sidney Skolsky said, "She was always talking loudly about the morons in the picture business. She refused to wear undergarments in scenes after being directed to do so, and went far past the line of duty and good behavior in the fight sequence with Sherry O'Neil. Jane bloodied Miss O'Neil's nose, hurt other important parts of Miss O'Neil, and caused one of the production staff to remark to me, 'Her performance didn't help the Fonda name.'"

Jane admitted at the time that "There was a lot of stir because I had Andreas working with me. But I feel you have to learn as much as you can. If you're not good, people turn against you, but if you try to be good in a way that doesn't seem to be necessary, they lash out at you anyway. I don't like the idea of turning people against me, but I've gotten over the feeling that everybody has to love me."

Jane was pleased with her performance in the film, but the critics did not agree when it was released the following year. The general tone of the reviews was reflected by Bosley Crowther in the *New York Times*: "As the heroine, the tall, thin actress who calls herself Capucine is as crystalline and icy as her elegant nomonym. Laurence Harvey is barely one-dimensional, and Barbara Stanwyck is like something out of mothballs. Jane Fonda is elaborately saucy and shrill (a poor exposure for a highly touted talent). Edward Dmytryk's direction makes you wonder whether he read the script before he started shooting. If he did, he should have yelled."

Nevertheless, Jane professed to enjoy making the picture. "The director and I waged a little secret fight to get Nelson Algren's book, which I knew so well, back into the picture. I think we did, too." Under Voutsinas' guidance, "I got a little humor into my role. People will remember Kitty Twist." The rest of the critics joined Crowther in finding Kitty less than memorable.

Jane continued to mine the press in order to transform her image. She still answered questions about what it was like to be Henry Fonda's daughter but made it clear that she was getting bored with them. She soon began to make irreverent jabs at her father in print, perhaps because he had publicly revealed his unhappiness over the direction in which his daughter was going. "I know it's very strange that a girl should feel competitive against her father, but that's the way I feel. I always feel that I have to prove to him that I'm right. Somehow he can't seem to separate my being a daughter from my being an actress."

chapter 12

FONDA
VS. FONDA

If Henry Fonda had been troubled by Jane's relationship with Timmy Everett, he was infuriated over her attachment to Voutsinas. Earlier, when she was still with Everett, Fonda had read about Jane's psychoanalysis in a newspaper article. "You need it like you need a hole in the head," he told her, but she had ignored his demand to give it up. Now she was talking publicly about her analysis, and out of her pronouncements about its virtues came veiled hints that life with father was what had driven her into it in the first place. "Daddy should have been analyzed forty years ago," was one of the quotes attributed to her.

During the filming of *A Walk on the Wild Side*, Jane was shown a script for the forthcoming film version of Irving Wallace's best seller *The Chapman Report*, which was due to be directed by the veteran George Cukor for Warner Brothers. Earlier she had been offered the lead in a new Broadway play by Garson Kanin, *Sunday in New York*. The opportunity to play a nymphomaniac housewife in *The Chapman Report* impelled her to decline the *Sunday in New York* offer, in which she would have had to play another vapid, well-scrubbed ingenue. Voutsinas persuaded her that to develop her dramatic potential, she should seek more roles with heavy overtones of sexuality. This in his view, was how reputations were made.

"My friends told me I was crazy to say no to *Sunday in New York*," Jane said at the time. "But I could see why they wanted me for it, and I didn't feel like doing that part again. When I was sent the script of *The Chapman Report*, people said, 'Why do it?' My reason was that I wanted to play the nymphomaniac, which I'd heard was the only good part in it. So I dressed up in my best nympho style and went to see George Cukor, the director. He looked at me and laughed. 'You are going to play the frigid widow,' he said. I was disappointed. But it was George Cukor, and you can wait a lifetime to work with him, so I took the part."

Jane leased a swank apartment just off Wilshire Boulevard in Beverly Hills. Once she knew she was going to be in *The Chapman Report*, she told an interviewer, "I didn't think I'd ever feel this way about Hollywood, but I really love it now and may be here all summer. I never enjoyed working so much before. It's partly that I've changed and partly the town. There's something different about this place. Maybe I know different people, but there's more new blood, more people willing to try new things and responsive to new ideas."

She remained publicly uncertain about her acting ability, despite her growing private confidence. But because of Voutsinas and, she claimed, her analysis, she was considerably braver than she'd once been. "I'm always in a panic. And I'm always ready to go out and make a mistake, even though I know I may be criticized. I do it because I'm always thinking my life will be over before I have a chance to do some of these crazy things. For instance, I knew that playing Kitty Twist would make me look very ugly. I thought that my career might be ended because of it, but I went and did it anyway."

There had been considerable controversy in Hollywood over the propriety of filming *The Chapman Report*, a steamy novel about a Kinseylike team conducting a survey of the sex habits of American women in Los Angeles. It was considered racy fare for the Hollywood of 1961. But despite the public arguments the making of the film generated, on release it seemed tame, and the problems of the women involved, which ranged from nymphomania to frigidity, were presented with relatively little sensationalism. All four of the female stars—Shelley Winters, Claire Bloom, Glynis Johns, and Jane—played their roles adequately.

For Jane, though, making the film was a milestone experience. The reason was George Cukor, who had directed some of the greatest film actresses of the thirties and forties. "There aren't words to describe what it means to work with him," Jane said. "He's a mystical character. He creates a woman. When you're working with him, it's like an aura wrapping you and the character and him together. He goes through the whole thing. He shoots everything fifteen or sixteen times. You know he'll protect you. He has impeccable taste and a sense of subtlety. He forces himself to love and believe in you. He's interested in talent. He had me out to his house and told me, 'I've let you do certain things now that if you did them three years from now, I'd knock your teeth in.' He teaches you discipline as an actress. I don't mean arriving on the set on time. I mean how to play in front of a camera and get the most out of a character."

Cukor was equally glowing in his assessment of Jane. "I think the only thing she has to watch is that she has such an abundance of talent she must learn to hold it in. She is an American original."

In order to do *The Chapman Report*, Jane was forced finally to confront Joshua Logan about the matter of her contract. The confrontation ended on an unhappy note. Logan later told me that the problems over the contract stemmed from the fact that he had guaranteed her one movie a year but had been unable to come up with another picture after *Tall Story.* "I tested her for *Fanny*, and although the test was delightful, she just wasn't right for the part." He also said that he had received a very high bid from producer Ray Stark for Jane's contract. He told Jane about it and offered to let her buy back her contract for a like amount, rather than sell it to Stark.

Jane said she asked Logan as a family friend simply to release her from the contract. Logan declined, but he made a counterproposal that would allow Jane to buy her contract out at a price lower than Stark's offer. "I was kind of hurt for a while by Josh's attitude," Jane told Hedda Hopper. "All that baloney about his being my godfather, that was just publicity. I grew up around him, so somebody decided it would be a good gimmick. He's just a friend of the family who was not enough of a friend to let me pay less money to get free. It was then I realized that you can't count on friendship when it comes to business dealings."

According to Ray Powers, negotiations were conducted and

Logan eventually was persuaded to accept $100,000 to release Jane. "I feel fortunate at my age," Jane said afterward, "to have been able to buy out. I paid for my freedom, but freedom is the most important thing."

Joshua Logan denied Jane's version of their contract differences, but he evinced no bitterness toward her. His bitterness was reserved for Andreas Voutsinas, who he claimed caused all the trouble. "I wasn't fighting Jane, I was fighting that so-called friend of hers, Voutsinas. I was trying to protect her from him."

When I asked Logan if he had been acting on behalf of his friend Henry Fonda, he replied, "Now, I can't comment on that. That's a confidence."

Apparently Jane was still feeling acrimonious toward Logan when she returned to New York after completing *The Chapman Report*. Henry Fonda was in Europe filming *The Longest Day*, but the word was around New York that he was extremely displeased with some of the statements Jane had made about Logan. What's more, he was by then downright furious about her relationship with Voutsinas. Peter Fonda, who was living in New York at their father's house, filled Jane in on her father's mood. Jane later said to a reporter, "Don't mention Andreas when you talk to my father. It will bring your conversation to an abrupt end."

Although Voutsinas was the number one man in Jane's life, Timmy Everett continued to hover on the fringes. "By that time I was an emotional wreck," he told me. "I was still hanging on, even though she'd made it clear that she only wanted to be friends. I was drinking heavily and generally feeling very self-destructive. One night, around Christmas, I went up to her apartment to talk to her. Voutsinas was installed there, and seeing them together after the two great Christmases she and I had—well, it just blew my mind. I was pretty drunk. I don't know what made me do it, but I rushed into the kitchen, grabbed a knife and started hacking at my wrist and hand. By the time they got into the kitchen there was blood all over the place.

"I know there are better ways to try to kill yourself, but I was so blind I couldn't even see what I was doing. Jane wrapped my hand in a towel and took me in a cab to Roosevelt Hospital. I called her the next day to apologize, and she said she didn't want to see me anymore.

"I saw her later that week at a New Year's Eve party at the

Strasbergs. We talked for a minute, but after that I never really talked to her again. Afterward, I mean for about three or four years, life was pretty rough for me. I continued to drink and finally ended up with a nervous breakdown. I just couldn't get her out of my system. It took six months in a mental hospital before I got back on my feet again."

Jane returned to Hollywood with Voutsinas in the spring of 1962 to play the female lead in the movie version of Tennessee Williams' Broadway comedy *Period of Adjustment*. She had auditioned for the play the year before when it was being cast. "At that time it was Greek to me—I didn't understand it at all. I didn't know whether it was a comedy or what. I'm sure I gave a bad reading. Then, when I was offered the movie and saw the script, I was frightened. But after I read it, I liked it. I was too young to know what it was all about when I first read the play, but since then I've learned a few things."

Nobody would include *Period of Adjustment* among Tennessee Williams' major works. But had it been written by a less celebrated playwright, it's debatable whether it would have been dismissed by the critics and public as abruptly as it was when it opened on Broadway in 1961. The plot explored the "period of adjustment" in the marriages of two couples—a nervous pair of newlyweds and a longer-married twosome on the verge of breaking up—and when it was adapted for the screen by scriptwriter Isobel Lennart, it remained a perceptive and intelligent comedy.

Jane had her hair cut and dyed blond for her role. "As a bride who cries most of the time throughout *Adjustment*," she said about herself, "I don't know how pretty I'll look. The whole story covers a period of twenty-four hours following the wedding and everything goes wrong. It's a story about the lack of communication between male and female—the old idea that a man must show off his masculinity and a girl must be dainty and weak. They're both so busy living in this framework that they go right past each other."

Of the four movies Jane had done, this, she said later, was her favorite. Directed by George Roy Hill, who had mounted the Broadway production, she enjoyed playing the nervous, nubile Southern bride in a cast made up mostly of Actors Studio people. "It was an enormous challenge for me, especially because with my two previous films, I felt I had tried but not gotten a good grasp on the characters I was playing. That was partly the fault of the scripts, but I knew I had made a lot of mistakes too. With *Adjustment* I felt that I finally got hold of a character and . . . well, I liked what I did. I became an actress because I needed love and support from a lot of people, but at the beginning I never dreamed I'd end up in the movies. A stage career is what I wanted. But somehow making movies gets to you. It's ego battering—you're up one day and down the next—and it's much tougher work for an actor, because with all the various things involved it's harder to create a performance. When I did *Adjustment*, I finally began to feel like an experienced film actress, and I decided movies were for me."

During her stay in California, Jane was offered a part in another play. It was a comedy called *The Fun Couple*, about a young married couple who are terrified that if they grow up and assume responsibility, they won't have fun anymore. The role of the wife was not unlike that of the bride Jane was playing in *Period of Adjustment*. The play was fast-paced and called for youth, freshness, fantasy, farce and tenderness. As a friend of hers told me, "Voutsinas convinced Jane that with the experience she was gaining as a comedienne in *Adjustment*, the role of the young wife in *The Fun Couple* would suit her perfectly and would give her first genuine opportunity to star in a hit play on Broadway. He also convinced her that it would be an excellent vehicle for his own debut as a Broadway director."

Jane agreed to star in the play provided Voutsinas was allowed to direct it. If it was the hit everyone expected, it would be a feather in both their caps. Jane was especially anxious that Voutsinas' directorial talent finally be recognized. She was tired of hearing him constantly denigrated by people like her father and others in the business.

The producers accepted her conditions and contracts were signed. Jane and Andreas spent most of their spare time in Hollywood during the filming of *Period of Adjustment* preparing for *The Fun Couple*, which was scheduled to open on Broadway later in the fall.

Jane also kept busy cultivating her image as the irrepressible and outspoken daughter of Henry Fonda by continuing to distribute controversial quotes to the press. Her statement of the year before about marriage being obsolete still followed her around, and she was afforded numerous opportunities to embellish on it, which she did. She also began to pontificate more caustically about her father. Even her brother wasn't spared. She criticized her father's marital record—he had just broken up with Afdera—and called him an unhappy, unfulfilled man. With equal fervor she criticized her brother's materialism and characterized him as a hapless neurotic forever trying to find himself.

Peter Fonda was appalled—he thought he *had* found himself. He had come into his share of his inheritance from his mother, had recently married, and had moved with his wealthy young bride to California. There he began to pursue an acting career of his own. "I was a conservative, a registered Republican," he says about his first years in Los Angeles. "Short hair, wearing business suits all the time, fur coat for my wife, house in Beverly Hills, tennis court, a garageful of fine cars. I thought of myself as one hundred percent upright—American and straight. I was into acting out other people's notions about who I should be—doing the right thing, being a member of the right clubs, joining the right party, meeting the right people. Being a socialite, the Blue Book thing—I believed in it, I accepted it."

When Jane's remarks about him were printed, reporters came to him for a reaction. "To each his own," he would say with a leering glance, making certain the reporters read in his face his disapproval of his sister's relationship with Voutsinas. The press sensed a war brewing and made the most of it. As a result, before he had gotten a single acting job, Peter was a minor celebrity in his own right. But he was hurt by his sister's condescension.

Nineteen sixty-two was another miserable year for Henry Fonda. His marriage to Afdera had failed. He had missed getting the lead in the stage hit *Who's Afraid of Virginia Woolf* because of an agent's misunderstanding. There was no other decent stage role available for him. He had been talked into making *Spencer's Mountain*, in his view an utterly worthless movie. His bile over Jane and Voutsinas was turning more and more sour, and now he was being called by friends to be told about her latest press utterances, which were generally aimed at him.

Jane was not surprised at the breakup of her father's marriage to Afdera. She had seen it coming—his long silences, his quickened temper, his wandering eye. But it angered her that he continued to disapprove of her personal life when his own was such a mess. Now publicly committed to a life without hypocrisy and unable, she claimed, to communicate with her father on any but the most superficial level, she continued to voice her feelings about him in the press. Then Peter began to add his voice to Jane's. "The only difference is," he once announced, "that living out in Malibu, my father sent his chicks home at night. His duplicity blew our minds."

Fonda at first kept a public facade of calm in the face of the blasts. He was proud of his children, he said repeatedly, especially Jane. "But now she is a bigger star than I ever was and has an unlimited future. And Peter seems to have settled down and has a good chance for an acting career."

But gradually his facade dropped. "I'm between planes somewhere," he told a magazine, "and before long there's a reporter to interview me, and he has a clipping that says Jane Fonda thinks her parents led a phony life. Or that she thinks her father should have been psychoanalyzed thirty-five years ago. Now it's all right for her to think it, but I don't think it's all right for her to say so in interviews. After all, I *am* her father. I mean, that's disrespectful. And some of the things she's been saying—well, they just aren't true."

By mid-1962 Jane's personal style had changed radically from that of the uncertain schoolgirl of five years before. She was an outgoing, opinionated, freewheeling woman who seemed, on the surface anyway, to have exorcised all her insecurities. She attributed her transformation to psychoanalysis and to Voutsinas, in that order, and fully enjoyed the attention she was getting. "I'm not at all like my father," she said. "I like fame. I don't go along with this stuff of hating to be recognized. I like to be recognized. I like to give autographs. My father always hated it. I never understood that. If you want privacy, you can make it for yourself.

"I used to think I was an introvert. Now I know I was just a shy extrovert. When I first went to Hollywood, I wasn't sure of my ability. I lacked confidence, so I said provocative things to create attention. Thanks to analysis, what I say now is really me.

"Before I went into analysis, I told everyone lies. But when you spend all that money, you learn to tell the truth. I learned that I had grown up in an atmosphere where nobody told the truth. Everyone was so concerned with appearances that life was just one big lie. Now all I want to do is live a life of truth. Analysis has also taught me that you should know who to love and who to hate and who to just plain like, and it's important to know the difference. Because then you learn to really love some people, really hate some people and just become passive about others."

While in Los Angeles, Jane had an ugly shock. It had been a particularly dry year in the Los Angeles area, and huge brush fires broke out in the hills and canyons above Sunset Boulevard. Scores of homes in Bel Air and Brentwood were consumed in the flames, and hundreds of others were severely damaged. The original Fonda homestead on Tigertail Road was one of those destroyed. Jane's grandmother and grandfather—the Seymours—had taken it over and had lived there for several years. "My whole childhood went up in smoke," Jane said. "When my grandmother got on the phone to tell me about it, I was more emotional than she."

According to Voutsinas, the incident proved to be a great emotional release for Jane. "It's like with her mother," he said. "When I became close with Jane, I waited and waited for a burst of emotion about her mother. But she had it sidetracked. When Jane would talk about anything in her past, in some strange way her memory would not include her mother. When we went up to see the place in Brentwood, she was upset. But then she packed all her memories about growing up there away. It was like her life started from twelve years old on."

Filming on *Period of Adjustment* was completed toward the end of June, but there would be no rest for Jane. In the expectation that she and Voutsinas would have an opportunity to share a working holiday in Greece and also, according to Ray Powers, to help pay off her financial debt to Joshua Logan, she accepted a leading role in a motion picture called *In the Cool of the Day*, which was scheduled to start shooting in Greece in July. A snag developed, however. Voutsinas, a Greek national, had never done military service. He had been promised a part in the movie, but then he discovered that he would be drafted immediately into the Greek army if he accompanied Jane to Greece.

At first Jane refused to go without him, and her agents tried to get her out of the movie. But it was an MGM picture for which its producer and director, John Houseman and Robert Stevens, claimed they had high hopes. They insisted that Jane fulfill her obligations. So, with her hair dyed dark brown and styled in severe bangs by the MGM hairdressers, she flew to Athens without Voutsinas to get it over with. Some location filming was scheduled for London in August, and she planned to meet him there. Afterward, they would return together to New York to start rehearsals for *The Fun Couple*.

Once in Greece, it quickly became apparent to Jane that *In the Cool of the Day* was one of those movie productions put together more out of a desire to provide its principals with an exotic holiday than out of any ambition to accomplish something worthwhile. The film was a turgid, sententiously romantic soap opera which featured—besides Jane in the role of a tubercular young lady—Angela Lansbury, Australian actor Peter Finch and an endless supply of Greek scenery. It would prove to be a low point in Jane's career.

Happy to have it over, Jane returned to New York to start preparations for *The Fun Couple* and was promptly honored by the Defense Department by being named "Miss Army Recruiting of 1962." She appeared at a ceremony of Army recruiters, decked out in a satin sash that read MISS ARMY RECRUITING, and delivered an animated speech about the virtues of army life and the need for a strong military force to deter America's enemies. Given her new commitment to honesty, she obviously meant every word of it, although the entire event had been arranged by her publicity agents.

chapter 13

THE FUN
COUPLE

Any hopes Jane had that *The Fun Couple* would finally give her a hit play to boast about were quickly dashed. There was trouble from the beginning, and the other three cast members— Ben Piazza, Bradford Dillman, and Dyan Cannon—grew progressively more desperate through rehearsals as director Voutsinas called for rewrite after rewrite from the novice authors.

"We started with a lot of enthusiasm and talented people involved," Jane recalled later. "But the two authors had never written a play before, and when it came to rewrites, the thing got worse instead of better."

Others connected with the production felt that Jane had suspended her critical faculties for the sake of Voutsinas, and that Voutsinas, anxious to have a Broadway credit at any cost, pressed on in the face of disaster. Says one, "the thing should never have opened. They all should have chalked it up to experience. The writing was inept and amateurish. Voutsinas' direction was murky and unresolved. It was as if he were using the production as his own personal toy. He obviously thrived on playing the great director. But he was directing a Broadway production the way he might direct an experimental scene for the Actors Studio. It was tentative and at the same time bizarre."

The Fun Couple opened the night of October 26, 1962. It was an unmitigated disaster. The audience, many of them Actors Studio friends of Voutsinas, Jane and the rest of the cast, hooted and snickered. The comments of Richard Watts in the next day's *New York Post* were typical of the reviews: "The most incredible thing about the play is that two such talented young performers as Jane Fonda and Bradford Dillman were willing to appear in the title roles. Even the sight of Miss Fonda in a bikini doesn't rescue *The Fun Couple* from being an epic bore."

"There's no use doing a play in New York unless it's a good one," Jane bitterly rationalized afterward. "It takes too much out of you. So far, I've never been in a successful play. I guess I'm doomed to flops."

Although it was true that the play was inept, Jane might have known better than to use it as an excuse for her failure. The real blame lay with Voutsinas for exploiting Jane to advance his career, and partly with Jane herself for being blind to his motives. "Voutsinas' hold over Jane was complete," says Peter Basch, who saw them often during the rehearsals for *The Fun Couple*. "She was a sweet and lovely girl and an enchanting actress, but she was tough and uncompromising when it came to defending Andreas, which she always seemed to be doing. She had put herself completely into his hands, and she was terribly unhappy over the fact that so many people thought ill of him. It's my guess that her pride kept her with Andreas long after she began to lose faith in him."

"What can I tell you about Andreas and Jane?" says an actress who knew them both. "He was the weirdest character— he gave me the willies. He looked like Satan incarnate, which I think is what got him the reputation he had. He had this accent and a kind of mad scientist aura. And he really worked at being mysterious and hypnotic. But there was something pitiful about him. I don't know if Jane dug him because he was pitiful— she had this thing about underdogs, you know—or because he was exotic and had a veneer of Oriental mystery. Or maybe he was just a fantastic lover, who knows? Whatever it was, they made the most unlikely pair—she with her sexy, aristocratic American beauty; he with his wizened features and his Transylvanian manner."

Jane's dismay over *The Fun Couple* found little relief over the next month or so. The three movies she had made in Hollywood during the previous year and a half had all been released. *A Walk on the Wild Side* was unanimously denounced by the critics, although some saw promise in Jane's performance. And *The Chapman Report* was greeted with a universal yawn; Jane was noticed, but barely. Only *Period of Adjustment* elicited positive comments.

Stanley Kauffmann, film critic for the *New Republic*, wrote about movies with deep seriousness. He was the first to examine Jane's work as a whole and in the light of high standards. "A new talent is rising," he wrote in November of 1962. "I have now seen Miss Fonda in three films. In all of them she gives performances that are not only fundamentally different from one another but are conceived without acting cliché and executed with skill. Through them all can be heard, figuratively, the hum of that magnetism without which acting intelligence and technique are admirable but not compelling. . . . Her comic touch is as sure as her serious one. Besides the gift of timing, she has what lies below all comedy, confidence in one's perception of the humorous—where it begins and, especially where it ends. Her performance is full of delights. . . . It would be unfair to Miss Fonda and the reader to skimp her sex appeal. Not conventionally pretty, she has the kind of blunt, startling features and generous mouth that can be charged with passion or the cartoon of passion as she chooses. Her slim, tall figure has thoroughbred's gawky grace. Her voice is attractive and versatile; her ear for inflections is secure. What lies ahead of this appealing and gifted young actress in our theatre and film world? Does she stand a chance of fulfillment, or is she condemned—more by our environment than by managers—to mere success? With good parts in good plays and films, she could develop into a first-rate artist. Meanwhile, it would be a pity if her gifts were not fully appreciated in these lesser, though large, roles."*

Kauffmann's article was a godsend, and although the *New Republic* was read by few people, the Famous Artists agency made sure that every important producer and director in Hollywood received a copy. Copies were sent also to the *Harvard Lampoon*, an undergraduate humor magazine that had given Jane its annual "Worst Actress of the Year" award for her performance in *The Chapman Report*. Kauffmann's article was also a vindication of sorts for Voutsinas, who was beginning to be nervous about his position in Jane's life. And for Jane, it had a special appeal over and above its favorable appraisal

New Republic, November, 1962.

of her acting talents. It had contained no mention of her father.

Jane and Voutsinas continued to live in her apartment on Fifty-fifth Street. The apartment had been decorated to the last detail and was filled with Regency and Louis XV antiques. Her bedroom was sumptuously European in style and was dominated by a huge brass four-poster bed framed by acres of gold satin canopy and covered with a huge fur rug. In the living room, one's eye was immediately drawn to a tiger and a leopard which lay silently on guard, mouths open and fangs bared, on the polished wood floor—a pair of rugs chosen for her by Voutsinas.

As a result of her favorable reviews for *Period of Adjustment*, Jane was besieged with new movie offers. She was urged by her agency to stick to comedy roles of the type she had played in *Adjustment* for it was these that audiences obviously enjoyed. She came over as bright, energetic, vibrant and sincere, and she projected sexuality and innocence with equal appeal. All were qualities audiences wanted to see, for they played on their own fantasies and sent them home happy.

Jane followed her agents' advice and signed with MGM, at a salary of $100,000, to play the lead in the film version of *Sunday in New York*, a frothy sex comedy by Norman Krasna that was enjoying a profitable run on Broadway that year. But first there was another project—an all-star Actors Studio revival of Eugene O'Neill's *Strange Interlude*.

At twenty-five, Jane seemed completely her own person to the public. True, she had inherited much of her father's looks and mannerisms. But her own distinct individuality made them only vague reminders of her provenance. Where her father spoke slowly, with a kind of throwaway inflection, she spoke in rapid-fire bursts, her voice a curious mixture of finishing-school detachment and thrumming conviction. Her eyes darted, where her father's remained fixed and distant. Her movements were purposeful and quick, with a dancer's grace and complexity, while her father's were at once shambling and economical. In conversation she had a way of ducking her head and then sliding it up and forward for emphasis, whereas her father, except for the use of his hands, remained Buddha-like. Her laugh was full-blown, nervous, deep-throated, while her father's, which seemed to come from no deeper than his teeth, was scratchy and tentative.

Jane seemed to follow some secret print in her genes that

had forged a nature totally different from that of her father. Henry Fonda had drifted into his late fifties with a rock-ribbed Midwestern consistency. Although he was an actor bedeviled by the usual actor's insecurities (how could he be an actor otherwise?), he stubbornly denied his neuroses and clung to his belief in himself as a self-contained fortress of sanity in the less than sane world he inhabited. For Fonda, acting served as a safety valve for his neuroses, a distraction not unlike farming and painting—a form of occupational therapy that enabled him to keep his anxieties at a safe distance from himself.

Jane, on the other hand, found in acting a way of coming to terms with her insecurities. She did not believe in the separation of woman from actress; indeed, her underlying goal was to unite the two. She was convinced the actor acts because of his neuroses, not in spite of it. Thus, she thought the more of herself she was able to expose on a personal level, the better a person she would be because of the expansion of her acting sensibilities. She used acting not as an occupational therapy to divert her neuroses but as a form of analysis to confront them. To her, on-stage acting and off-stage living were synergistic— although they had different forms of expression—the two worked together like gas vapors and sparks in the piston of an engine. Her job was to keep the engine as finely tuned as possible so as to ensure perfect combustion.

And combustive Jane had become. Although she'd managed to bring many of her insecurities to the surface, she was not yet able to resolve them. She'd freed one hand from the bonds that tied her to her past and was desperately wriggling the other loose. As she did so, her father sought to keep the tie bound.

Henry Fonda was interviewed early in 1963 and was asked about Jane's statement: "Don't mention Andreas when you talk to my father—it will bring the conversation to an abrupt end." Fonda responded by saying, "Well, it won't come to an abrupt end, but we'd have a short pause until we got to another subject." When Fonda talked privately about Voutsinas, however, he cursed him, characterizing him as an unwholesome influence on Jane. He held him responsible for the incomprehensible change that she had gone through and refused to have him in his house. "I couldn't talk enough about Jane and the good things she has," her father said. "But in one area she has a blind spot." This area was her choice of men. "She's going to get hurt," he concluded bitterly.

Voutsinas readily admitted that he had fantasies of becoming what he called "the power behind the throne." But on the other hand, he said, "I can't be that much of a Svengali, I really can't, you know. And I'm hurt, very hurt by Jane's father's rejection of me. And so is Jane."

Jane decided to maintain silence in the face of the growing criticisms of Voutsinas from her friends and father. She grew more furious with her father but could not discuss her feelings with him—he would simply turn away with an angry, sarcastic remark about the fool she was making of herself. Finally, in a mood of resentful despair, she gave up her attempts to win him over and turned more avidly than ever to Voutsinas for solace.

Together they continued to get their theatrical nourishment from Lee Strasberg. In addition they underwent further psychotherapy and strove to marry the esoteric perceptions of analysis with the imperatives of the Method, convinced that such a union would elevate them into the rarefied atmosphere of true artists. Most stars learn early in their careers that merely to be a performer creates its own torment. To be a performer and an artist somehow doubles the burden. As did Marilyn Monroe before her, Jane Fonda agonized before the mirror and ached through her entire body before each public appearance, even if it was only in a scene at the Actors Studio. After the praise that was heaped on her for *Period of Adjustment*, she had found that success, rather than providing security, gave birth to new insecurities.

"It's become much harder for me now," she said early in 1963. "Just to get up in the Actors Studio and do a scene is so hard. Mainly because I know that there are people there who have far more talent than I do. I know that I do have something else. I have star quality. I have presence on the stage, which may make me more important than they are. What I have is obvious, it's like a commodity and it's in demand. But in terms of acting ability, they have more. That's why it's so hard."

She was not boasting about her star quality, nor was she being modest about her acting ability. She was hardheaded and practical enough to recognize the signs of her success and what they meant, and realistic enough to comprehend her limitations. But as happens with most stars, the middle ground between her public image and private reality became a swamp of self-doubt. The questions Stanley Kauffmann had posed—does she stand a chance of fulfillment, or is she condemned to mere success?—haunted her. Under the prodding of Strasberg and Voutsinas, she aspired to art. But her knowledge of herself and her awe of what she considered the true art of the actor made that higher ground seem unreachable.

The production of *Strange Interlude* provided a particularly trying test of Jane's inner confidence. Although the Actors Studio was basically a noncommercial workshop where projects were put together and performed exclusively for members and friends, it occasionally gave birth to productions that its directors thought suitable for full-scale presentation on the commercial stage. *Strange Interlude* was such a project. It had started as an acting exercise for Geraldine Page, a Studio member who was considered one of the finest actresses in the American theater, and had evolved into a full-scale production directed by José Quintero. With Miss Page starring as the troubled Nina Leeds, Jane won the part of Madeline Arnold, the girl with whom Nina Leeds' son falls in love.

Geraldine Page, an actress of diverse and powerful colors, had practically cornered Broadway's neurotic-leading-lady market. She was no longer just another capable performer. She had become a larger-than-life type in the minds of many playwrights, directors and producers. The scope of her talent was vast, and the intensity and daring of her performances invariably stunned other actors. Jane Fonda was in awe of her. Page's ability to dominate a stage, and to plumb emotions Jane had never conceived of, gave Jane feelings of profound inadequacy.

Rehearsals for the long and taxing play lasted through the winter, and the production opened to enthusiastic reviews on March 12, 1963. The cast also included Betty Field, Ben Gazzara, Pat Hingle, Geoffrey Horne, William Prince, Franchot Tone and Richard Thomas, all members of the Actors Studio. Howard Taubman in the *New York Times* called it a "brilliant revival" and declared that "Jane Fonda happily contributed her vivacity and beauty to the final two acts."

Jane, though disappointed by the blandness of her personal notices, realistically acknowledged that she could hardly expect more while sharing the stage with Geraldine Page, who gave a bravura performance. She was content with the opportunity to perform with a superb ensemble of actors in a professional production—"an atmosphere in which art had a chance to happen," she said. She realized, nevertheless, that she was not about to gain the acclaim as a stage actress she had dreamed of.

Jane had once remarked, "I'd like someday to be as great an actress as Geraldine Page or Kim Stanley." Now that she had seen what it took to be a Geraldine Page or a Kim Stanley, she felt slightly foolish for ever having had such a dream for herself. She felt young, inexperienced and profoundly distanced from achieving the kind of controlled virtuosity they were capable of. There were too many Geraldine Pages in the New York theater—actresses who had the magic gift of ripping a character apart, then putting it back together with a uniqueness that made it their exclusive property. It had to do with that mysterious gift of intuition a great actor possesses, the ability to perceive totally the truth of a character and bring it out with full-bodied and unerring certainty. Jane had been intellectualizing for two years about making art, but art in acting had nothing to do with the intellect. It was pure and simple instinct coupled with the emotional depth and intellectual intuition she did not possess. She had talent, yes, and she had an actress' temperament—in short, she could act. But the sobering experience of *Strange Interlude* convinced her that she did not have the sort of acting genius that made art possible.

Shortly after the opening of *Strange Interlude*, the first revealing, in-depth story about Jane appeared in the *Saturday Evening Post* under the byline of Alfred Aronowitz. The article probed beneath Jane's public image and presented a fairly accurate picture of her joys and her torments.

The same issue of the *Post* contained the first article to be published in the popular American press about the United States' growing involvement in Vietnam. Entitled "The Long and Lonely War in South Vietnam," it described in alarming terms, with pictures, what was happening in the Vietnam of 1963. An accompanying editorial warned: "Americans are going to have to get accustomed to the fact that the war will be a long one."

Jane in the meantime was busy adjusting her sights. She went directly from *Strange Interlude* into the filming of *Sunday in New York*, the picture that would finally establish her in the eyes of the American public as a full-fledged movie star. *Strange Interlude* was the last play in which she would appear.

Although Jane despaired of ever possessing the monumental

emotional resources of someone like Geraldine Page, she was, at twenty-five, a highly charged young woman who exuded a smoldering sensual urgency that registered well on the screen. Coached by Voutsinas, she used this quality to good advantage in the filming of *Sunday in New York*, a picture that was to become the template of her movie future as a clean-cut sex symbol.

Sunday in New York, most of which was filmed in Manhattan with Cliff Robertson and Rod Taylor in costarring roles, had been a minor, trite Broadway sex comedy. It was transformed for the screen by director Peter Tewkesbury into a stylish but still trite Hollywood sex gambol—a bit more daring than similar comedies of previous years, but cut from the same cloth. Jane played a single girl living in New York who was caught in a web of farcical sexual intrigue. The story was necessarily short on frankness and long on innuendo, and the stock salaciousness of its dialogue gave the script whatever humor it had. In many respects, Jane's character of Eileen Tyler was the most difficult she'd ever had to play because of her one-dimensional mock innocence. The character was cousin to the cheerleader in *Tall Story*—Jane's intervening film roles had been more on the order of character parts—but she managed to infuse it with an amusing credibility. "Making the picture was completely fun from start to finish," she said, "which is more than I can say for the other films I've made. The part could have been boring, but it wasn't. I'm sure this movie will help my career."

It did. When the picture was released in February 1964, her reviews were unanimously favorable, even though the film itself was dismissed as inconsequential. Stanley Kauffmann came in with another commendation for Jane, somewhat mitigating the lingering effects of the reviews she had received earlier for the dud she had made in Greece. "Jane Fona's last film, *In the Cool of the Day*, was an unsurmountable disaster," Kauffmann wrote, "but it does not disprove her comic powers in *Period of Adjustment* and the current *Sunday in New York*. Miss Fonda has wit.... It is in the immediacy of her voice, her readings of lines, her sharp sense of timing. The combination of her slightly coltish movements and her unpretty but attractive face gives her a quality that cuts agreeably across the soft grain of other young actresses. Her presence has the instant incisiveness and interest that are usually summed up in the term 'Personality.' This last is certainly not identical with talent.

Alex Guinness has large talent, but little personality. Miss Fonda has considerable of both. It is still worth wondering—up to now, anyway—what will become of her?"

By the time Kauffmann reasked the question he had first posed a year and a half before, Jane was well on her way to providing the answer.

chapter 14

PARIS
REDUX

Along with its other effects, the assassination of John F. Kennedy on November 22, 1963, was a particularly demoralizing event for millions of progressive Americans of increasingly libertarian instincts. Kennedy was their demigod. His youthful, wry style of leadership and his sophisticated but wittily self-effacing manner created an appeal that ignited the idealism and the imagination of a generation of people hungry for the promise of a new national lifestyle. Dwight Eisenhower, with his down-home grin and his look of eternal befuddlement, belonged to the older generation. Now, with Kennedy at the nation's helm, it was young America's turn.

When Kennedy was assassinated, the youth of America aged overnight. No matter how false the myth of Camelot might eventually turn out to be it was as if their life-sustaining juices had been extracted through the barrel of a rifle and replaced with the anguished fluids of despair.

Kennedy's murder was the watershed experience of the new American consciousness that had been evolving out of the do-nothing fifties. That consciousness had already drawn the plans for a reinvigorated society and was merely waiting for Kennedy to implement them. When he was killed, the already growing reaction against commercialism and materialism surged forward with the driving inevitability of an express train. This was the new America, and as it evolved over the next ten years it would pass through three basic, overlapping phases.

The first was the love-and-flower phase, a reaction against the violence symbolized by the assassination and the shattered promise of the Kennedy years. The second was the drug-sex-violence phase, which sought to create and define an alternative worldview representing the millions of disenfranchised young—and not-so-young—of America. The third was the activist phase, the frantic application of that worldview to the monolith of America's hypocritical respectability. Bound together by the communicative power of music, fueled by the escalating Vietnam War, and promoted by the media's pandering to the country's vicarious yet often self-righteous fascination for the startling and outrageous, the three phases eventually became one—a diffuse yet loosely unified subculture that dubbed itself the counterculture movement. Primarily the manifestation of white, educated, middle-class youth, along the road the movement picked up others among the more seriously alienated and socially or politically oppressed—Blacks, Indians, socialists, anarchists, women, the poor.

As the popular mirror of both the conventions and aberrations of America, Hollywood, with its financial appreciation for the nation's taste for the bizarre, quickly began to exploit and reflect the new culture. At the time of Kennedy's assassination, Hollywood had already embarked on a desperate effort to become Europeanized. The French New Wave had begun to have a serious impact on the American movie industry. Television was sucking movie audiences away from the theaters in droves, and what was left of the market for motion pictures largely ignored the traditional Hollywood "product" and flocked to see the "more honest" films from Europe. In an attempt to recover their audiences, American films rapidly became infused by the cinematic techniques and mannerisms of the European cinematic style—blurry, slow-motion love scenes, split-second flashbacks, improvised dialogue, the roller-coaster effects of the handheld camera, nudity and sexual frankness, and a taste for closeups of glamorless, proletarian faces. The European influence, coupled with the movie industry's concern to exploit young America's rapidly expanding interest in film as a serious art form, helped shape a new Hollywood. It was a Hollywood that would eventually become a major outpost of the counterculture, as that movement attempted to transform the values and life-style of much of America to conform to its radical, hedonistic, hypocrisy-free vision.

Having decided to concentrate exclusively on advancing herself as a major film actress, Jane Fonda's aspirations meshed well with those of the new Hollywood, which was about to find its evolution accelerated by the Kennedy assassination. Where else could Hollywood go to learn the popular new French film techniques at first hand than to the successful French film producers and directors? And where else could Jane Fonda go to expose herself to these techniques than to Paris?

After finishing *Sunday in New York*, Jane left with Voutsinas for Paris in the early fall of 1963 to star in an MGM-sponsored picture by the well-known French director Réné Clément. The film, called *Joy House*, costarred the popular French actor Alain Delon and was one of Hollywood's first attempts to capitalize on America's fascination with the New Wave. Characteristically, as in most attempts to make quick capital of a misunderstood mass enthusiasm, the picture would turn out to be a dismal failure.

Jane's trip to Paris was carefully planned by the experienced MGM image makers, and she arrived in a fanfare of publicity. It was quite a switch for the girl who had arrived there five years before as a lonely, unhappy student inept in the language and feeling like a fish out of water. "This time I had a girl linguist with me, and I didn't speak one word of English for two months. And all that publicity, with reporters constantly crowding in—they adore my father in Europe. All this, mind you, in my French. It was wonderful. I never felt so good."

She was an instant celebrity and could not go anywhere without being recognized. During the next few months most of the French magazines published feature stories about her. The press delighted in her technically correct but idiomatically fractured French, and it printed her wisecracks and malapropisms as rapidly as they rolled off her tongue. She captured the French fancy even further with a dazzling performance on a television interview show. She covered her hair with an old straw hat but wore a revealing blouse and bikini that showed off her long, shapely legs to advantage. She amused her viewers by calling everybody "thou," a rare form of address in France, and by making such remarks as, "I sent a check to my father recently—he spent a lot of money on me, and it's only natural that I should help him out."

Jane gained even more frenzied publicity when it was reported that she was the reason for the breakup of her costar Alain Delon's much-publicized romance with actress Romy Schneider. Delon, one of France's most adored heartthrobs and a young man with a reputation as a Peck's Bad Boy—he was poor-born and was rumored to have connections to the French underworld—was intrigued by the aristocratic, outspoken Jane. She, in turn, was captivated by Delon's limpid good looks and his cocky self-assurance. "I will undoubtedly fall in love with Delon," she announced to the press. "I can only play love scenes well when I am in love with my partner."

Film flackery, to be sure, but Jane thoroughly enjoyed her new sex-and-sin image and cooperated willingly in expanding it. She knew she wasn't like that—she was still Jane Fonda, after all, the well-mannered young woman of impeccable background. But being in France and speaking the language somehow made the whole business more fun than it would have been in America. She discovered she could say things that would be inappropriate vulgarities in English but had a delicious drollery in French. As her French became more proficient, she delighted in trying them out.

Joy House, which was called *Ni Soufs* (*Neither Saints nor Saviors*) in French, was conceived as a taut suspense thriller in the Hitchcock vein. It turned out to be an absurd, contrived melodrama. The story has Alain Delon as a small-time mobster on the lam from some underworld cohorts he had cheated. Pursued to the Riviera, he is saved by Lola Albright, playing a Salvation Army-type angel of mercy, and Jane Fonda, an expatriate Cinderella. From there the plot twisted and turned, alternating implausible sexual intrigues with absurd mysterious horrors.

When *Joy House* opened some months later, critics and public alike howled. The gumbo of a plot was thickened by the grafting on of bizarre chase music. Clément's script tried to be clever, witty and offbeat but succeeded only in being ridiculous. Jane didn't fare well with the critics either. "Miss Fonda has some mysterious hold over Miss Albright," Judith Crist wrote in one of the kinder reviews. "It's not all Miss Fonda has—or at least she so attempts to indicate by alternatively impersonating the Madwoman of Chaillot, Baby Doll and her father Henry; she's a sick kid, this one."

Jane knew she was in a clinker well before the film was

released. "As usual in Europe, there was no script and very little organization," she said, anticipating the reviews. "It sort of threw me because I'm used to working within a structured framework. There was just too much playing it by ear for my taste."

During the filming, the publicity Jane had generated on her arrival in France intensified, largely because of her reputed affair with Delon. A pop song likened Jane to a gazelle, and the editors of the elitist magazine *Cahiers du Cinéma* put her on its cover and interviewed her for eight pages—coverage usually reserved for the haughtiest of film directors. Comparisons to Brigitte Bardot became more and more frequent. "La BB Americaine," Jane was called, and from a physical point of view the characterization was not far off the mark. Jane was not beautiful in the classic sense, but her striking face, her lithe, boyish body, and her flippant sensuality sparked the French imagination. With her long hair dyed blonde for the movie, and with the natural pout of her mouth emphasized by lipstick, she bore a resemblance in photographs to Bardot that was sometimes uncanny.

The French saw in Jane if not another Bardot, some exotic combination of Annie Oakley and Sheena, Queen of the Jungle, and the press fell all over its inkpots attempting to describe her. Most of the prose came out purple. "A young wild thing galloping too fast, bursting into flame too easily . . . a revelation," went one account. "A super BB, a cyclone of femininity, a marvelous baby doll," went another. "On the outside, she's true to her image," wrote journalist Georges Belmont, "tall, blonde, the perfect American, with long, flexible movements. Inside she is sultry and dangerous, like a caged animal. . . . I watched her move and thought in a flash of the black panther I used to watch in the zoo."

Under the circumstances, Jane was a dead cinch to gain the attention of France's leading public fancier of feline women, director Roger Vadim. Vadim had "discovered" a large number of the nation's most celebrated sex stars, among them Bardot, Annette Stroyberg, and Catherine Deneuve, and had more or less married most of them.

Vadim was about to start a remake of the postwar French film classic *La Ronde*. It had been based on the German play *Reigen*, a sly comedy of errors revolving around sex, by Arthur Schnitzler. Vadim intended to take advantage of the increased permissiveness toward sex and nudity on film, much of which he had been responsible for, and shoot *La Ronde* in a contemporary, freewheeling style. When he saw the impact Jane Fonda was having on the French public, he decided to add her to the picture.

Vadim's real name was Roger Vladimir Plemiannikov. His father was a Russian refugee from Bolshevism who became a French citizen and died when Vadim was nine. Born in the early 1920s of a French mother, Vadim studied for the French consular service until the war and the German occupation interrupted his education. After the war he worked as a journalist before trying his luck as an actor. By 1950 he had given up acting for more mental off-camera chores when he encountered Brigitte Bardot on a movie lot. Others may have seen her first, but none showed the enterprise of Vadim. He staked his claim by moving into the home of Bardot's prosperous middle-class parents. She was sixteen at the time and had been trying to break into movies by doing bit parts. When she was eighteen and still an unknown brunette, she and Vadim were married.

By the time Bardot became twenty-one she was blonde and, if not famous, at least notorious—thanks to Vadim. He took photos of her scantily clad and distributed them to agents and movie scouts. He got her parts in nine movies within a three-year period and established her in the public eye as an amoral child-woman. Not satisfied with her progress, or his, he decided to direct her himself in a film designed to make her "the unattainable dream of every man."

The picture, *And God Created Woman*, achieved the image he was after for Bardot and did almost as much for him. But the movie destroyed their marriage. During the filming of the picture's key lovemaking scene, Vadim ordered Bardot's leading man, Jean-Louis Trintignant, to act as if he meant it. The actor did as he was told, and Bardot discovered that she meant it, too.

While their divorce was in the works, Vadim directed Bardot in *The Night Heaven Fell*. During the shooting Vadim's new love, a Danish model named Annette Stroyberg, was in constant attendance. At dinner every night, Vadim was said to treat his wife as a younger sister and Annette as a lover. Everyone appeared happy with the arrangement, and when news of it reached the press, the three were heralded as examples of the new carefree morality.

Bardot got her divorce in December 1957. The next day, Vadim became the father of a daughter, Nathalie, born to Annette Stroyberg on her twenty-first birthday. "What is there to be ashamed of," Annette demanded to know when the news was treated as a scandal. "I love Roger." Brigitte offered to be the baby's godmother but was graciously turned down.

Stroyberg and Vadim finally got married in June 1958. Then he revealed his plan to transform her into another Bardot. He changed her screen name to Annette Vadim and starred her in a slapdash movie about a vampire woman. Just as the picture was about to be released, French newspapers broke another scandal. Annette, they reported, was having an affair with French singer-guitarist Sasha Distel, who had enjoyed brief fame as one of Brigitte Bardot's lovers during the later stages of her marriage to Vadim. An exchange of letters between Vadim and Distel was leaked to the press, reportedly by Vadim himself, and the vampire movie opened to standing-room-only crowds.

In his next picture, Vadim went all out to establish Annette as Bardot's successor. He starred her in the nude opposite Trintignant in a film entitled *Les Liaisons Dangereuses*. The picture was held up for two years due to financial and censorship problems, but when it was finally released, it cemented Vadim's reputation as a shameless, free-living, naughty-erotic Pygmalion. In the meantime in 1960, he divorced Annette, claiming that Distel was still hanging around and that "I want to escape the ridiculous situation of the cuckold." In France, where cuckoldry was viewed as a serious matter, the masses sympathized with him. He managed to retain custody of his daughter.

When Vadim traveled to the United States in December 1961 for the delayed opening of *Les Liaisons Dangereuses* (it was generally panned), he brought along his new mistress and protégé, Catherine Deneuve, a delicate eighteen-year-old Parisian blonde. "She is my fiancée," he announced, "and when I have a fiancée, I marry her." He also vowed that he would make Deneuve as big a star as Bardot and Stroyberg. When Vadim failed to marry her after she gave birth to his son, Deneuve declared that it was all right with her. "I'm against marriage," she told the press. The two lived together for another year or so, then went their separate ways—she to become a star on her own, he to seek another Galatea.

Vadim, tall and stoop-shouldered, had the magnetism and high-voltage charm of a star himself, although he lacked the standard matinee idol's good looks. His long mournful face, generous nose and seemingly tombstone-sized teeth gave him a strong resemblance to the French comic actor Jacques Tati. Nevertheless, he had a commanding way with impressionable young women and a reputation as an accomplished lover. He effectively mixed quiet self-assurance with shy, boyish vulnerability and was well liked by almost everyone who knew him—except for many of those who had to deal with him financially. His reputation as a man with an insatiable sexual appetite was overblown by the press, but he did have an abiding need for regularity and variety, and he obviously enjoyed playing sexual teacher to a series of invariably beautiful and obliging students. By 1963 he was something of an envied hero in France. Consequently, when it became known that he had turned his attentions to Jane Fonda, the entire nation, with the help of the press, held its collective breath.

"I met Vadim that first time in Paris when I went to study painting," Jane recalled later. "I heard things about him then that would curl your hair. That he was sadistic, vicious, cynical, perverted, that he was a manipulator of women, *et cetera*. . . . Then I saw him again in Hollywood a couple of years later. He asked me to meet him for a drink to talk about doing a picture. I went, but I was terrified. Like I thought he was going to rape me right there in the Polo Lounge. But he was terribly quiet and polite. I thought, 'Boy, what a clever act.' Then back in Paris the second time, he wanted to talk to me about doing *La Ronde*. Okay, I'm older, and I think, 'Christ, I never gave the guy a chance.' This time—well, I was absolutely floored. He was the antithesis of what I'd been told. I found a shyness. . . ."

Celebrated as a bon vivant, Vadim also had a *petit bourgeois* side that amused his friends. He enjoyed nothing more than presiding over a house with wife and children and having friends in for dinner and informal salons. A witty, intelligent conversationalist—he spoke several languages—including Russian, he suffered fools patiently and was considerate of anyone who sought his company. By the time he met Jane, he was more a wry observer than a participant in the freewheeling life around him, and he usually behaved with a remote dignity—even in sexual matters—that belied his public image. In many ways, not just physically, he bore a startling resemblance to Henry Fonda.

Whether it was because she thought her part in *La Ronde* was an exceptional one or simply because the moth could not resist the flame, Jane agreed to work with Vadim. His personal authority, sophistication and self-assurance, which he mixed like a master alchemist with his sad-eyed vulnerability, further captured Jane's fancy once she started filming. "I began making the film, and I fell in love with him. I was terrified. I thought, 'My God, he's going to roll over me like a bulldozer. . . . I'll be destroyed. . . . My heart will be cut out. . . . But I've got to do it.' And I discovered a very gentle man. So many men in America are . . . men-men, always having to prove their strength and masculinity. Vadim was not afraid to be vulnerable—even feminine, in a way. And I was terrified of being vulnerable."

The relationship that ensued was inevitable. Vadim was a man who held the view that modern society's conventions were outmoded and hypocritical, especially those dealing with sexuality and marriage. He had promoted his convictions through his work and life until they were of a piece in the public mind with the man himself. He was also a man who relied on the largesse of others; he was hardly wealthy and depended on the generosity of friends, often women, to see him over financial rough spots. No man approaching forty, with two marriages, two children and countless affairs behind him, falls helplessly in love. There is invariably a certain strategy and design in his response to the woman who attracts him. With his career becalmed by a string of flops, he saw in Jane an opportunity to revive it, not only with *La Ronde* but in the long term as well.

For her part, Jane was in the process still of questioning the attitudes and values of her upbringing. In Vadim's discourses on decadence—it was his contention that conventionality was what made society decadent, not freedom and sensuality—she found comfortable support for her continuing need to rebel against what she felt was society's hypocrisy. In addition, she required a strong man in her life—not a repressive one like her father, but one who would control and direct her while at the same time encouraging the expansion of her spirit and broadening her ability to live without the guilt and recrimination with which she had been raised.

Her role in *La Ronde* required Jane to spend most of her time in bed, alternating between her character's lover and husband. The film was being shot in French (it would be dubbed into English for its American release), and Vadim spent a great deal of his spare time patiently coaching Jane on her accent. Since the picture was designed to exploit its sexual content, he also coached her in the techniques and subtleties of lovemaking. Studio technicians said that they watched the Fonda-Vadim love affair develop right before their eyes, and that Jane proved to be an eager and pliant student.

Jane acquired a luxurious apartment in a seventeenth-century house on the Rue Seguier, close by the left bank of the Seine. It did not take long before Vadim moved in. *La Ronde* was completed in January 1964, and thereafter the two conducted their affair in strictest privacy, much to the dismay of the press. They frequently dropped out of sight for days while newspaper speculation mounted. Occasionally the press was able to confirm—with conveniently available photos—that they had spent a couple of weeks skiing together in some remote village of the French Savoy or had stayed with friends in a town on the Atlantic, but mostly the stories concerned the secrecy of the Fonda-Vadim romance. This was not like Vadim at all, the newspapers contended; he must be doing it out of deference to "La BB Americaine" (Americans, after all, were not as liberated as the French).

The concept of vulnerability seemed to be the key to their mutual attraction. Of the beginnings of their romance, Vadim later said, "Like all the women I have been involved with, she had a... vulnerability. Nothing is more attractive than vulnerability in a woman. She wants to be beautiful but is not sure that she is. She wants to be happy but manages always to be unhappy. Jane always thought that to be happy you must build walls to protect yourself from unhappiness. If I taught her anything it was to be more herself, not to be afraid. Later, she became more open. But in the beginning... you ask if the walls were high? They were a fortress! The Great Wall of China! She was very afraid of me, but attracted too. So she decided, 'Okay, I will do what I feel and then leave and never see him again, and the problem will be over.' So it was an easy conquest for the first few days. She was fighting the enemy by running out of the citadel and into his arms. But then, she discovered it was not over, and she retreated again behind her walls.

"Living with her was difficult in the beginning. One can

fall in love fast. But to know if you can live with some-one . . . that takes longer. She had so many—how do you say?—bachelor habits. Too much organization. Time is her enemy. She cannot relax. Always there is something to do—the work, the appointment, the telephone call. She cannot say, 'Oh, well, I'll do it tomorrow.' This is her weakness.

"Her strength? Jane has a fantastic capacity for surviving. She learned long ago how to be lonely. She can be very—in French we say *solide*. For me, what was attractive was her attention to other people. She knows how to listen. This is so rare, especially for a woman. She opens her mind, tries to understand. Others try to change a man. Jane accepts him for what he is."

chapter 15

LA LIAISON DANGEREUSE

Jane returned to the United States in mid-February to do a series of publicity promotions for the opening of *Sunday in New York*, leaving Vadim in France to wrap up the technical work on *La Ronde*. Although she was in love with him, she was careful to avoid all mention of Vadim to anyone but her closest friends, since she wanted more time to test the validity of her feelings before confirming them publicly. Besides, she knew what the American press would do if it got wind of the affair. They were still writing about her romance with Alain Delon, and Jane did nothing to discourage their conclusions that she was pining for Delon.

Her reviews for *Sunday in New York* were unanimously favorable. She went through a round of interviews in which she claimed she would never appear in a nude scene ("Personally, I couldn't appear nude—I'm too modest"); commented on some of the stories that had surfaced about her in her absence ("It doesn't surprise me to find a lack of good in people—it neither surprises me to find betrayal from friends"); and conceded that she and Voutsinas had broken up but still remained friends. And she philosophized on the mores of life, sex and marriage, unconsciously revealing the effects her secret affair with Vadim had had on her thinking.

Jane also debunked some of Hollywood's anxiety over European films. "After being in France, I realize how much we take our movies for granted," she said. "The French really

know and love American movies. They have a set of American
directors they really flip over—Hitchcock, Cukor, Stevens,
Kazan, Sturges . . . to me it was incredible. And it's no superficial appreciation. They can discuss American films in detail,
and a lot of movies that open and close in a week in the United
States are considered masterpieces there. There's a certain fla-
vor and type of thing we do here that is unique to them. Most
of our producers and directors put a feeling of virility into their
films. Eurpoeans like our Westerns because they express masculinity and strength. You hear the most arty, highbrow talk,
the most cerebral discussions about our Westerns. It's funny—
for ages the Europeans have wanted to make movies the way
we do, and now Hollywood is trying to imitate the Europeans."

She was glad, however, that American moviemaking was
no longer centered in Hollywood. "I enjoy making pictures
abroad, but I'm no runaway actress and wouldn't want to live
there permanently. My home is New York."

When asked how she would enjoy acting in a play or movie
with her father and brother—Peter had by then made four
pictures—she said, "Good God, no. It would be awful. I couldn't
stand it, and neither could they. First, Peter's still got to find
himself as an actor, and it would hurt him to be subjected to
both of us—Dad and me—at the same time. Maybe Dad and
me in television, but only maybe. The filming could be done
in two weeks. I guess we could stand each other that long."

After a month in the States, Jane was anxious to get back
to Paris and Vadim. Her first tasks on her return were to make
an English sound track for *La Ronde*, which was now being
called *Circle of Love*, and to dub *Joy House* into French. Completing these, she and Vadim left Paris for a quick trip to
Moscow, a first visit for both. Vadim had long wanted to see
the land of his paternal forebears. His feelings for Jane had
given him the impetus to go.

Jane was reluctant to make the trip at first—she still had
the typical American's prejudice against Russia. Once she got
there, however, she couldn't have been more astounded. She
found Moscow completely different from what she'd imagined
and discovered the Russian people to be almost the total opposite of what she had been led to expect. When she returned,
she said, "I couldn't believe it. All my life I've been brought
up to believe the Russians were some alien, hostile people
sitting over there just waiting to swallow up America. Nothing

could be further from the truth. I was amazed how friendly and kind and helpful they were. My eyes were really opened to the kind of propaganda we've been exposed to in America. Every American should go to Russia to see for himself. They'd have a completely different idea of the people."

In interviews over the next few months she never failed to mention her discovery, but few reporters or publications printed her thoughts. As one editor said later, "Who cared what Jane Fonda thought about Russia? We did her a favor by keeping that stuff out of print. The American people wanted to know about her sex life, not how noble she thought the Russians were. If we'd printed that stuff, she would have turned into box-office poison."

No one who visited Jane in France that summer came away without an earnest lecture about how the American people were being deceived by their government, their schools and their press. In her first venture into political commentary, she was feverish in her condemnation of America's ignorance of Russia. She claimed that the United States' phobia was being fostered by the government solely in order to keep incumbent politicians and military people in power. She saw America's paranoia over Russia and Communism—a paranoia that she admitted she herself had long suffered—as a giant hoax. In her view, Russians weren't aggressive at all. Yes, their government was just as guilty as the United States' in creating international tension and distrust. But after all, the Russians had more reason to feel that way after what had happened to them in two world wars. If only the people could make decisions about how they were supposed to feel toward each other, instead of governments!

It was the summer of the notorious Tonkin Gulf incident in the Far East. In May 1964, President Johnson had received a secret thirty-day scenario from his advisers for graduated military pressure against North Vietnam that would culminate in full-scale bombing attacks. The scenario included a draft for a joint Congressional resolution that would authorize the President to use "whatever is necessary" with respect to Vietnam. The measure, known as the Tonkin Gulf Resolution, was overwhelmingly approved by Congress. It opened the way for major escalation of the war, and it effectively gave the President the power to wage war without any further Congressional approval.

Jane, who had just returned from Russia with somewhat of a convert's passion, was exposed daily to the cynicism of the

French, themselves veterans of the Vietnamese conflict, over America's inability to grasp the dimensions of the conflict. The Tonkin Gulf Resolution presented her with a real snag. Up to that point in her life she had developed no strong political consciousness. Except for her natural compassion for the oppressed and her lingering schoolgirl's idealistic desire for justice and equality, she had never thought or acted in political terms. Suddenly she felt the stirrings of political awareness. But unread and uneducated in contemporary events, she was at a loss over what to do about them.

Jane and Vadim spent most of the summer of 1964 in St. Tropez, the old Mediterranean fishing port that had become the fashionable resort of French cinema celebrities. Jane learned quickly to overcome her natural possessiveness as various ex-wives and mistresses of Vadim trooped in and out of town. She became a surrogate mother to Vadim's daughter, Nathalie, almost seven, and was soon inducted as a fullfledged member of the fast-living international film set that headquartered itself at the Hotel Tahiti. She loved the ease with which people moved in and out of one another's lives and admired their lack of shame or embarrassment in sexual matters. In the context of her strongly puritanical upbringing, this was a revelation. To be able to express oneself on any level without fear of rebuke was the sort of freedom she had been seeking for years. The honesty and directness of the life—no matter how neurotic or maniacal it sometimes became—impressed her. Most of the Ten Commandments were in a state of suspension in St. Tropez, but the Golden Rule prevailed. If someone coveted someone else's mate, more often than not the someone else would step aside with gracious Gallic civility.

"I'm terribly relaxed with Vadim," Jane said at the time, referring to him as always by his last name. "He is not a man who has to prove himself with women. He's known beautiful women; he was married to beautiful women. I would feel insecure with a man who had to prove himself, who was restless, who had things he hadn't done."

The French press was undone with excitement over what it punningly called "*La Liaison Dangereuse*." Soon it demanded to know when Jane and Vadim would marry. Jane had retracted her "marriage is obsolete" pronouncement of three years before and now conceded that she intended to marry sometime. But she denied any desire to marry Vadim. "I love Vadim," she said. "He's wonderful fun to be with. He's taught me enormously, but why in heck should I marry him? His two marriages ended badly. I'm not at all sure he's made for family life, and I'm not sure of myself either, at this stage. So why spoil an almost perfect relationship by introducing a new element into it, such as the official ties of marriage?"

Her friends believed that Jane was sincere, but the press remained unconvinced. *La Ronde* was due to open soon in France. The premiere of every one of Vadim's pictures had been preceded by a spate of publicity, and the news-hawks were sure that an official Fonda-Vadim union would be the launching pad for *La Ronde*. Actually Vadim wanted Jane to marry him. She still did not trust her feelings about him, however—she needed more time. Vadim had to be content to wait.

"I told Jane," Vadim has said of their early days together, "that I am incapable of making love to one woman all my life. 'If I have a sex adventure,' I said, 'I will not lie to you. But one thing I promise you—it will not be important. I could not have a mistress. Also I will not behave in public in such a way as to embarrass you, because it will not be an elegance to you.'"

Jane not only accepted this, she made a similar vow. Vadim, with his abiding need for sexual variety and his detached, professorial approach to sexual experimentation, set out to teach Jane how to rid herself of her American preoccupation with the deeper meaning and significance of the sex act and to enjoy it for its own sake. To him, a lover of expertly prepared and leisurely taken meals, a sexual encounter was like sitting down to a fine dinner; it should be anticipated and enjoyed with the same delectation. It was not long before Jane, her enthusiasm for rooting out all the inhibitions of her psyche still at high pitch, adopted Vadim's hedonistic philosophy as her own.

Although she didn't want to marry, Jane was by then in love with Vadim and was willing to suffer his idiosyncrasies— his financial irresponsibility and his sexual adventurism—in exchange for the emotional security and authority he provided her. She foresaw a long if not lasting relationship and found no impediment to sharing a household with him. Once her love was in high gear, her domestic juices began to flow. Like any young woman who believes she has found the first genuine love of her life, Jane felt the instinctive need to wrap it in domesticity. This meant a home, a place where she and her

man could live—not as two lovers having an affair, but as
mates and partners embarking on a long life together. But they
would need space, a house with plenty of extra rooms where
friends and family could stay, and land to give them seclusion.

Since both were animal lovers, Jane convinced Vadim of
the desirability of living the rural life. In August she found a
small, unkempt old farm for sale at the edge of the tiny town
of St.-Ouen-Marchefroy in the countryside west of Paris. The
house, a quaint, run-down stone and tile-roofed cottage, was
set on three acres of land. Jane fell in love with the setting and
the picturesque village nearby and immediately bought the
property. Then she set out to restore the house to her own
specifications and landscape the surrounding acreage. She
worked at it with her characteristic energy and impatience,
driving out from Paris almost every day to supervise the work-
men and often lending a hand herself.

"The house had been built around 1830, and what really
sold me on it was the color of the stone walls—a kind of beige
honey color like an Andrew Wyeth drawing. I left the walls
up but completely gutted the inside and modernized it. I had
to be there all the time to make sure everything was done right.
But sometimes it got frustrating. Just try telling ten French
workers, in your French, how to modernize a place and yet
keep its original beauty. The land was flat, and there weren't
any trees, so I had a bulldozer come in to move the earth
around and give it a more rolling effect, and I had dozens of
full-grown trees brought out from Paris and planted. It was
wild—every morning you could see these lines of trees advancing up the road like Birnam Wood coming to Dunsinane."

Work on the farm was interrupted in November by a summons from Hollywood. Jane had signed earlier with Columbia
Pictures to star in the film version of a little-known comic novel
by Roy Chanslor called *Cat Ballou*. Production was ready to
start, so Jane dropped everything at St.-Ouen and, with Vadim,
left for California.

Cat Ballou might have been notable enough for the boost
it gave to the career of Lee Marvin, up to then a good, reliable
secondary screen villain. But it also proved to be the first
unqualified hit for Jane Fonda. The picture was a raucous,
freewheeling Western that spoofed every Western cliché its
makers could think of. Marvin was cast as the most sinister
badman of them all—a hard-drinking outlaw with a silver nose

(his own having been bitten off in a fight) and a drunken horse.
As Kid Shelleen, the hollow shell of a once-feared gunfighter,
he would win movie stardom and an Academy Award for his
performance. Jane played Cat Ballou, the very model of a
demure Old West heroine—except that the sweet schoolmarm
turned out to be as handy with her guns as any Wyatt Earp
when she teamed up with the Kid to avenge her father's murder
at the hands of local landbusters.

Jane acquired a house in Malibu and moved in with Vadim
while the picture was being shot. When the company traveled
to Colorado for location filming, Vadim went along. It was
the first hard knowledge Hollywood had that Jane was living
with Vadim, and the film community was abuzz with gossip.
"Jane Fonda and Roger Vadim are an item," Hedda Hopper
wrote, a bit belated. "The British would discreetly refer to them
as 'Jane Fonda and friend,' but Hollywood calls Vadim 'Jane
Fonda's boy friend.'" Most of the gossip was not that benign,
however. People who cared about such things recalled Jane's
strange relationship with Andreas Voutsinas during her last
prolonged stay in California. Stories quickly began to circulate
describing weird, erotic, nocturnal goings-on at Jane's beach
house.

Most of Hollywood was convinced that Jane had brought
Vadim with her to promote him to the American film industry
and try to get him work as a director. *Joy House*, the picture
she had made with René Clément, had been released with Jane
being thoroughly roasted by the critics. A budding resentment
grew toward her in Hollywood—on the part of the younger
generation because of her easy success as the daughter of Henry
Fonda; on the part of the film capital's older denizens because
of her fierce independence and continuing castigation of her
father. Her few critical successes had been dismissed, while
her more frequent failures were secretly applauded. The debacle
of *Joy House* vindicated those who wished Jane ill. Because
the film was French and laden with murky sexuality, the gossip-
mongers were more than willing to believe that Jane had allowed herself to be seduced into a life that was as aberrant as
that shown on the screen. Jane, of course, still thin-skinned
when it came to gossip, grew angry and defensive, claiming
that her relationship with Vadim was "nobody's damn business
but my own."

Those who were close to Jane at the time—mostly actors

she had known during her Strasberg days who were now working in movies—drew another picture. "Jane and Vadim were
really in love," says one, recalling a visit with them. "He treated
her with deference and affection, and she was prouder than a
peacock of him. From the stories I'd heard, I expected to walk
in on an orgy, and to tell the truth I was a little disappointed
to find everything so quiet and domesticated. Jane was into
cooking, in the French style, and I envied the kind of relaxed,
European ambience she created. Vadim was lovely—quiet,
but with lots of personality and charm."

"I hadn't seen Jane in some time," remembers another. "I
was surprised at the changes she had gone through. She was
still high-strung and nervous, she still had that quiver in her
voice, but she was much more open than before, and she had
a kind of serenity that I'd never seen. I'd say the reason she
was so good in *Cat Ballou* was because she was really grooving
on Vadim. She was enthusiastic about the picture, she was
talking about herself and Vadim doing a film together here,
and she was just very up about everything."

"There we were on location in the hills of Colorado," said
one of the actors in *Cat Ballou*. "And here was this Frenchman
in hornrimmed glasses reading *Mad* magazine—all by himself,
sitting on a camp chair on the mountainside while Jane was
filming. They weren't standoffish at all. Between scenes, at
lunch, they joked around with everyone. Vadim's a very friendly
guy."

Jane's stay in California during *Cat Ballou* was uneventful.
She gave few interviews and spent most of her free time introducing Vadim to the Hollywood she knew and liked. She
had been surprised on her arrival in October to find how much
the film community had changed since she'd been there last.
There had been an influx of youth into all areas of the movie
industry. Moreover, Hollywood was rapidly becoming the West
Coast headquarters of the American pop music scene. Legions
of young performers and musicians, all apostles of the increasingly popular rock music, along with additional thousands of
youthful hangers-on, had flocked to Los Angeles during the
previous year. An amorphous subculture, based on the yet-to-
be-articulated gospel of peace, love and psychedelics, was just
starting to form in late 1964. Jane and Vadim were fascinated
by it.

chapter 16

NAKED
ON BROADWAY

Filming of *Cat Ballou* ended in December, just before Jane's twenty-seventh birthday. She and Vadim hurried back to France—she to check on the progress of the renovations at St.-Ouen, he to do preparatory work on a new film he hoped to make with Jane under the auspices of MGM. Operating out of Jane's Paris apartment—she was determined to have the farm ready for occupancy by spring—they started the new year quietly. Vadim watched Jane attack the completion of the farm with amusement. He cared little for houses and surroundings and possessions. Wherever he was, as long as he had friends, good food and wine and conversation, he was content. But he indulged Jane's impatient perfectionism in organizing the farm and marveled at her industriousness.

However quietly 1965 started for Jane, it would become the most tumultuous year of her life. Vadim's French producers had found an American distributor for *La Ronde*—Walter Reade-Sterling, Inc.—and the film was due to be released late in March under the title *Circle of Love*. In February Jane was called back to Hollywood to discuss the possibility of making a film with Marlon Brando. Had it been any other project, she probably would have passed it up. But she had been eager to work with the mercurial Brando since her start as an actress. When her agent Dick Clayton, who had succeeded Ray Powers, told her that she had a chance to get the female lead in Brando's forthcoming movie, she rushed back to California to lobby producer Sam Spiegel for the part. Spiegel had announced plans to make a picture called *The Chase*, with Brando as his male star. He was using the time-honored publicity device of conducting a "nationwide search" for the right actress—known or unknown—to play opposite Brando in the picture.

While Jane was preoccupied in Hollywood, the Reade-Sterling organization was preparing for the premiere in New York of *Circle of Love*. The opening was scheduled for March 24 at the DeMille Theater on Broadway. During the first week of March, the distributors unveiled an eight-story-high billboard over the theater to announce the movie. On the billboard was a huge, lifelike figure of Jane, hair tousled, lying on a bed in the nude and gazing seductively across Broadway at another billboard advertising the film *The Bible*.

Stories about the billboard immediately hit the newspapers and newsmagazines. Humorous or outraged articles and editorials, often illustrated with pictures, were printed throughout the nation. Earl Wilson, the syndicated show-business gossip columnist, adopted a particularly scandalized tone when he described it: "You don't often hear a sophisticated Broadwayite shout 'THAT'S DISGRACEFUL!' But an old and trusted friend of mine . . . protested in those words when he saw the painting of Jane Fonda—her derriere amazingly bare—covering the front of the DeMille Theater. . . . Numerous people—mostly women—have phoned in protests."

Wilson went on to wonder "what middle-westerner Henry Fonda thought about his daughter's nakedness. Father Fonda flew to Spain the other day . . . just in time to avoid getting involved. Anyway, the word is around that oversexed movies are fighting for their life—that in films, at least, S-E-X is not here to stay."

Aside from revealing a dubious gift for prophecy, Wilson succeeded in providing Reade-Sterling with the kind of publicity movie distributors otherwise have to pay millions for. And Jane, when she heard of the billboard, instantly threw more oil on the fire. She announced that she was suing Reade-Sterling.

Dorothy Kilgallen, another columnist, accused Jane of being party to the whole business and clucked her tongue disapprovingly over what she claimed was Jane's indulgence in cheap

stunts. The fact is that Jane was genuinely shocked by the
billboard—not so much because she was portrayed in the nude,
but because the distributors were promoting *Circle of Love*
exclusively as a sex picture. At no time in the movie did she
appear nude. True, she was often in and out of bed, and there
were considerable suggestions of nudity, but she was never
actually seen in the buff.

"To me," she said later, "*Circle of Love* had been a great
opportunity to do a beautiful visual comedy and my first costume picture. They ruined it here—first that awful dubbed
English, and then that big poster of me nude! There was no
such scene in the picture. In fact, I was never nude at all in
the film. I resent that misleading and dishonest kind of pro-
motion. Vadim resented it too."

Jane hired the prestigious law firm of Paul, Weiss, Rifkind,
Wharton and Garrison to press her suit against Reade-Sterling.
It was the same firm that would later represent Jacqueline
Kennedy in her imbroglio over the publication of a book about
John F. Kennedy's assassination. Jane's action did not take as
long to resolve as the former First Lady's would, but the public
followed it with almost as much interest. Jane's attorneys claimed
that she had suffered extreme "anguish and shame" as a result
of the billboard and demanded compensatory and punitive damages in the combined sum of $3,000,000. When Walter Reade,
Jr., chairman of Reade-Sterling, was served with the complaint,
he declared that he could "not understand what all the fuss is
about."

Reade, making the most of the publicity bonanza, announced that "despite the legal differences existing between
Jane Fonda and Reade-Sterling," he intended to host a champagne party in her honor following the press preview of *Circle
of Love* and had invited both Jane and Vadim to come to New
York for the event. He referred to Jane's lawsuit as "a woman's
prerogative" and characterized the nude billboard as "an effort
on the company's part to capture some of the adult sophistication contained in the film. We consider *Circle of Love* to be
a brilliant adult motion picture and we were anxious that the
sign convey this image."

In a humorous effort to forestall Jane's suit and to milk the
event for even more publicity, Reade had a large, square patch
of canvas draped across Jane's exposed derriere, thus drawing

further attention to it and getting another round of pictures in the newspapers.

Jane was unamused. "It's more ridiculous than ever with that Band-Aid," she exclaimed. Reade was left with nothing to do but take the billboard down altogether, something he knew he'd have to do in the first place. The billboard came down, the dispute was eventually settled and the movie died a quick death, with Jane receiving no better reviews than she had for *Joy House*. It's doubtful that more than a few hundred thousand people saw *Circle of Love*. Those who did pay to see it, drawn by hopes of catching Jane in the nude, were sorely disappointed. Yet the billboard remained fresh in everyone's mind. It was that, more than anything else, that established Jane as America's new sex symbol.

Jane was still in Hollywood angling for the costarring role in Spiegel's *The Chase*. After *Circle of Love* was released, and with two consecutive critical and box-office flops to her credit— flops for which she had been assigned a good deal of the blame—one might have thought that Jane was in trouble as an employable actress. But Spiegel's interest in Jane was stimulated by the publicity over the billboard. He liked controversial actors, even difficult ones. He dismissed Jane's bad reviews for *Joy House* and *Circle of Love*, contending that she had been misused and misguided by her French friends. When he saw a rough print of her performance in the yet-to-be-released *Cat Ballou*, he was convinced that she was right for *The Chase*. Spiegel offered her a contract early in April. Delighted, Jane immediately called Hedda Hopper to announce that she had just gotten the part of her life.

Spiegel's reputation around Hollywood was that of a producer who made few pictures but who, when he did, skimped on nothing. The screenplay for *The Chase* was written by Lillian Hellman and was based on a series of stories and a play by Horton Foote about intolerance and provincialism in Texas. Hellman and Foote were distinguished writers. Spiegel had hired the tasteful Arthur Penn to direct the film. He had Brando as his star. And he would be operating with a large budget, so that the film would be rich in production values. Now he had in Jane Fonda, as he declared, "the right person for the right part."

"It's the most exciting and sexiest part any actress has ever had," he said at a press conference to announce Jane's signing. "Lillian Hellman has written many great roles for women, but she believes this is her best." Seldom had a Hollywood film project promised so much.

Filming was not due to begin for another month, so Jane returned to New York with Vadim to confer with her lawyers about the Reade-Sterling suit and to arrange to sell her apartment on Fifty-fifth Street. She'd decided to make France her home and to keep her house in Malibu as her American residence when working in Hollywood. While they were in New York she, Vadim and his daughter—who was visiting from France—stayed at Jane's father's house. Henry Fonda was in Europe filming *The Battle of the Bulge*.

Anxious to counteract the effects of the billboard controversy, Jane gave a few selected interviews while she was in New York. A different, more reflective Jane Fonda emerged. When asked about her relationship with Vadim, she clammed up, but one reporter raised her hackles with the suggestion that Marlon Brando would not like having Vadim on the set during the filming of *The Chase*. "That's a lot of bullshit," Jane replied in her first public use of a vulgarity. "First of all, Vadim wouldn't come on a set where I was working unless he was wanted. Second, he's a very close friend of Marlon's."

"You wouldn't characterize Vadim, then, as your coach—such as Andreas Voutsinas used to be?"

"No, I wouldn't," Jane answered curtly.

"Won't you say something about your relationship with Vadim?"

"No."

"You won't discuss it?"

"No."

When asked if she was going to get married, Jane said, "No, not at the moment. I don't guarantee that might not change tomorrow." The fact is that Vadim was by then pressing Jane to get married, and she was wavering in her determination to stay single.

What about her attitudes? Was she still an untrammeled freethinker, not above trying to shock people? "There certainly was a time when I tried," she said, "partly to rebel against being my father's daughter and wanting to be accepted in my own right. But now I think I've made it on my own right. I don't feel the pressure to strike out with wild remarks. I feel more relaxed and tranquil than I did two years ago.

"I'm not a freethinker, I've never been particularly involved with bourgeois attitudes toward life, so I didn't have to rebel against them. Well, I guess I have them to some extent as far as money is concerned. I wish I didn't. I dislike it—the general attitude in America that having money is sacred. It's like a disease, and it's something that bothers me about myself."

With these thoughts, Jane was reflecting some of Vadim's ideas, although her interviewer didn't realize it. Vadim was not a man of strong political convictions. His view of the world was more a cultural one. He disliked societies built on an obsession with money. He saw America as being the epitome of such societies and had often held forth at length on the subject in discussions with Jane. He did not deny the virtues of modest luxury and leisure time, but he felt that these could be achieved in ways other than by mass enslavement to the ideal of money. It was for this reason that he was intrigued by the growing undercurrent of antimaterialism among American youth.

"What's the most important thing for a woman to remember in her relationship with a man?" Jane was asked.

She waxed long and pensively on this: "I think honesty is the most important thing, and the thing that is most rare and difficult to have. So many of the relationships I've had and seen others have are really based on dishonest premises. It's the first thing to kill a relationship.

"From the beginning with a man," she went on, unwittingly defining her relationship with Vadim, "to be able to say anything, to be able to hear everything, to talk about everything, that's the secret. It's when you don't communicate, when you don't exchange, when you start sitting on grudges, that you start harboring anger. Then the little things build up and really make it false. I see so many people living together where there is no love anymore. They just stay together and there is no spark of communication on any level. I find it absolutely appalling."

Explaining her reluctance to marry, she said, "I think a lot of the problem comes from women. . . . Women want to possess somebody, particularly in marriage. It's one of the main reasons I'm not married. I don't want to possess anyone . . . and I don't want to be possessed.

"I think the difference between a man and a woman is the difference between two stars that are as far apart as two different worlds. Women's concerns are quite different from those of men, who are much more abstract in every way. And this is one of the basic reasons for so much ill will between wives and husbands. It's very different to get these two worlds to meet. The ideal relationship is to recognize that you can't change it.

"A woman wants it there... wants everything in relationship to herself. I think it's glandular. We give birth to man, and we want him to come back to us.... Women don't have the kind of ambitions men do. When they feel a man is escaping from them they panic, they want to bring him back. The moment this happens the man feels trapped, and the woman feels frustrated. They drift apart, fighting it all the time. Yet you can become much closer in the natural apartness that exists if you know how to work at it. But it's difficult for me because I have that possessive instinct in me. I am always much happier, however, when I am able to truly—not just intellectually— respect that aspect of the man I love and not feel frustrated by it."

Jane's philosophy, derivative and half-baked as it might have been in the opinion of some, impressed many people when it appeared in print. It also confused them, fogging the image they had of a wild and reckless sex kitten.

In spite of the allegedly stratospheric IQ attributed to her by her press agents—a bit of sleight-of-hand puffery to which Hollywood press agents habitually resort to give their glamorous clients credibility as superhumans, she was not really an original thinker, as much as inclined to say the unexpected. Much of what Jane expressed was the result of her own introspection and experience. She was certainly intelligent, but her intelligence was considerably more derivative than unique, which is the case with most mortals. She had a quick, pragmatic mind and a humanistic sensibility that made her sensitive to the plights of others. She believed in neither religion nor God and found what little spiritual nourishment she needed in rationalistic interpretations of the universe. Her concerns were almost exclusively with the physical, and her principal private concern was to have a tangible grasp of the dimension of her mysterious, elusive emotions.

Her curiosity was almost boundless. But if experience and information equal knowledge, and if experience and knowledge equal wisdom, Jane was still working, at twenty-seven, on the front end of the equation. Admittedly late-blooming and under-educated, she was a sponge for new information and experi-ence. Her sense of discovery was keen and highly developed. With her character solidly cemented to her instincts, however, and her enthusiasm usually more certain than her knowledge, it often led her down the path of dogmatic reliance on the ideas of those to whom she was emotionally tied. This had become a pattern in her life—she had exhibited it as a youngster with her father, then with Strasberg, Everett, her analysts, Voutsinas and others. It found its fullest expression with Vadim, who seemed to embody a smattering of each of the men who had been important to Jane.

The irony would be, in a life filled with ironies, that the very questing nature that drove Jane into her intellectual and emotional dependence on Vadim would eventually drive her out of it. But not before a painful apprenticeship in the me-chanics of self-awareness.

chapter 17

BAREFOOT
IN MALIBU

The beach community at Malibu is half an hour and several light years away from the suburban splendor of Beverly Hills. In 1965 it was a sort of West Coast St. Tropez where life proceeded with the barefoot and faintly bohemian insouciance that characterized "hip" beach colonies all over the world. The town of Malibu is situated on the busy Pacific Coast Highway, but an access road leads from the highway past a small shopping center to the beach itself. Along this road, which runs close and parallel to the curving Pacific shoreline, is the private Malibu Colony—a long row of smallish, tightly crowded houses of varying designs and styles that look out on the narrow strip of sand to the rim of the world beyond. When they returned from New York in May, Jane and Vadim, along with Nathalie, settled into her modest house in the Colony.

With "the part of her life," and playing in a cast of top professionals, Jane knew that she would have to give her most accomplished performance of her career in *The Chase*. She was both intrigued and terrified by the prospect of acting with Brando. She found him "just about the sexiest man of all time," but she knew that appearing in the same film with him was, from a career point of view, difficult and dangerous. He had a way of filling up the screen and making whoever else was in his films appear wooden and inconsequential. He was a master of

148

stillness. Other actors acted; Brando simply existed as a monumental, riveting presence on the screen. The expressiveness and delicacy of his emotions were without peer, but his forte was his indelible magnetism and identity. Jane not only would be acting with him; she would be competing against him.

Brando was the most universally admired of all American film actors, but in 1965 his career was in decline. Following his early successes, he had left behind a more recent string of pictures which were interesting for his presence in them but otherwise of little consequence. The better part of screen acting is in the reacting, and Brando's performances were often blurred by his having so little to work against. His depictions of grief, anguish, despair, humor, and violence often seemed isolated and without any reference outside his own personality. With his powerful naturalism confined to a vacuum, his acting had become hollow and narcissistic.

Yet he was still a magnetic and beguiling performer, and in 1965 he was desperate for a film role that would revitalize his career. As the idealistic, tragic Texas sheriff in *The Chase*—a role that fitted his private character like a glove—he thought he had found it. He was determined to make the most of it, and soon his demanding, eccentric perfectionism dominated the preparations and filming of the picture.

When they first met to discuss *The Chase*, Jane was awed by Brando's authoritative confidence. "I was there when he came in for the first time to discuss the script. He will not settle for anything less than the truth. He wants to get at the root of something—not in the way most actors do, in terms of their own part, but in terms of the entire script. If he senses something is wrong, he cannot agree to do it. People say he's difficult. . . . I suppose he is sometimes, but he won't settle for something less than what he feels is right. I don't have that kind of courage, and that's why I admire him so much."

Admire him she did, but she was unable to quell the sense of inadequacy she felt playing opposite him. As filming progressed into the summer, she grew less and less happy with her role and was increasingly unsettled by an undercurrent of helplessness building up in her. Away from the cameras, Brando was sociable and sympathetic, and Jane was particularly attracted by his complexly articulated social concerns—he was already involved in the movement to restore the civil rights of American Indians. But on the set he was no help to her at all with his critical, fussy, convoluted approach to their scenes.

The Chase was an allegory, heavily larded with symbolism, about the greed and hypocrisy of American society as reflected in a small, contemporary Texas town. The central character was a reluctant sheriff—Brando—who sought to bring in alive, against the will of the bigoted, lynch-minded townspeople, a local escaped convict falsely accused of murder. Jane Fonda was cast as Anne Reeves, the young low-life wife of the convict, who was played by Robert Redford. She was having an affair with the weakling son of the town's richest oligarch. Her paramour, acted by James Fox, was also an old school friend of Anne Reeves' convict-husband. As the story unfolded, she and her lover were persuaded by the sheriff into trying to talk her husband into surrendering peacefully. In the ensuing action, which was thick with bloody violence and embellished by a symbolic holocaust (America consuming itself in the flames of its own provincial lust), the woman lost both her lover, who was killed in the fire, and her husband, who was shot down in cold blood by a local bigot on the steps of the jail as the heroic, battered Brando brought him in.

Despite the promise the film held, which was on the order of a classic like Henry Fonda's *The Ox-Bow Incident*, it became bogged down in literary melodrama, complete with a modern-day version of an ancient Greek chorus. From a production point of view it was first-class and was filled with rich detail, but its dices-loaded, shortcut appeal to liberal sympathies was as transparent and predictable as its characters were sterotyped. Jane's role was less than what it had seemed when she had signed for it, and in the end she became nothing more than a featured player with only a few fleeting scenes with Brando.

In June, while Jane was making *The Chase*, *Cat Ballou* opened. It was the first time such a satirical, irreverent movie had been made. Along with almost everyone else connected with it, Jane feared that its Tom Jones approach to the Old West might not sit well with critics and audiences. Her fears were erased by the torrent of critical acclaim. The picture was hailed as a masterpiece of cinema satire. Lee Marvin's notices were practically delirious in their unqualified praise of his performance, and Jane's were almost as glowing.

"In a performance that nails down her reputation as a girl worth singing about," wrote the reviewer for *Time* magazine, "actress Fonda does every preposterous thing demanded of her with a giddy sincerity that is at once beguiling, poignant and hilarious." It was the first performance in the nine films Jane had made that earned her the unqualified approval of *Time*. Even Judith Crist, up till now one of Jane's most caustic critics, smiled on her. "Well, let's get those old superlatives out," she wrote in the New York *Herald Tribune*. "Jane Fonda is just marvelous as the wide-eyed Cat, exuding sweet feminine sex-appeal every sway of the way. . . . This *Cat Ballou* is a honey."

Jane's agents were delighted, for *Cat Ballou* turned her into a full-fledged box-office star and elevated her future worth into the $300,000-per-picture range. Vadim was delighted, not just for Jane but because her success was sure to pave the way with MGM for the picture he was trying to organize with Jane as star. Sam Spiegel and Columbia were delighted, because it meant that Jane would be almost as big a draw as Brando when it came time to release *The Chase*.

But for Jane, still trying to keep up with Brando and master her role in *The Chase*, the praise was anticlimactic. She had known all along that she was a first-rate film actress, and she was by then too much of a veteran to be overly impressed by reviews. She perceived herself as a full-fledged professional now, and she adopted the typical professional's detachment about her performances. She had done things in *Cat Ballou* that she hadn't liked, she said, and her discussions were devoted more to these than to what she had done so well.

When Jane and Vadim settled at Malibu in May, their life together started off quietly enough. It was not long, however, before they were fully embraced by the Colony. At first Vadim was more of an attraction than Jane. With his Bardot-Stroyberg-Deneuve legend, his notoriety was more interesting than the rather conventional fame of the many film celebrities who lived in Malibu. Everyone was anxious to get to know him, and he obliged by being friendly and gregarious. He was naturally more outgoing than Jane, and since he enjoyed nothing more than a houseful of fun-loving people, Jane was soon hostess to the same kind of perpetual party she remembered the Strasbergs having seven years before. By July, much of Malibu's social life centered on Jane's house, and the beach community soon became the primary outpost of the foreign film set. Jane and Vadim had a constant stream of visitors, both from along the beach and from abroad, and on weekends the house overflowed with people.

One visitor to the house, though not a frequent one, was Jane's father. In Hollywood to make a new picture, he was angry about the malicious gossip floating around among his acquaintances about Jane's living arrangements with Vadim. He and Jane had had limited communication during the previous few years. He had tried gamely to ignore the jibes of his two children and had stopped talking to the press about them. But now, having learned about his son Peter's public conversion to marijuana and Jane's romance with Vadim, he was nettled once again. And curious.

"One day the phone rang," Jane later recalled, "and it was Dad saying he wanted to come over. He had never met Vadim, and he wanted to dislike him. He came into our house expecting God knows what after all the things he had heard, an orgy, I suppose. But there I was slopping around in blue jeans and Vadim was sitting on the deck fishing, one of Father's passions in life." Fonda was as surprised as everyone else to find Vadim friendly and likable. But he was still of another generation, and he could not countenance Jane *and* Vadim's living together without being married.

Jane had at last reached a tentative accommodation with life, at least as far as her feelings about her father were concerned. Much of this was due to the influence of Vadim. She no longer felt the need to strike back against Henry Fonda's disapproval, and she even began to feel some sympathy for him. Looking back on it, she said, "You're an adult when you can see the very definite stages in the relationship with your parent. First of all, there is complete worship, when you believe everything he says. Second is the time when you discover, 'My God, he makes so many mistakes,' and you start blaming him for the trouble you have. Third is the period you go through, at least I went through, of absolute rigid condemnation, which is a justification of having to find your own identity. Fourth, maturity comes when you can look at the relationship with your parent objectively. Mistakes were made, but, hell, nobody's perfect."

Throughout the summer Jane was increasingly touched by Vadim's empathy for her father and by his efforts to bring her closer to him. A father himself, Vadim admired Henry Fonda and found his alienation from his children sad. He philosophized about Jane and her father in such a melancholy way that Jane began to take part of the blame for their estrangement.

She also began to view her father differently. She realized that she loved him a great deal more than she had been willing to admit, and that she'd outgrown much of her earlier rancor and resentment without even realizing it.

Jane had not given up analysis, but by now she was much less dependent on it and visited her Los Angeles therapist only on occasion. She had achieved a certain level of confidence and assertiveness in her life (which was what most people seek from psychotherapy), and her relationship with Vadim had had a much healthier effect on her state of mind than the probing of analysis. She had been taking a steady diet of addictive pills, all properly prescribed, during the previous few years—amphetamines for energy and weight control, antidepressants for psychic support—but she had grown much less dependent on these as well.

Jane's serenity during the summer of 1965, once filming of *The Chase* was finished, coupled with her newly discovered feelings about her father, were such that she became increasingly amenable to the idea of marrying Vadim. Her decision to do so, when she finally made it, was more impulsive than considered, however. In late July Vadim left her in California and returned to Paris. She was to follow him in another month, after her post-production work on *The Chase* was finished. Vadim wasn't gone for more than a few days before Jane found herself moody and depressed. She missed him terribly.

Before he left, Vadim had again urged Jane to marry him. At the end of her lonely week she phoned him in Paris and told him that she was ready. But, she said, their wedding would have to take place in the United States so that certain friends could be on hand to celebrate with them. Vadim flew back to California immediately, bringing his mother with him. On Saturday, August 15, he and Jane chartered a private plane and flew to Las Vegas with a load of friends. Among those on the plane were Vadim's mother, Peter Fonda, Brooke Hayward and Dennis Hopper, French actor Christian Marquand, Vadim's best friend, and Marquand's wife, Tina Aumont, the daughter of actor Jean-Pierre Aumont. Also aboard were Robert Walker, Jr., and his wife, who lived down the beach from Jane, actor James Fox from *The Chase*, Jane's cousin George Seymour, Dick Clayton, her agent, and the left-wing Italian journalist Oriana Fallaci.

The marriage was performed by Justice of the Peace James

Brennan (the same man who had married Cary Grant and Dyan Cannon a few weeks before) in a plush six-room suite on the twentieth floor of the Dunes Hotel. Marquand was best man, and Tina Aumont and Brooke Hopper were bridesmaids. Peter Fonda played his guitar. Henry Fonda sent his regrets from New York, where he was starting rehearsals for a new play.

The ceremony was conducted in a tongue-in-cheek style appropriate to its setting, according to *Look* magazine. "It was not just an ordinary wedding. An orchestra of female violinists undulating in skin-tight blue-sequined gowns played the wedding music. The judge was so disappointed when he heard the groom had not bought a ring that Vadim borrowed one from Christian Marquand. Jane had to hold her finger upright to keep the ring from slipping off. Vadim's mother, an energetic photographer, missed the ceremony because she spent her whole time taking pictures of Las Vegas.

After the ceremony, the members of the wedding attended a striptease version of the French Revolution in which a naked woman was mock-guillotined to the music of Ravel's "Bolero." They all stayed up the rest of the night gambling, then watched the sun rise over the desert through a haze of marijuana smoke, according to Peter Fonda.

To the press, which gave the wedding wide coverage— "JANE WEDS BB'S EX" read one headline—Jane attributed her decision to marry to the fact-that it made it easier to travel with Vadim's children, to register at hotels and, "Well, I guess because of my father. I knew I was hurting him." More recently, she has said that she felt weak and lost at the time. "I remember the day very well. I felt out of place. I had always thought that I would never marry, and instead, here I was, getting married, and saying to myself, 'I honestly don't know why I'm doing it.' I'll tell you, I was sleeping."

The newlyweds returned to Malibu the day after the wedding. Jane spent the following week finishing her work on *The Chase*. Then, early in September, she and Vadim packed up and flew to France, where they installed themselves in the refurbished farmhouse at St.-Ouen and continued preparations for their new picture—a film version of Emile Zola's novel *La Curée*.

Called *The Game Is Over* in English, the story was a probing character study of the pampered and selfish young wife of a middle-aged French businessman who falls in love with her

JANE FONDA
HEROINE FOR OUR TIME

Relaxing between takes on her first movie, *Tall Story*,
Hollywood 1959.

Twenty-two and starring in *Tall Story*, directed by her father's friend,
Joshua Logan. *COLLECTION NEAL PETERS*

Henry visits Jane before going back East to do a Broadway play, 1959.
WIDE WORLD PHOTOS

A bit of cheesecake as Kitty Twist in *Walk on the Wild Side*, 1962.
COLLECTION NEAL PETERS

With co-star Peter Finch, on location in Greece for *In the Cool of the Day*, 1963. Jane played Christine Bonner.

Cat Ballou, 1965. Lee Marvin won the Oscar for Best Actor in 1965 for his portrayal of the acerbic, noseless Kid Shelleen. *KOBAL COLLECTION*

Cat Ballou. COLLECTION NEAL PETERS

In Vadim's *La Curée (The Game is Over)*, 1966, playing Renée Saccard.
KOBAL COLLECTION

With the international set at a gala ball in Venice, 1967.
WIDE WORLD PHOTOS

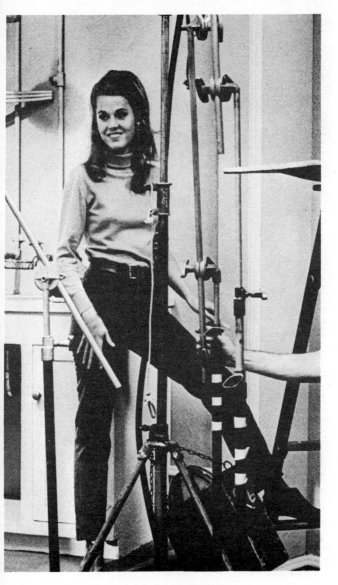

As Corie Bratter in *Barefoot in the Park*, 1967. Her husband in the movie was Robert Redford.

Barbarella, 1967. COLLECTION NEAL PETERS

Outside the Belvedere Hospital in Paris with daughter Vanessa Vadim, who was born on Brigitte Bardot's birthday, September 28, in 1968. The baby was named for Vanessa Redgrave. *RON GALELLA*

The downtrodden Gloria in 1969's *They Shoot Horses, Don't They?*

With Donald Sutherland in their famous Free Theater Associates (FTA) show which toured American Army camps in 1971. *STEVE JAFFE*

Holding her Oscar for Best Actress in the role of Bree Daniels,
the resourceful prostitute, in *Klute*, 1972. *RON GALELLA*

With Donald Sutherland in *Klute*.

Bree Daniels in *Klute*. COLLECTION NEAL PETERS

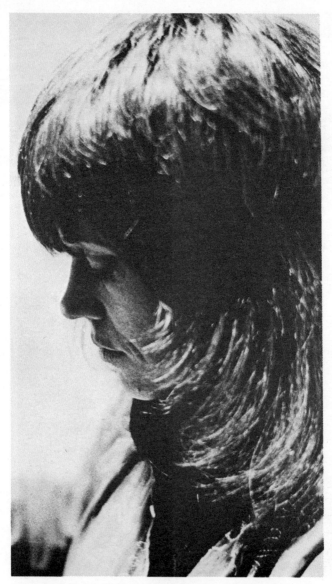

Campaigning for George McGovern at Brandeis University,
October 1972. *ALBERT SPEVAK*

At an anti-aircraft gun position outside Hanoi during her controversial trip to North Vietnam, July 1972. *WIDE WORLD PHOTOS*

A black wig for *Steelyard Blues*, 1972. In this, her next movie after *Klute*, Jane again played a prostitute and co-starred with Donald Sutherland, but the film was not a success. *KOBAL COLLECTION*

RON GALELLA

In character as Lillian Hellman in *Julia*, co-starring Vanessa Redgrave. This shot was taken at the Winterbourne Hotel on the Isle of Wight in September 1976. *RON GALELLA*

Urging British support of American farm workers while on
location in England to make *Julia*, October 1976. RON GALELLA

With Bruce Dern in *Coming Home*, 1978.

Both Jane and Jon Voight won Oscars as Best Actress/
Best Actor in *Coming Home*.

The determined cattle rancher Ella Connors in 1978's *Comes A Horseman*.

TV reporter Kimberly Wells witnesses a potential nuclear disaster in *The China Syndrome*, 1979.

Daughter Vanessa and son Troy in matching tuxedo outfits accompany Jane and her husband, Tom Hayden, to the 1980 Academy Awards presentations. Jane was nominated for Best Actress in *The China Syndrome*. WIDE WORLD PHOTOS

At a Fitness Benefit for the ERA, Jane demonstrates stretching
exercises at her "Workout" studio in Beverly Hills, January 1980.
WIDE WORLD PHOTOS

Lily Tomlin, Dolly Parton and Jane share a laugh with director
Colin Higgins on the set of *Nine to Five*, 1980.

With brother Peter, Jane attends Henry Fonda's seventy-fifth birthday
celebration at the Wilshire Theater in Los Angeles, where he was
starring in *The Oldest Living Graduate*, May 16, 1980. *WIDE WORLD PHOTOS*

On Golden Pond, 1981. Jane, playing the daughter of Henry Fonda and Katharine Hepburn, confronts her life-long estrangement from her father (perhaps drawing parallels to their real-life relationship), and they eventually reach a tentative yet heart-felt reconciliation.

The opening of her exercise studio, "Jane Fonda's Workout." At age forty-two, Jane is an inspiration to women and proof that it's possible to be lean and lithe at any age. *RON GALELLA*

stepson, a young man about her own age. Vadim saw the film as an opportunity to do his first really profound work, and he toiled round the clock to perfect the script. He planned a picture lush with color and lavish with scenic decor. There would, of course, be plenty of sensuality, as there always was in Vadim's films, but for the first time in his career he was going beyond mere sex-and-nudity entertainment. He intended to use the picture to transform his reputation into that of a serious filmmaker.

With her attachment to Vadim complete, Jane approached *The Game Is Over* with more dedication than she had evinced for any of her previous films. It was a family affair. Vadim gave her a generous voice in the preparation of the script and convinced her that her role as Renée Saccard, as he intended to shape it on film, would establish her at last as the topflight dramatic actress she had always dreamed of being.

The role was a magnet to anyone of Jane's aspirations. She had proved herself as a comedic performer but had yet to play a successful dramatic part. Renée Saccard was an opportunity to get away from the hackneyed dramatic heroines—the flashy trollop, the frigid wife—she had portrayed in her American movies. It was a chance to sink her teeth into a full-blown dramatic character, to paint a heightened and comprehensive portrait of a woman in love—her joys, her sorrows, her hopes, her fears.

The film nevertheless was to contain several extensive nude scenes. At first, Jane was apprehensive about them, not because she didn't trust her husband, but because she knew they would represent a contradiction of her earlier proclamations about never appearing nude. She had had a fleeting moment of semi-nudity in *The Chase*, but the scene had been shot from behind and was more teasing than revealing—besides, in the Hollywood of 1965 it couldn't have been filmed any other way. She had been reluctant even about that, but at Vadim's urging she had gone through with it. Among others, the scenes in *The Game Is Over* called for her to be filmed fully nude with co-star Peter McEnery during a swimming-pool scene and a bedroom lovemaking encounter.

When it came time to film the swimming-pool sequence, Vadim closed the set at Jane's insistence. Unknown to her, however, a freelance French photographer was secreted on a catwalk above the set. As Jane doffed her robe to do a run-through of the scene with Vadim and McEnery, the photog-

rapher started snapping pictures. Whether he was there with
Vadim's secret consent, as he later claimed, has never been
determined. But when Jane later found out about it, she was
livid. She was even more furious when she learned that *Playboy*
magazine had gotten the photos and intended to publish them.

Vadim, some of his friends later said, was not beyond col-
laborating in such a stunt. Once he knew that *Playboy* had the
pictures, he decided to exploit the event for all it was worth
for the sake of the publicity it would provide *The Game Is
Over*. Accordingly, his friends suggested, he feigned outrage.
He and Jane then consulted her lawyers and shot off a letter
to *Playboy* warning the magazine not to publish the photos.
She claimed the pictures had been taken without her consent;
if they were used, she would seek an injunction and hold the
magazine liable for damages.

chapter 18

HURRY
SUNDOWN

During her stay in France for *The Game Is Over*, Jane grew increasingly aware of the political and social unrest that was spreading through the Western world. With the crumbling of the French empire in Africa and the Far East, the voice of the proletarian intelligentsia of France—led by old-guard Soviet-oriented Marxists and augmented by the newer student movement which derived its ideological inspiration from the Chinese Communist Revolution—found sympathetic ears throughout the country. In the early sixties the Communists and Socialists had taken much of the credit for the downfall of French colonialism. They transformed themselves—especially those of the student generation—from being the self-appointed conscience of France into the conscience of the entire West. They railed against the imperialism, racism and oppression they claimed were endemic to Western civilization and called for worldwide revolution and the liberation of all oppressed peoples from the undemocratic bondage of capitalism, which rewarded few and exploited and enslaved many. Out of this mix of political radicalism and opportunism was born the French New Left, whose ideological champions were—in addition to the Chinese—the Cubans, the North Vietnamese and Vietcong, the revolutionary blacks of North America and the homeless Palestinians of the Middle East. The radical impulse soon manifested itself in the French film industry as more and more filmmakers sought to couple the pathos and violence of social revolution with their own romantic visions. *La lutte*, or "the struggle," became the focus of much of the new filmmaking being done in France by the midsixties.

Jane Fonda, who through her relationship to Vadim had already become friendly with many of the French cinema's leading left-wing celebrities—Simone Signoret and Yves Montand were two of her closer friends—was sympathetic to the passion and conviction of their developing commitment to social justice. Nevertheless Jane was an American, and she found it difficult to reconcile her friends' political idealism with their virulent anti-Americanism. Their tendency to blame the United States for all the ills of the world disturbed her, but her attempts to defend her homeland from their condemnation were no match for their sophisticated and fact-filled arguments. Of course, there were inequities and stupidities in the American system, but there were many good things too, she would argue—only to have the good things discredited in a whorl of clever, rapid-fire logic. Jane was accused of having a provincial's view of her country; she did not possess the insight to see through her own nationalistic conditioning and perceive the evils the American system visited on the rest of the world. Hurt by their condescension, Jane took less to talking and more to listening during the long discussions that raged among the friends who visited the farm. On her own, she began to read some of the books whose authors she heard praised.

The second half of 1966 saw the first mass demonstrations against the Vietnam War in the United States. Inspired by youthful America's civil rights passion during the late fifties, an American New Left had been born earlier in the sixties. In 1962, a group of radical thinking undergraduates and postgraduates from colleges and universities throughout America had convened in Port Huron, Michigan. From this convention sprang an organization called Students for a Democratic Society—SDS, for short. Among others, SDS was the brainchild of a recent University of Michigan graduate named Thomas Hayden. Hayden was the principal author of the organization's manifesto, called the Port Huron Statement, which claimed a close cause-and-effect relationship between American capitalism and society's ills. He was elected the first president of SDS and quickly became one of the principal theorists of the

New Left movement, as well as tireless activist and demonstrator. Reform, rather than revolution, was the motto of the early New Left, and the organizing of economically oppressed classes and racial minorities was the methodology.

But then, during the summer of 1963, two Buddhist monks had burned themselves to death in Saigon to dramatize local resistance to the repressive policies of the Diem regime. Pictures of the monks sitting stoically in pillars of self-inflicted fire repulsed much of America and turned the New Left's attention almost exclusively to the United States' involvement in Vietnam. Shortly thereafter, Diem declared martial law throughout South Vietnam. Hundreds of Vietnamese students were beaten when they protested, further stirring the ire of the young American reformers. During the year after Kennedy was assassinated and the entire fabric of American life threatened to unravel, the New Left further concentrated its focus on Vietnam, growing more impassioned and radical as it did so. And as President Johnson promised to contain American involvement in the war, all the while secretly escalating it and promoting an atmosphere of government dissembling, the Left considered itself the voice of truth and conscience in America.

Jane Fonda, then filming *The Game Is Over* in France, had seen the mushrooming undercurrent of protest and disaffection during her stay in California the previous summer. Much of her exposure to it came through her brother and his friends. In November, two young American pacifists, emulating the Buddhist monks of Saigon, burned themselves to death in full view of the public at the Pentagon and the United Nations. Concurrently, the first large antiwar march was held in Washington.

As these events were reported in France, Jane's circle softened its criticisms of America—at least of its youth. An atmosphere of celebration and congratulation permeated discussions among Jane's leftist French friends. The events in the United States did not yet mean revolution was at hand, but at least it was a beginning. Jane suddenly found herself praised for being an American. Delighted, she began to sympathize and identify with the furiously expanding American political conscience she was reading and hearing about. She looked forward to her return to the States in the spring to make a new film, so that she could observe at first-hand what was happening and learn more about it.

The new film was *Any Wednesday*, another coy bedroom comedy from Broadway. Jane played the young East Side mistress of a philandering, aging New York corporation executive, a role she could walk through blindfolded by then. Shooting was divided between New York and Hollywood, and when she arrived in California, she was astonished at the rapidity of the changes that had occurred in her six-month absence. The pop music scene had become preeminent, practically everyone in the film industry under forty was growing long hair and experimenting with drugs, and Sunset Boulevard looked like the Main Street of a vast hippie commune.

When asked to compare the new young-American lifestyle to that of France, Jane said, "It's inconceivable that anything like this could happen in France. Whatever happens in Paris just happens in an intellectual way, it never goes public. Maybe the whole thing is just too far away from French culture and existence. In France, the middle class is everything. Everyone is essentially an individual. What's happening here springs quite naturally from a commercial culture. France couldn't and doesn't lend itself to what's happening here. Maybe the language has something to do with it. I come back here after a short time and everybody's talking differently. 'Scene' is out and 'bag' is in, or things are 'groovy.' Can you imagine French accommodating itself to that sort of change? In French, argot is argot. It doesn't change."

Jane left no doubt in anyone's mind that she liked what was going on in California. It was youthful, energetic, rebellious— all qualities that appealed to her. She and Vadim lost no time in exploring the new scene, with her brother as chief tour guide.

Since Jane had seen him last, Peter Fonda's transformation had been startling. A few years before, Peter had settled in Los Angeles to pursue an acting career of his own. He had married Susan Brewer, the stepdaughter of businessman Noah Dietrich, an associate of Howard Hughes, and set out on a Beverly Hills life in the tradition of his wealthy father-in-law—three-piece suits, manicured lawns, expensive cars. But the winds of social change soon blew his way, and by 1966 he had turned his back completely on his earlier lifestyle. Peter was now acting in low-budget motorcycle movies advocating the use of LSD, mescaline and psilocybin. He claimed that the use of hallucinogens had helped him exorcise his demons and set him on the road to self-fulfillment. "As that first [LSD] trip progressed," he said later, "I thought about my father and about my relationship with him and my mother and my sister. And suddenly I busted through the whole thing and related to everything. There was no more worry about my father, mother and sister. I began to feel really on top of all my problems. I had no further relationship with the past; I'd kicked it."

Jane's traditional pity for Peter turned into admiration bordering on envy. Her brother was expunging his guilt and anxiety more radically than she had ever imagined possible. He pursued his metamorphosis with a single-minded intensity that left her agog. Where she had once had contempt for his haplessness, she now praised him for being stronger and braver than she was. She was proud of the initiative and leadership he displayed among his friends and admired the cool authority of his newly acquired manner. He was fast becoming one of the leaders of the new, youth-oriented Hollywood. His and Jane's roles were reversed: He became the teacher, she the student.

Peter and his wife had had their first child in 1964. They named her Bridget, after Bridget Hayward, who had committed suicide in 1960. By spring of 1966, Susan Fonda was expecting again. She resolutely kept up with Peter and remained devoted to him. The only one in the family unhappy about Peter was, as usual, his father.

Jane and Vadim were hoping to take life easy for a while and sample a little more of the new Hollywood after she finished *Any Wednesday* in May. But their plans were diverted by a call from Otto Preminger. Preminger was about to make a film from the best-selling novel *Hurry Sundown* and wanted Jane for the female lead. *Hurry Sundown* was a huge book—a multi-charactered story about poor black sharecroppers and wealthy, paternalistic white landowners in Georgia. Its themes were race relations and civil rights in the changing South. Preminger had seen Jane in *The Chase*—in intention not very different from *Hurry Sundown*—and liked the way she had handled her Southern accent. Jane leaped at the chance to work with the controversial Preminger in what she was sure would be a major motion picture. Vadim was no less enthusiastic. "Both of us consider Preminger enormously talented, dynamic, charming," Jane said. "He's one of the rare ones who can be a showman and an artist at the same time." She signed for the role of Julie Ann Warren, the dissatisfied, oversexed wife of the rich landowner who, as a result of a typical Preminger casting error, was to be played by the English actor Michael Caine.

Preminger, after encountering some difficulties in finding a place in the South to do his location filming, settled on an area near Baton Rouge, Louisiana. Along with the rest of the company, Jane arrived in sweltering Baton Rouge at the beginning of June. Rooms and offices for more than a hundred people were taken at the Bellemont, a colonial-style motel with a Confederate flag hanging in the shimmering heat above its entrance and a reputation for hospitality to movie people. But *Hurry Sundown* was the first film ever to be made in the South with black actors in leading roles (the two black leads were played by Robert Hooks and Diahann Carroll). Rumor quickly spread that Preminger was there to make a film, as one local put it, about "niggers gettin' the best of us white folk." Troubles immediately started. Tires were slashed on company cars. Several cast members received telephoned threats. The section of the motel where the picture's stars were housed was like an armed camp, guarded around the clock by shotgun-toting state troopers. The actors, black and white, felt like the poor relations of an aristocratic family, hidden away on the plantation in seclusion and shame. Diahann Carroll, who rarely journeyed out after dark, said, "You could cut the hostility with a knife. I'm not a fighter. I usually smile, then go into my room and cry my eyes out. But down there the terror killed my taste for going anywhere. Everything was supposed to be checked out before we got there. That was the company's responsibility. But they blew it."

Nearby St. Francisville, Louisiana, was chosen as the "typical Southern town" for the movie. With a population of less than a thousand, it was the kind of place where ladies still wore gardenia corsages to the drugstore, where men in ice-cream suits still sipped bourbon on their porches at sundown, and where no one counted for anything unless his family had lived there for at least a hundred years. A fading remnant of the antebellum period, it was white-Protestant, old-guard and crumbling. It was also a center of Ku Klux Klan activity in Louisiana.

To this town Preminger brought his integrated cast to film the story of a post-World War II Southern white oligarchy being outsmarted by poor-but-honest blacks—a subject about which most white Louisianians were anything but sanguine. Attitudes ranged from unfriendly to violent. On most film locations, policemen are needed to hold back curious onlookers. Such was not the case on the location of *Hurry Sundown*. "You never saw anybody," said Robert Hooks, who kept a diary of his experiences. "You could feel their eyes watching you behind lace curtains, though. Like they could cut your heart out."

For Jane, the experience was an eye-opener. Although she had already made a movie about Southern bigotry and had heard plenty about it from others, she had never experienced it at first-hand. Visited only twice by Vadim, she spent two tense, lonely months in Baton Rouge having her already liberal consciousness raised. "I kissed a little Negro boy on the street in front of the courthouse and the sheriff asked us to finish the scene, get out of town and never come back," she recalled.

Compounding the cast's tension was the autocratic Preminger, who treated his actors like lowly soldiers in some grand combat scheme. Preminger thrived on his reputation as a cinematic tyrant. Unfortunately, his directorial techniques were equally heavy-handed. A trademark of the many films he had made over the years was an excruciating tendency to underline and belabor dramatic ideas and textual subtleties by means of self-conscious visual juxtapositions and symbols. As one critic said, "He makes films with a convoluted German syntax, the way Kant wrote philosophy."

For Jane, *Hurry Sundown* represented an interesting acting challenge despite the conditions under which she had to work. The part of Julie Ann Warren was her old nemesis, the sensual, highly charged dramatic character she had unsuccessfully wrestled with before in pictures like *A Walk on the Wild Side*. Under Preminger's weighty, humorless direction, she quickly realized that her character would be as obvious and stereotypical as in her previous American embodiments of it—unless she added some colors to it other than those Preminger had in mind. She worked hard on her characterization, consulting Vadim almost nightly by telephone in Hollywood. In the end Jane produced a performance that managed at least partially to transcend Preminger's ponderous style. She was helped considerably by what she had learned playing the role of Renée in *The Game Is Over*, and she invested Julie Ann Warren with about the only credibility of any of the film's characters.

Although her big scene, regretfully the scene for which the picture would be remembered, was a kind of lascivious encounter between her and Michael Caine in which she simulated fellatio on a phallic saxophone between his legs (an example of Preminger's simplistic style of symbolism), she gave Julie Ann a sympathetic believability that held an otherwise fragmented and misconceived film together. It was by far the best acting she had done so far, with the possible exception of *The Game Is Over*, and Jane credited it to what Vadim had brought out in her.

While Jane was in Louisiana, the August 1966 issue of *Playboy* came out with six pages of the nude photographs taken of her on the set of *The Game Is Over*. They showed Jane, bare except for a flesh-colored bikini bottom, cavorting around the swimming pool with costar McEnery, who was dressed. The photos, in black and white, were obviously candid-camera shots. The credibility of Jane's well-publicized ire was compromised somewhat by the fact that the magazine also published, as part of the same feature, a posed, filtered, full-color nude photo of her that might have come from Vadim's own files. Jane was furious. As soon as filming on *Hurry Sundown* was completed in mid-August, she fled Louisiana and rushed back to Los Angeles to do something about it.

Her anger was due mainly to the fact that in *The Game Is Over* only her nude back was intended to be seen in the swimming pool sequence, whereas the *Playboy* pictures exposed her frontally to the full view of the public. In the multimillion-dollar lawsuit she brought against Hugh Hefner, publisher of *Playboy*, her lawyers claimed that "she has withheld from the public glare her nude person and likeness, and refused to permit any photography which used the exposed portion of her body." The suit claimed, among other things, invasion of privacy. Jane argued that when an actress appears naked on the screen, she does so as a fictional personality. But an actress appearing unclad and against her will in a publication—well, that was something else again. The suit was destined to drag on for months in the courts, both American and French, and Vadim happily found himself on the receiving end of another publicity bonanza for one of his forthcoming films.

chapter 19

THE ANTIWAR
FEVER

Jane and Vadim had to remain in Los Angeles to be on hand
for depositions. While they waited, they planned their next
joint film project, a segment in a three-part French film based
on the horror stories of Edgar Allan Poe. They also tried to
interest Hollywood studios in a film version of *Barbarella*—a
popular and saucily erotic French comic strip.

Jane was anxious to return to her farm in France. She was
drained emotionally by her stay in Louisiana and the litigation
over the *Playboy* pictures, and she was looking forward to the
"joy of doing absolutely nothing until after the first of the year."
Her father was in California with his new wife to make another
Western, *Welcome to Hard Times*.

Henry Fonda had married for the fifth time the previous
December. His new wife, Shirlee Adams, was a young airline
stewardess and model, and like her husband's two previous
wives, just a few years older than Jane. A pretty, uncomplicated
Midwestern young woman, she was "completely without the
usual phoniness of most stars' wives," according to one of
Henry Fonda's friends. When she and Jane had a chance to
get to know one another, Jane concluded that her father had
finally found the ideal wife. Shirlee was socially gregarious,
and in eight months of marriage she had loosened up Henry to
the point that he began to appear more and more often at parties
and other social events.

Henry Fonda's new contentment was soon to be tested, though. On August 22, just after Jane had returned from Louisiana, Peter Fonda was arrested with three friends for possession of eight pounds of marijuana and nine marijuana plants, which were seized in a raid on a house he had rented in Tarzana. He was released on $2,000 bail pending a jury trial. With Jane's nude-picture imbroglio already front-page news, the newspapers jumped eagerly on Peter's troubles with the law. Again, Henry Fonda's two offspring were the talk of Hollywood.

Peter was tried with three other defendants. His defense was that he wasn't aware of the presence of the drugs in the raided house. His case ended in a hung jury, although one of his friends, John B. Haeberlin, was convicted. At the trial Peter kept his hair long, wore funky clothes and tinted sunglasses— everything his lawyer told him not to do. "I knew I wasn't guilty, but all my principles were at stake," he later said.

Two women on the jury voted against him. He was not acquitted, because a felony charge required a unanimous jury vote; he could have been retried, but the prosecution decided not to pursue the case, primarily because of the disappearance of an essential witness. The implication was left that the judge thought Peter was guilty, but that to retry him would be foolhardy in the absence of a vital witness.

The younger Fondas' legal problems in the fall of 1966— Jane's civil, Peter's criminal—at first had the usual disheartening effect on their father. But with his new young wife's help, he soon came to realize that the problems were at least partially his as well as theirs. He understood, finally, that his children's rebelliousness was not some kind of isolated aberration that existed without cause; it was an expression of their natures, and their natures were refractions of his. He began to acknowledge publicly that he hadn't been a good father. And without compromising his own principles, he endeavored to understand Jane and Peter's attitudes and actions in terms of the effects he had had on them. His marriage to Shirlee had humanized him considerably in the past year, and he surprised Jane and Peter, as much as himself, by standing up for them in their legal difficulties.

Peter's arrest and trial, for all their gravity, had the salutary effect of bringing the entire family closer together than it had been since the early Brentwood days. Henry Fonda showed up at Peter's trial and said, "I'm here to give moral support and any other support I can to my son." And he meant it. He still disapproved vigorously of Peter's lifestyle, but he hoped the trial would be an object lesson that would serve to straighten him out. Although Peter still couldn't talk to his father in any meaningful way, he perceived that the senior Fonda's support represented the beginning, possibly, of a new era in their relations.

Peter was even more pleased at the way his trial had brought Jane and him together. Jane had zealously defended him in the press. She declared her belief in his innocence and announced that she was willing to back him financially for another trial, if necessary. "I really dig my sister," Peter said shortly after his dismissal. "Probably a great deal more than she digs me, and she digs me."

During Peter's tribulations, Jane traveled back and forth between France and the United States. She and Vadim discovered in September that their marriage was not legal in France because he had failed to register it with a French consul in the United States, so they planned to remarry in France the following spring. *Any Wednesday* was released while Jane was pressing her lawsuit against *Playboy*, and she was praised once again by the critics for her comedic talents. The movie cemented her reputation as an outstanding comedy actress, and she was immediately offered the female lead in the forthcoming film version of Neil Simon's hit Broadway comedy *Barefoot in the Park*.

Shortly after she returned to California in the late fall to begin filming the Simon movie at Paramount Studios, *The Game Is Over* was released. The reviews were lyrical in their praise of her characterization of Renée Saccard and were no less praiseworthy of Vadim's contribution. "The performance by Jane Fonda is one of her very best," wrote Archer Winsten in the New York *Post*. "*The Game Is Over* is a film of uncompromising artistry and originality," said Dale Monroe in the Hollywood *Citizen-News*." It is Vadim's best picture to date and is unquestionably Miss Fonda's finest screen portrayal. The actress has of late demonstrated her agility as a light comedienne in Hollywood films. *The Game Is Over* is the first opportunity she has had . . . to display her intense dramatic ability with such a probing, in-depth characterization. . . ." "Miss Fonda . . . has never looked so beautiful nor acted so well— and in undubbed French, at that," Gene Youngblood observed in the Los Angeles *Herald Examiner*.

The redoubtable Judith Crist was one of the few who disagreed: "Roger Vadim firmly establishes Jane Fonda as Miss Screen Nude of '67 while equally firmly setting the intellectual cause of cinema back some 40 years. Seldom has such lavish and lush scenery, decor, flesh and photography been used to encompass such vapidity and slush. . . ."

Miss Crist notwithstanding, Vadim's promise to Jane that the role of Renée would establish her as an important dramatic actress had been fulfilled. Yet Jane's achievement was indeed compromised by the film's nudity; she discovered in short order that it was her nude body that audiences were flocking to see, not her dramatic talents, and it made her openly sarcastic about the intelligence of American movie audiences. As a result, she found it easier than ever to agree with Vadim's philosophy about giving people visually provocative images and hedonistic themes. Accordingly, while she was involved in the making of *Barefoot in the Park*, she and Vadim intensified their plans to make a film version of the highly erotic *Barbarella*.

To the press, Jane had become an enigma. Reporters and gossip columnists had difficulty reconciling the Jane Fonda of American movies with the Jane Fonda of French films. An article by Gerald Jonas that appeared in the *New York Times* on January 22, 1967, reflected this. "Jane Fonda has managed to maintain two entirely different public images simultaneously between France and the United States," Jonas wrote. "Over here she appears in movies like *Barefoot in the Park* and *Any Wednesday*; she sounds and dresses like the pretty roommate of the girl you dated in college, and most people still think of her as Henry Fonda's daughter. Over there she stars in movies like *The Circle of Love* and the just released *The Game Is Over*. She sounds like the girl you eavesdropped on in Paris cafes; she undresses like Brigitte Bardot, and everyone knows her as the latest wife . . . of Roger Vadim."

Meanwhile, Peter Fonda had become a popular symbol of the New Hollywood, and a poster of him on a motorcycle became the bestselling example of this new media form. All the long-accepted barriers of guilt and shame were coming down, and curiosity about drugs and uninhibited sexuality was given full rein. The time was ripe, Vadim and Jane thought, for a film that would repudiate the Christian sense of sin, celebrate and legitimize the new eroticism, and depict a futuristic morality that would make the current concern over present-day morals seem absurd. *Barbarella* was the ideal vehicle, and as a result of the glowing reviews Jane and Vadim received for *The Game Is Over*, Paramount Pictures agreed to finance it. Dino De Laurentiis would be the producer, and filming would begin in the fall in France and Italy.

By 1967 the war in Vietnam had become the burning central issue in American life. Youthful reaction to it had hardened into widespread anger and frustration, rapidly polarizing American society. When Jane returned to France after finishing *Barefoot in the Park*, she was beginning to subscribe to the rising antiwar sentiments like most of her Malibu film-industry friends. Commuting almost daily between St.-Ouen and Paris for ballet lessons and production meetings for *Barbarella*, she saw evidence that the antiwar fever was not just an American phenomenon but was equally intense in France. Left-sponsored student marches and demonstrations denouncing the United States erupted in Paris after each Anerican escalation of the war. Committees to aid American military deserters were formed, peace rallies were organized, political seminars convened, and anti-Americanism rose to a high pitch. As Jane listened to the speeches, arguments and diatribes, she began to view the United States in an increasingly critical light.

The Battle of Algiers, a left-wing movie celebrating the liberation of Algeria from French imperial rule a few years before, had become a popular manual of revolution and possessed an irresistible appeal for anyone who believed that colonialism was a corrupt, anachronistic, enslaving system. Jean-Luc Godard and other well-known figures of the French cinema were participating in rallies and turning into film propagandists for various liberation movements. Much of the artistic and literati population of Paris was fervent with revolutionary ardor.

The same was true elsewhere in Europe. In England, actress Vanessa Redgrave made speeches denouncing American imperialism and joined mobs that stormed the American embassy in London's Grosvenor Square. Jane, long an admirer of Redgrave's acting and of her independence as a woman, was deeply impressed by her uninhibited militancy and activism. Also the daughter of a famous theatrical family, Vanessa Redgrave was soon to become the inspiration for Jane's first ventures into antiwar activism, which were limited to attending a few Parisian rallies and listening to statistics-filled litanies about the numbers of Vietnamese the United States was killing, burning and maiming.

Vadim and Jane began to have long discussions about the war among friends like Oriana Fallaci, the socialist journalist who had witnessed their wedding, and Elizabeth Vailland, a French writer committed to communism. Vadim had caught the French antiwar fever, and he too grew harshly critical of the United States. At first, Jane deflected his criticisms. But then, as she later said, "He brought things to my attention. For instance, when the Americans evacuated the village of Ben Suc in Vietnam and put the people in a concentration camp and completely demolished the town, Vadim said, 'Look what they're doing.' And I said, 'If they're doing it, they must have a reason.' So he gave me a book to read, a book on Ben Suc, and it upset me terribly."

Jane and Vadim were remarried in a French civil ceremony at the town hall of St.-Ouen on May 18, 1967. Jane turned down starring roles in *Bonnie and Clyde* and Roman Polanski's *Rosemary's Baby* so that she could remain in France to prepare for *Barbarella*.

But there was disturbing news from home. Her father had gone to South Vietnam on a USO-sponsored tour to entertain troops. When he returned, he told a reporter, "Before I went, I wasn't anti-Vietnam—although I'm anti-card burning and flag burning, and I think a lot of the unwashed who go into these demonstrations are protesting for the sake of protest—but I was apathetic. Well, my eyes were opened. I discovered it was my morale, and America's morale, that needed strengthening, not the troops'. This has been said before—and I couldn't agree more—that every time there's a parade or peace rally in this country it will make the war that much longer, because it doesn't escape the attention of Ho Chi Minh. But I'm still a liberal. I don't feel I'm a hawk because I'm for our involvement in Vietnam, and I don't agree that we should bomb the hell out of them. But you can't be there and come away and not at least feel, well, obviously we should be there and the job is being done and it's a good job."

When Jane read her father's remarks, she was deeply distressed. She had tried to talk to him about Vietnam during her last stay in California, but he'd dismissed her ideas with his characteristic refusal to discuss anything he felt sure she was uninformed about. He was convinced that her growing sympathy toward the antiwar movement was just another manifestation of her rebellious nature. She had tried to tell him what was going on in France and how the French felt about the United States' role in Vietnam. Not only hadn't he been interested in hearing about it, he had shouted, "You don't know what the hell you're talking about." Now, reading her father's remarks—and they sounded just like him—she resolved to learn more about Vietnam so that she could speak with authority, the next time she saw him.

If Jane was an enigma to the press as an actress—the sweet, amusing girl-next-door in American movies, the sultry sex symbol in French films—her private image was equally baffling. Her marriage to Vadim seemed to absorb her. The relationship had transformed her from an anxious, flighty American girl to a calm, sophisticated, Europeanized woman. Although she had learned to adapt to the sexual adventurism of Vadim and their friends, she was still basically a one-man woman and found it difficult to derive much lasting pleasure from a life of extramarital liaisons, no matter how routine it became, according to Vadim's hints to the press. "There are women who can make love and forget about it in the morning," Vadim said about her. "But not Jane. She is too . . . sentimental."

Her deepest happiness came from her farm. Like her beach house at Malibu, Jane's home in St.-Ouen rapidly became open house to the international film set. She loved playing the busy hostess. A visitor would be greeted by a howling pack of animals: several dogs, even more cats and a yardful of ducks, rabbits and a pony. When Jane returned from trips, the dogs would leap on her in a scene that, as one friend said, "Would have had Albert Payson Terhune on his knees, sobbing."

Inside the ancient farmhouse, Jane had created a modern tasteful home with but one mild touch of the bizarre—a wall of glass that separated the low-beamed master bedroom from the bathroom, giving occupants of either chamber a clear view of what was happening in the other. "I almost drowned in the bathtub one day," Jane recalled to an interviewer. "Vadim came running in wearing one of my miniskirts, and it was a disaster."

Vadim's sense of satire delighted most in visual incongruity. To him nothing was more deliciously incongruous than the sight of Jane entertaining Brigitte Bardot, Annette Stroyberg and Catherine Deneuve. Jane appreciated the irony too, and she claimed to enjoy the company of all three. "I know all

Vadim's women," she said. "I like Annette. I like Bardot. I especially like Catherine. Her little boy comes to visit us, often at the same time Nathalie's here. It's marvelous, having the children together."

It was the frequent presence of the Vadim children that got Jane to thinking about having a child of her own. She saw the farm as a perfect place to raise a child—it was much like the Brentwood estate of her own childhood. Although she and Vadim had decided when they first started living together that she wasn't cut out to be a mother, her continuing exposure to Vadim's children made her feel differently. "I was always terrified of having children. Being in analysis made me very aware of all the kinds of mistakes parents can make, and I was afraid I'd make them all too. But then I thought, well, at forty you may be pretty damned sorry you didn't."

By the summer of 1967 Jane was determined to have a child. Vadim, who loved children, was all for it. But first they had to make *Barbarella*.

chapter 20

BARBARELLA AND BEYOND

Movies based on well-known American comic strips were seldom as successful or as appealing as their models. Aside from the fact that cartoon characters do not lend themselves well to real-people portrayals, one box-office element that was lacking in all such pictures was sex—with the exception, possibly, of the harmlessly seductive glances of Appassionata von Climax in *Li'l Abner*.

European comic strips were something else again where erotic innuendoes were common. The strip most familiar to Americans in 1967 was one that had been published for some time in the avant-garde New York magazine *Evergreen Review*. This was "Barbarella," a sleek, audacious combination of science fiction and soft-core pornography.

Jane Fonda had grown accustomed to answering questions about being a sex symbol by disclaiming any interest in the office and denying that she ever thought of herself as one. "The overemphasis on identifying me with sex is pretty silly," she said. "I'm no sex siren just because I believe in approaching sex and the human body with honesty. Most of the women who've been big sex symbols have had problems in their own sex lives. They weren't so much women as female impersonators. It was a caricature. Look at Marilyn Monroe. She parodied femininity. I'd hate to think that my appeal was based

on that kind of abnormality. I think the whole obsession with
sex, and with the size of a girl's breasts, is a perversion—it's
a sad comment on the state of manhood in America. The real
homosexuals are the big tough guys who think they're so manly.
All they're doing is hiding behind their fears. They all want
to go back to their mothers' breasts, that's all. If you ask me,
the whole business about sex is sickness because it's dishonest.
Everyone fantasizes about doing things that they would be
afraid to do in reality. That's not for me."

In *Barbarella*, Vadim and Jane saw a handy opportunity to
exploit American movie audiences' sexual obsessions and parody their fantasies. According to Vadim, Jane would play "a
kind of sexual Alice in Wonderland of the future." The picture
would give them the license to make a kind of joint philo-
sophical statement about the ridiculousness of the old-fashioned
sexual and moral preoccupations of contemporary society. At
the same time it would allow Vadim daringly to glorify Jane
"as the ultimate sex symbol" and provide "a whimsical, lyrical
outlook toward sex in the year 40,000 A.D."

Vadim put together an international cast and started filming
in Rome during the summer. John Phillip Law, an ethereal
young American actor who had played in *Hurry Sundown* and
was a Malibu neighbor, was cast as the pure, blind Guardian
Angel who looks after Barbarella as she gallivants from galaxy
to galaxy in pursuit of righteous pleasure. With its far-out story
and otherworldly setting, the film required a great deal of in-
genious and expensive technical effects to make it work. Not
the least of these involved the picture's opening sequence,
which required Jane to do an elaborate, sinuous strip in a state
of zero gravity while the film's credits were run off.

"I was completely naked under the titles," Jane said, "and
there's a funny story about how that happened. We were supposed to have a costume, but it didn't arrive. So we sat down
and Vadim said, 'Listen, anyone who's read "Barbarella" ex-
pects her to be naked all the way through. And we're doing
this as a spoof of the sort of pictures people think I make. So
let's start out naked.' I agreed to do the scene naked, but Vadim
promised that he'd cover my nudity with the titles. He did the
titles once and I said, 'That's not covered enough.' So he did
them again."

It was the most difficult and complicated film Jane had ever
worked on. Rather than attempt to portray Barbarella in some

surrealistic way, she played her as straight Jane Fonda—as American, one might say, as apple pie. She underlined the parody by taking things seriously rather than acting for laughs. The resulting contradiction between her fresh, bouncy innocence and the picture's lewd cartoon world of the future gave the character of Barbarella an unexpectedly fey sexuality that would have been mere lewdness in the hands of another, less subtle actress.

For Jane, the acting was easy but the filming itself was filled with perils. The sets were complex, and the special-effects machinery often broke down at crucial, dangerous times. One scene called for 2,000 wrens to be blown by giant fans into a cage occupied by Jane, whereupon the birds were to become so excited by the wind currents that they would pick off her clothes. For four days the fans whirred, the birds swooped, Jane emoted—but nothing happened. In desperation, Vadim jammed birdseed into Jane's scanty costume and fired guns in the air. This bothered the birds not at all, but it drove Jane into the hospital with hypertension, a fever and acute nausea. After three days of rest, she returned to work and finally completed the scene with the aid of even larger fans and a flock of peckish lovebirds.

It is a curious fact of movie-industry life that most arty, breakthrough films fail at the box office but have what their makers like to call a *succès d'estime*. Just the opposite would happen with *Barbarella*—when it was released, the public lined up to see it while the critics, except for a few who interpreted it as an amusing reflection of the high campiness that marked the times, lambasted it. "You could subtitle the film, *2001, A Space Idiocy*," Charles Champlin wrote in the Los Angeles *Times*. "Miss Fonda plays what you might call Flesh Gordon." Others saw it as "glossy trash" or "beautifully photographed garbage" and considered its only saving grace to be Jane's extended nudity and a witty, futuristic copulation scene between her and actor David Hemmings. "Vadim is the screen's foremost celebrant of erotic trash," Pauline Kael remarked, "with the scandalous habit of turning each wife into a facsimile of the first and spreading her out for the camera. . . . *Barbarella* is disappointing after the expectations that one had of a film that would be good trashy, corrupt entertainment for a change. *Barbarella* isn't even good trash, but it's corrupt all right. . . ."

In an interview after *Barbarella* was released, at which

Vadim was present, Jane was asked outright if she was an exhibitionist. Vadim interjected. "In America you are all so Puritan, so prude. You worry so much about showing the body. All actors are exhibitionists. I know, for I was an actor. But I suffered agonies as an actor, because I am not an exhibitionist. A voyeur, perhaps, but not an exhibitionist."

"Vadim," Jane said as the interviewer recorded their exchange, "I don't think he means in a physical sense. He means, do I need attention?"

"Ah, yes," Vadim said. "Well, you do exhibit yourself, as a kind of . . . experiment. You would not need to do this if you knew, really, who you are. But you do not quite know who you are, so you make tests, as in chemistry, to find out."

Vadim's comment was apparently an insight for Jane: "Yes, wow!" she said excitedly. "You're absolutely right. I never realized that until this moment—that I do in life exactly what I do when I act. I go through this extroverted exhibitionistic period—talking like the character, and so on—as an experiment."

To the interviewer she said, ". . . The identity I found as an actress is desperately important to me. Oh, I do feel about two hundred times more pulled together since I met Vadim, but if I had not had that identity to begin with, it might not have worked out at all. I'm certain that deep down, I still have no confidence. Really, that's no bull. If a situation begins badly, if I feel I'm being boring, or that I don't look good, well, I crumble. You want to hide, but the old ego won't let you. So you go onto a stage, or a screen, and hide behind the mask of a character. You're safe, but people are still looking at you. My father is like that. It has got to be the prime motivation of every actor—this need to express yourself sort of fictionally because you don't have confidence in your real self. That, and a certain exhibitionism."

Physical exhibitionism, the interviewer wanted to know?

"I'm not a physical exhibitionist," Jane said firmly.

But what about the nudity in her films?

"It certainly is not something I get any kicks from. I agree with Vadim about it. In each picture that I have been nude, it was necessary to the text to achieve the proper dramatic effect."

The question of her public nudity was fast becoming a central issue in Jane's life. In November, while she was still making *Barbarella* in Europe, another controversy swirled in the

United States that contradicted her disclaimers about being an exhibitionist. *Newsweek* came out with a feature story on nudity and sex in movies. The magazine's cover was adorned with a seminude picture of Jane, although the story itself hardly mentioned her. The cover created a furor, especially among public school boards which approved the purchase of *Newsweek* for use in social studies courses. Cries of outrage were sounded throughout the country about the magazine's libidinous assault on the minds and sensibilities of innocent schoolchildren, and it was banned from many school libraries. Although Jane was somewhat of an innocent victim, the incident was another installment in the hardening of her sex-symbol image, as well as evidence of the country's increasing unrest.

The United States was becoming more intensely divided than ever. Martin Luther King's murder had inflamed the reformist antiwar spirit of young America, white *and* black. The huge march on the Pentagon in October 1967, carefully planned and orchestrated by the New Left leadership, was the first mass demonstration against the war to draw Americans from all walks of life, not just radicals. Hallucinogenized hippies marched arm in arm with Bergdorf-outfitted housewives; doctors and businessmen in ties and vests mingled with scruffy folk singers. The media focused on the march and from that point on sympathy for the antiwar movement began to permeate every level of American society. And as opposition to the war broadened—helped by the government's indictment in January 1968 of Benjamin Spock, the celebrated baby doctor whose child-rearing theories were embraced by millions of parents, on charges of counseling draft evasion—antiantiwar sentiments hardened as well.

In January, while completing work on *Barbarella*, Jane became pregnant. When she found out about it in February, she was at once elated and frightened. In March she canceled out of two Hollywood films she had agreed to star in, stocked up on copies of Dr. Spock's books and other guides, and settled in at her farm to prepare for the birth of her child in September.

Although for most pregnant women time usually slows to a crawl, for Jane it seemed to compress and speed up. Freed of further filmmaking responsibilities she became more sharply aware of what was happening in the world. During the early months of 1968, student agitation at the Sorbonne and other universities dominated the front pages of the French press.

Many of her friends were more actively involved than ever in the struggle against the French government's suppression of Left-inspired demonstrations against the American war in Vietnam and other student issues. As Jane saw evidence and heard tales of governmental brutality, she became increasingly incensed.

"I started reading the newspapers more carefully. I started watching the news on French TV; the B-52 bombers dropping their leftover bombs on the villages. I started following the testimony at the Bertrand Russell tribunal, understanding the split between what we were doing and what we said we were doing. A lot was happening inside me."

Peter Fonda arrived in Paris and brought vivid stories of the violence growing there over the war. Although he sympathized with the antiwar movement, his feelings transcended the war. Steeped in the antimaterialistic fervor of Hollywood's drug-and-love culture, he still envisioned the eventual transformation of America into a society of peace and universal love based on magical, mind-expanding drugs.

And he was full of talk of a low-budget movie he planned to make with Dennis Hopper about a pair of drug-dealing hippies on a motorcycle trip across America. Although Jane was unimpressed by his ideas for the film, she was pleased by his new ambition and sense of purpose. And even though she thought his notions about the transformation of American society unrealistic, she got caught up in his fervor, especially when he connected his dream to his own children and to the child she was expecting. Measured against her fears, Peter's daring and hope seemed at once reckless and admirable, and Jane envied him for his crazy pioneering determination.

With her maternal instincts ripening, Jane was repulsed and frightened by the violence in America and France. Robert Kennedy was assassinated. The Democratic Convention in Chicago was turned into a bloody battleground as Hubert Humphrey was nominated to run against Richard Nixon. In Paris, radical students and police fought pitched battles over students' rights to demonstrate against the war. She grew depressed over the prospect of bringing a child into a world that seemed to grow more and more discombobulated by the day. When she visualized her child having to grow up in the atmosphere of intergenerational hatred that seemed to have established itself as a permanent fact of life, she felt guilty for wishing to have a child at all.

Jane continued to be exposed to increasingly angry but highly rational criticism of the United States. She "met American deserters and Vietnamese of the National Liberation Front, who knew facts that I had not been aware of. Then I saw a movie on the Washington march, boys with long hair and professors and radicals putting flowers into the guns of the guards standing in front of the Pentagon. A lot was happening, and I learned. . . ."

Jane brooded extensively over deep contradictions she began to perceive in the American system. She was by then, like most young Americans, totally opposed to war, and she began to give financial and moral support to organizations in Paris that had been formed to help American deserters. In talking to some of these young men, she heard hair-raising tales of atrocities committed in Vietnam and secret weapons being used against the civilian population. She was shocked to discover that much of what she learned glaringly contradicted the official reports issued by Washington. For the first time she thought it likely that the United States government actually was lying to the American people about its conduct of the war, as well as about other foreign policy matters. It was her contact with the deserting GIs, more than anything else, that aroused Jane's ire about the American system.

One of the French radicals Jane got to know well during her pregnancy was Elisabeth Vailland. Roger Vailland, a well-known French Communist who was a hero of the Resistance in World War II and who had championed the Communist cause in France in the years thereafter, had recently died. Elisabeth, his fifty-year-old widow, was an Italian-born writer. She had become loyal to Communism during World War II as a young member of the partisan underground that fought against the fascism of Mussolini and the Nazi occupation of Italy. She married Roger Vailland in the early 1950s and, with him, had become an experienced political activist in France. After Vailland died, she carried on his work. She also deepened her friendship with Jane Fonda.

Although Jane had enjoyed her trip to Russia a few years before, mostly because she had been surprised to discover that the Russian people were as harmless as she had expected them to be malevolent, she remained unimpressed by the Soviet

brand of Communism. And in spite of her growing disenchantment with the United States in 1967 and 1968, her belief in
the American democratic ideal, with its built-in enmity toward
Communism, was still much too intact to be seriously compromised by the beguiling logic of her French leftist friends.
Nevertheless, she found a certain romance in their idealism
and a genuine humanitarian appeal in their lifelong struggle,
personal sacrifice and political activism. Jane determined that
they were not promoting violence, especially the women among
them, but were advocating humane change—a new world order
in which everyone would share in the riches of the planet. The
Communist rationale could hardly be called evil in itself, she
thought. If Communism in practice sometimes created violence
and suppression—well, that was because Communism's evolution was forever being challenged by the reactionism of the
capitalist world, and because of the natural bellicosity of the
universal male ego in whose mind Communism had been conceived and by whose hands it was molded.

Elisabeth Vailland was a different kind of Communist—an
activist, to be sure, but a pacifist with a woman's compassion
for the disenfranchised of the world. She was a tough-minded
intellectual whose knowledge was broad and whose sense of
injustice ran deep and fervent. At the same time she was a
woman who was alone in the world, weighted down by the
sadness caused by the recent loss of her husband. In Jane,
Vailland found a confused but eager student. Jane, for her part,
found in Vailland a sympathetic and understanding teacher.
Jane listened to Elisabeth Vailland's bitter but inspiring stories
of her thirty years of political activism with a growing admiration for what a woman could do in the world besides make
movies and keep house.

chapter 21

THEY SHOOT
HORSES

As Jane moved into the advanced stages of her pregnancy, she became much more subdued. A case of mumps kept her bedridden for more than a month. And when she was safely over it she became almost obsessively protective of herself fearing that because of the mumps episode, the baby might be born damaged. She spent most of the summer in St. Tropez with Vadim. She took long solitary walks on the beach and generally withdrew into herself.

Not all was quiet in St. Tropez, however. Again there was a steady stream of friends to and from the Vadim villa. Brigitte Bardot, who lived nearby, was especially solicitous of Jane. All summer long she had been predicting that Jane's baby would be born on September 28, her own birthday, and that it would be a girl. Jane and Vadim insisted it would be a boy, and many of their discussions revolved around the name they should give him. Catherine Deneuve insisted that Jane have her baby at the same hospital where she had given birth to her son by Vadim.

By mid-September Jane and Vadim were back in Paris. She was having nightmares about the baby being born in the form of a ten-year-old facsimile of Brigitte Bardot. As Vadim later told it, on the evening of September 28, he playfully put his hands on Jane's stomach and, mimicking a sorcerer, told her that she must start having the baby. "Forty minutes later, the labor pains began. I had remembered everything. I took scissors and string, in case the baby was born on the way to the hospital, and we started out. Fifty meters from the hospital the automobile stopped. Yes, I had remembered everything except to buy the gas. So I picked up Jane and carried her to the hospital—believe me, it was very dramatic—and one hour later she gave birth."

Jane had been hoping for a boy but she quickly got over her initial disappointment that the child was a girl. At least the baby didn't look like Bardot. She and Vadim named her Vanessa, partly in honor of Vanessa Redgrave and partly because they simply liked the name, which they thought went well with Vadim. "She will grow up to be 'VV'," boasted Vadim. The baby, unaffected by Jane's case of mumps, had Vadim's eyes and head, but the lower half of her face was all Fonda.

For Jane the birth was another epiphany in her life. "I had been wanting that child so much, for so long.... And something happened to me while she was growing inside my stomach. For the first time in my life, I felt confident as a human being and as a woman, and I'm sure it was because I was finally a mother. I began to feel a unity with people. I began to love people, to understand that we do not give life to a human being only to have it killed by B-52 bombs, or to have it jailed by fascists, or to have it destroyed by social injustice. When she was born—my baby—it was as if the sun had opened up for me. I felt whole. I became free."

A few weeks after Vanessa's arrival, *Barbarella* opened in the United States and established Jane more solidly than ever in the public mind as a symbol of wicked sexuality. What the public didn't know was that while her nude or scantily costumed image was cavorting with erotic abandon through the ethereal world of *Barbarella*, she was back on her farm in St.-Ouen nursing Vanessa, feeling decidedly unsexy, and trying to come to terms with an entirely new complex of emotions.

The baby quickly became the central focus of her life. "It's made my life completely different," she said a few months later. "I can't get over the miracle of giving birth. I feel fulfilled, rounder. Little things that used to bother me seem so unimportant now. I want more children. I miss being pregnant. I've never been so elated. The pleasure and pain were so extraordinary that I try to hang onto every memory of them."

Barbarella's release represented Jane's first appearance on screen in almost a year. When it became clear that it was going to be an international box-office success, she was flooded with scripts from Hollywood. One was an adaptation of a 1935 novel by the late Horace McCoy, a little-known Hollywood screenwriter, that had more recently surfaced in Europe as a cult book of the French left. It had been praised by such pillars of the French intelligentsia as Simone de Beauvoir, Jean-Paul Sartre and Albert Camus, who declared it "the first existential novel to come out of America." It was required reading—as an indictment of the American capitalist system—for any self-respecting, well-informed French revolutionary. The book's title was *They Shoot Horses, Don't They?* When Jane read the book and then the screenplay, which was a faithful rendition of the novel, she insisted on making it her next picture.

Jane's role was to be that of Gloria, a defeated, downtrodden American girl of the early 1930s who, in utter financial and spiritual desperation, signs up for a dance marathon. The marathon dance craze of the time, with its pain and suffering, was treated by McCoy as a metaphor for the Great Depression in America and the ingrained social ills that caused it. The screenplay captured the novel's burning despair perfectly, and the picture's producers hoped that the movie would serve as an effective symbol of the political poisons behind America's Vietnam experience. Director Sidney Pollack said, "Kids don't want to be entertained today. They're pretty cynical. Hopefully, they will find it interesting and enlightening to discover that there's been another bad time in America, even worse than it is now."

Jane saw in the film a threefold challenge. First, she felt that the role of Gloria, the marathon dancer, gave her the kind of dramatic opportunity she had never had before. The second lay in the script. With its straightforward, naturalistic, presentation of a slice of American life, it contained a searing indictment of the evils of American capitalism that coincided with Jane's rising political anger. It was a script with a heavy message. Yet it was not pedantic—laden with pointed, obvious speeches and dialogue that had made so many films of its type such a bore. Third, "I was sick and tired of being thought of as a sex symbol. I felt I had to start doing more serious work than *Barbarella*."

Jane returned to the United States at the end of the year to start preparing for *They Shoot Horses, Don't They?* By January

1969, she, Vadim and Vanessa were resettled in Malibu. After a year and a half in France, Jane was glad to be back. "When you come home," she said, "that aggressive American friendliness comes as such a shock after the coldness of the French. But it's a joy to come back. Life over there is entrenched. It's frozen. It's got arthritis. I adore it here. And all the things that are happening." If Jane seemed to have lost some of her affection for France, possibly it was because her feelings about Vadim were changing.

Jane was thirty-one. After giving birth to Vanessa, she had dieted down to her lowest weight ever and was immensely pleased with her leaner, more mature look. She was ecstatically happy with the baby and could feel her internal strength and confidence multiply as each day went by. She was a proud mother, and she delighted in showing Vanessa off to all her California friends. What pleased her almost as much were the signs that her father was becoming more tolerant of her.

Henry Fonda had bought a house in the exclusive Bel Air section of Los Angeles and spent much of his time there quietly with his wife and flower beds. He was proud of his new granddaughter, even more pleased by the positive effect motherhood seemed to have on Jane. "We're very close now," he boasted to a reporter, "closer than we've ever been. She doesn't talk about me the way she used to any more. She's got this marriage with Vadim, and the baby, and my God, that girl has maternal instincts she never knew she had. She's grown into an extremely intelligent, attractive woman. She's outgoing, not at all like me. . . . Look at the kind of home she's created, look at the life they lead out there in Malibu. People coming, people going, all day long, open house all the time, and Jane handling it all so beautifully, making people feel comfortable. . . ."

Fonda had even grown more tolerant of his son, although he still disapproved of much of what Peter was doing and who he was doing it with. When Fonda's adopted daughter Amy, by then an impressionable fifteen, visited him in Bel Air, he would not let her see any of Peter's motorcycle-and-drug films. He detested most of Peter's friends, and he particularly disliked Dennis Hopper, with whom Peter was filming the low-budget cross-country motorcycle movie that was to be *Easy Rider*. "The man is an idiot," Henry Fonda said. "He's a total freak-out, stoned out of his mind all the time."

It seemed that half of Hollywood was stoned out of its mind

all the time. But except for her consumption of tranquilizers, diet pills and, on occasion, marijuana and hashish, Jane Fonda stayed away from the more exotic drugs. The drug craze was in high gear in filmland, and many of her acquaintances were regular users of hallucinogens and cocaine. Jane was puzzled by the intense dependence on heavy drugs she saw all around her, and it was characteristic of her own sense of independence that she resisted numerous urgings to start using them. She accepted her brother's self-proclaimed "liberation" through LSD, but she was loath to try it herself. "I think proselytizers become as square as the people they're proselytizing," she said. "Why all this proselytizing by takers of LSD? An alcoholic drinks, but an alcoholic doesn't say, 'Come on, you have to be an alcoholic, too.' Sure, I've taken pot, but I prefer a good drink."

However, her brother Peter was on the verge of turning his spaced-out image into millions of dollars with *Easy Rider* which told the story of two hippie drug dealers who are senselessly murdered on their journey "in search of America." The film's grim ending reflected the confusion and violence of the day, as did Peter Fonda himself when he expressed his stylish disillusionment in the film. "I've always thought about suicide," he said. "I've popped pills and drove a car over a hundred miles an hour into a bridge." Fonda's death wish hit much closer to Hollywood's true feelings than did the love-and-flower-child myth to which many in California continued to cling.

Jane Fonda's role in *They Shoot Horses, Don't They?* was to become yet another symbol of Hollywood's increasing fascination with the new violence and despair. To underline the mood, Jane had her long blonde hair chopped off and tightly marcelled, thirties-style. "One of the reasons I took the part," she said, "is that I want to play something completely different, something that is not necessarily sympathetic in the conventional sense." She also wanted to get away from the bubble-headed comedy characters she was remembered for in Hollywood. To strengthen herself for the arduous role, she jogged every day along the beach, swam as much as she could in the chilly Pacific, and faithfully followed a high-protein diet. She also read everything she could find on the Depression, even seeking out her father to probe his memory of the period. He had created another hapless victim of American society twenty-five years earlier with his portrayal of Tom Joad. Jane envisioned *They Shoot Horses, Don't They?* as having the potential to become a modern day *Grapes of Wrath*.

"It's the most beautiful story I've read since I became an actress," she said. "My role is a girl who's really a loser. Men treat her badly, and she can never win. She's embittered and negative toward life. I want to make her a very real character.

"The war we're going through now—well, our country has never gone through such a long, agonizing experience, except for the Depression. The Depression is the closest America ever came before to a national disaster, the kind of thing that unites people and reduces everything to basic questions—eat or not, live or die. Perhaps audiences—especially kids—will be able to come away from seeing *They Shoot Horses* with the feeling that if we could pull out of the Depression, we can pull out of the mess we're in now. The picture may work on audiences the same way the marathons themselves did, letting people see people who were suffering even more than they are.

"Another thing I like about the film is that it's about people dealing with problems created by society rather than by themselves. They are dealing with them the best they can, yet they are condemned for their solutions."

The filming of *They Shoot Horses, Don't They?* during the spring of 1969 was the first in a series of events that year that would finally shatter Jane's residual inbred assumptions about America and launch her on a completely new course. It was a long, arduous picture, and as she delved deeper and deeper into the role of Gloria, the character's despair became her own; as she identified more intensively with the despondent Gloria, she grew despondent herself. Eventually the characterization absorbed her completely—so much so that she finally moved into a dressing room at the studio rather than stay at home in Malibu with Vadim. "I found I couldn't go to work in the morning as a happy woman and then step into that role. Gloria was such a desperate, negative, depressed person. Gradually, I let myself become that way too. How could I go home like that? I'd walk in the door and auuugh! So I stayed away. Of course, Vanessa would stay overnight with me every now and then. Still, it took me months to get over it."

Although she did get over it, playing that part in that particular movie at that particular time had a profound effect on Jane. As she looked around at the real world in which she lived from the perspective of the fictional but uncannily similar world Gloria inhabited, all distinctions blurred. Like the America of the thirties, America in the sixties was in a state of crisis, as desperate but more volatile.

Susannah York, who costarred in *They Shoot Horses*, recalls that Jane became increasingly moody and disturbed during the shooting of the picture. "Jane was very much into her role and working very, very hard on it. The few times we talked I could see she was having a problem with her part. I was, too, but she seemed particularly intense about it and upset most of the time."

Another member of the company says, "Jane worked like a demon on that character. I've been connected with a lot of films, and I've never seen anyone go through such agony to produce a performance. It was really frightening, sometimes, the way she'd come off the set after a scene. She'd hold onto that character like it was a priceless possession . . . no, it was like she was possessed, like the character had gotten thoroughly inside her and completely displaced Jane Fonda."

A third observer remembers that Jane became "a fanatic about Gloria. It was like an actor who guzzles a quart of vodka before going on to play a drunk scene, then afterwards remains drunk. Jane wore the role on her sleeve. She'd get away from it a little on weekends, but just a little. During the week it was hard to tell the difference between Jane and Gloria. Off the set she walked like her, talked like her, mumbled like her. She had this perpetual tired, vacuous expression on her face, and she'd go around with her body slumped over like a sapling in a heavy wind. She got thinner and thinner—you could almost see the weight melting away. Before long, everybody connected with the picture was worried about whether she was going to make it through."

The grueling shooting schedule lasted into May. Much of the movie was filmed inside an exact replica of the old, well-known Aragon Ballroom on Lick Pier in Ocean Park, an amusement center just south of Santa Monica. During the long, difficult location filming, Jane lived much of the time in a trailer adjacent to the pier.

"God, it was hard doing that part," she said later. "It was like walking a tightrope over Niagara Falls constantly. . . . When we finished the endurance race sequences, everybody would collapse, weeping hysterically. . . . It was the toughest thing I've had to do—ever.

"I'm opposed to taking your work home with you. That's

why the more I got into Gloria, I stayed away from home. . . . I became Gloria. She was uneducated, tough, bitter, cynical. It took me a long time to stop talking like her. Talking bad, using a lotta bad English, *et cetera*. . . . And feeling like her. Hard, rough, brittle . . . I was so miserable. How Vadim stuck with me I don't know. I discovered a black side to my character I didn't know about. . . . Gloria was hopeless, suicidal, and in the end she dies. In my performance there could not be an inkling, a ray of hope. It had to be that way; otherwise the ending wouldn't work."

When *They Shoot Horses, Don't They?* was released six months later, it was widely praised, with many critics predicting an Oscar for Jane. It was easily the best performance she had ever given. It was muscular and athletic, sensitive and knowing, totally devoid of the sex, nudity and coy naughtiness her reputation was built on. For this she was glad. But she was not particularly happy with the way the picture turned out.

Jane believed that *Horses* had the potential of being a truly great movie, a classic, but that something had been lost between the filming and the final editing. She disliked the misty opening-credit sequence with the galloping black horse; she was convinced that it was a misleadingly romantic softening of the picture's stark impact, a damaging compromise. She had pleaded for the removal of a slow-motion sequence of her falling down in a meadow—again, she said, film gimmickry that eroded the film's blunt honesty. And she was especially unhappy about the exclusion of a scene that provided a logical explanation for Gloria's quitting the marathon. She was convinced that Gloria's tragic fate lost some of its credibility as a result.

Jane was right, but try as she did to persuade director Pollack and the producers to make the changes she wanted after she saw a rough print, her feelings had no influence on the final cut. And by the time the picture was released in December, she was no longer emotionally involved in it. She had a myriad of other, more pressing concerns on her mind.

chapter 22

SYMPATHY
FOR THE DEVIL

Hollywood had always been an escapist milieu, but by early 1969 escapism had entered a new dimension. The hippie-oriented culture had blossomed into a full but sinister flower. The drug-suffused haze that permeated the flashy beach houses of Malibu, the sedate mansions of Beverly Hills, the spectacular cliff houses above Hollywood and the plain bungalows of the dreary San Fernando Valley was accented by a growing cynicism that rapidly transformed itself, for many, into a kind of doomsday mania. Hollywood, even more rapidly than the rest of the country, grew increasingly schizophrenic.

The innocence and optimism of the earlier, gentler hippie phase had given way to a wholesale fascination with demonism and violence. The Polish director Roman Polanski had whetted America's appetite for sexual and visual horror in films.

Polanski and his wife, the starlet Sharon Tate, were regular visitors at the Fonda-Vadim house in Malibu. Sharon had recently discovered that she was pregnant, and she looked forward eagerly to bearing Polanski's child late in the summer.

Polanski, an aggressive, competitive, cocksure European manchild with an insatiable sexual hunger, found his career as a director-writer-producer flourishing as a result of *Rosemary's Baby*. It seemed few tales about Roman Polanski's bizarre private life in Hollywood were exaggerations. He and his wife, at least through some of their associations, were at the epicenter of "Mondo Hollywood," as one writer described the film community. Because of Vadim's reputation, and because of his and Jane's relationship with Roman and Sharon, many of the rumors about the Polanskis spilled over onto them.

"You know," Jane said in an interview in the early spring of 1969, "since I've been with Vadim it doesn't matter what I say to writers. They always imply that we live in some kind of weird, perpetual orgy. Good God, we don't even go to Denise Minnelli's, much less to orgies. And we don't go in for that Hollywood jazz. I mean, people drop in here—Peter and his wife, Dennis Hopper, Christian Marquand, Roman Polanski. . . . It's very loose—I mean, casual—down here on the beach. . . . We had Simone Signoret over the other night . . . and we screened [Andy Warhol's] *Nude Restaurant and Flesh*. This is an orgy?"

Fanning the flames of gossip further was a book written by one of Warhol's most notorious film performers, Viva Superstar. Called *Superstar*, it was for the most part a semifictionalized journal-cum-anthology with various famous figures in Viva's life. Two of the figures echoed many aspects of the personality and rumored private activities of Jane Fonda, called "Jean La Fonce" in the book, and Roger Vadim, who was called "Robert." Needless to say the account of a weekend at La Fonce's house was replete with the most exotic forms of licentiousness.

When I asked Viva whether the Jean La Fonce of her book was based on Jane Fonda, she said, "It's all fiction." In fact, she responded to all my questions about the book with, "It's all fiction." And with a huge wink.

It is possible that in early 1969, Jane Fonda was not above indulging in such weekend sport as Viva described, but it's hardly likely that she was the perpetual orgiast the book and many gossip columnists implied that she was. In fact, the Jean La Fonce of *Superstar* confesses almost sheepishly that she is "too straight" a person to live up to the reputation that surrounds her.

That spring Peter Fonda and Dennis Hopper's *Easy Rider* was released. Not since James Dean in *Rebel without a Cause* or Marlon Brando in *The Wild One* had a movie actor so captured the imagination and admiration of a generation as did Peter Fonda in his role as Captain America. He projected the schizoid mood of young America with such forcefulness that the film's many inadequacies were overlooked. *Easy Rider* was an immediate box-office hit, and the movie made Peter Fonda not only a genuine star, but a man to be reckoned with in the executive suites of the movie industry. Suddenly the studios began to fall all over themselves to sign up young filmmakers who, they hoped, would capture the Fonda financial magic.

The success of *Easy Rider* brought Jane and Peter closer during the summer of 1969. Each was full of praise for the other in the press. Peter declared he had stopped taking LSD and other hallucinogens. He limited himself almost exclusively to marijuana, as did Jane, he said, and he planned to use his new national stature to become a spokesman for the antiwar and ecology movements. In interviews he decried the waste and hypocrisy of American society and championed the drive for radical change.

Despite her pleasure over Peter's success, Jane grew more moody and depressed during the summer. Much of her bleakness was the result of her spiritual hangover from playing Gloria in *They Shoot Horses, Don't They?* She seemed unable to shake the deep feelings of pessimism that haunted her as a result of her immersion in the character and in the gloomy period in which the picture was set. Gloria had been able to find release from her misery only through death. Once filming was over Jane was left with Gloria's interior misery but without any mode of release.

But what affected her more profoundly was the continuing escalation of the war in Vietnam and the American government's often brutal suppression of reaction to it. President Nixon had announced after his inauguration that he would start withdrawing troops in small increments from Vietnam. But he had compromised the effects of his declaration immediately by stepping up American bombing.

The antiwar movement had reacted with a new outcry. The more vocal and active the dissent became, the more assiduously the Nixon administration tried to stifle it. Federal trials were being conducted all over the country against activists who were putting their bodies, their careers, their futures and sometimes their lives on the line. "Conspiracies" were being uncovered and announced almost weekly by the government. The FBI, the CIA, the Army Counterintelligence Corps and other agencies had been turned into a massive combined political police

force that infiltrated, spied on and sometimes actually engi-
neered the activities of the "subversives who sought to under-
mine the American way," as one high government official
described the militant proponents of peace. Antiwar hysteria
was countered by prowar paranoia, and traditional concepts of
patriotism and moral responsibility were being blurred by vi-
olently contradictory interpretations.

Jane watched the turmoil grow from the comfortable sanctuary of her Malibu home with an increasing sense of unease,
frustration and guilt. She had been sufficiently disabused of
her residual beliefs in the efficacy of the American dream to
have grown cynical and disbelieving about the true intentions
of flagwaving politicians. As visions of Vietnamese women
and children consumed by napalm flashed more frequently in
her mind's eye, she grew at once more angry and anxious. She
realized that she had lived in an ivory tower for the thirty-two
years of her life, no matter how sophisticated she thought herself. Like many privileged, liberally reared people, she felt
deep pangs of self-betrayal for having clung so long to beliefs
that were being contradicted daily by the current events.

Two of Jane's neighbors in Malibu were Donald and Shirley
Sutherland. He was the little-known Canadian who would soon
achieve acting stardom for his role in the satirical antiwar movie
M★A★S★H. Shirley Sutherland, his wife, was the daughter
of a luminary of left-wing Canadian politics. She had long been
an outspoken critic of the war in Vietnam, as well as of other
manifestations of what she called the corruption of the American system, which included racism and sexism. Indeed, she
was Malibu's resident political and feminist philosopher and
the beach colony's chief organizer of local celebrity support
for Indians, antiwar protesters, draft resisters, women's lib-
erationists, Black Panthers, and other components of the American radical movement. She had been proselytizing for months
up and down the beach on behalf of her various causes. Soon
she had a more than interested listener in Jane Fonda. Jane's
vision of her own role in the scheme of things was becoming
more unsettled and she was anxiously starting to look for a
way to expiate her guilt and redefine herself.

One of the most resoundingly popular music hits of 1969
was the Rolling Stones' "Sympathy for the Devil," a throbbing,
sardonic celebration of the satanic forces at work in the world—
a devil's-eye view of history, so to speak. The devil of the

song's title, in the eyes of composer-singer Mick Jagger, was responsible for all the violent and cataclysmic events of the past, and sympathy was demanded because all of us were personifications of Satan. *They shouted out/Who killed the Kennedys?* went one of the song's lines. *Well, after all/It was you and me.* . . . It was no small irony that Roman Polanski had been Robert Kennedy's dinner companion the night Kennedy was shot. Like Polanski, Sirhan Sirhan, Kennedy's murderer, was a foreigner who had been involved in certain occult and Luciferian pursuits around the Los Angeles area. So had another local figure—Charles Manson. "Sympathy for the Devil" and other popular rock recordings had become the leitmotif of the darkening mood of young America. Indeed rock music, with its harsh tones and violent rhythms, was no longer simply a reflection of the times. It was prophecy, and the counterculture became infected by its increasingly obsessive doomsday messages.

During the early summer of 1969, Jane became increasingly friendly with the Sutherlands. She grew particularly attracted to Shirley Sutherland's political brilliance and articulateness. At the end of June she went back to France with Vadim and Vanessa to spend a month on business there. She returned to Hollywood at the end of July. During the first week in August, she attended a small party given by the pregnant Sharon Tate. A few days later, Hollywood and the world woke up to learn that Sharon Tate and three of her houseguests had been slaughtered. Doomsday had truly arrived.

The murders had a further demoralizing effect on Jane. The things she had learned about herself while playing in *They Shoot Horses* had cracked open a door in her sensibility through which a whole new batch of stimuli poured. Her involvement in motherhood, her growing awareness of the violence that was raging throughout the country, and finally, Sharon Tate's brutal, senseless murder—all combined to provoke an intensifying storm of indignation, anxiety, guilt and fear in her.

Jane had already started to question the meaning of her relationship with Vadim. The more deeply immersed in the character of Gloria she had become earlier in the year, the more she had grown unsettled by Vadim's preoccupation with sensual pleasure. For Vadim, life was almost exclusively the sybaritic pursuit of money and erotic diversion, and Jane began to realize that his diversions were achieved too frequently at the expense of others. She brooded about the lack of seriousness in his life and work. Her exposure to progressive people like Shirley Sutherland and her identification with Gloria—a woman who had all her life been exploited and abused by men—made Jane increasingly aware of her own exploitability. When she began to examine her role in her husband's life, she realized angrily that she had often allowed herself to be used solely for his pleasure or business advantage. She had spent almost four years trying to live up to his image of the perfect mate, and although there had been good times, she now felt deprived of an identity of her own. Sharon Tate's murder became in her mind a symbol of the utter pointlessness of the libertine lifestyle. Sharon's slaughter was indirectly the result of the beautiful actress's willingness, in fact her need, to be used by the men in her life. Jane was shaken by the realization, yet in it she recognized her own vulnerability to the same kind of exploitation. And when, later, she learned that Charles Manson and his devout crew of drug-crazed killers had been stalking the beach houses of Malibu that summer, she was repulsed. That knowledge was a dramatically chilling insight into the fact that what had happened to Sharon might just as easily have happened to her.

chapter 23

GETTING THE
RADICAL HEAT

In September, Jane returned with Vanessa to her farm in France in a deeply unsettled state of mind. Although she had recovered physically from the grind of filming *They Shoot Horses*, she was still trapped in a web of conflicting emotions. For a while she devoted herself to a variety of self-improvement projects— a speed-reading course so that she could race through the many political books she wanted to catch up on, lessons in self-hypnosis in an attempt to defeat her smoking habit—but nothing seemed to divert her from her growing spiritual malaise.

Sharon Tate's murder continued to weigh heavily on her. The lifestyle Jane and Sharon had shared now seemed utterly vacuous, even sinister. Vadim, more fascinated than repelled by the events of August, provided her with little emotional support. He continued to approach life as if nothing had changed and had little patience for Jane's searching questions about the meaning of their lives. Indeed, he bitterly resented Jane's growing preoccupation. Jane knew that things had changed. What she didn't know yet was the extent of the change.

Since her beginnings as an actress, Jane had always done things with extreme passion and commitment. Whether it was preparing for a part, trying to make her marriage work, bearing a child, or restoring the farm, she had pursued such activities with a determination that generally left her both fulfilled and hungry for new projects to realize. But now, everything she had poured her energies into previously seemed unimportant. What was important was coming to terms with her confusion.

"I needed to go away and put myself in a totally new environment—in order to understand myself and what was going on inside me," she later said. During the previous year, she had listened to her brother talk about the changes he had gone through as a result of his exposure to the Indian philosopher Krishnamurti. Meeting Krishnamurti was, to Peter, "Like meeting Jesus. He insists that people ask themselves—not him—the questions."

Jane decided that she wanted to know more about India and Indian philosophy. Many youths she had met had gone to India and come back totally transformed. She knew others from Hollywood—notably her friend Mia Farrow, who had returned from a pilgrimage to India shining with a luminescent aura of peacefulness and self-esteem. India seemed the logical place for Jane to go to seek a resolution of her confusion.

"I chose India because I knew nothing about it," she said. "But I knew that by going there I could be completely isolated." She departed from Paris shortly after Vanessa's birthday. Once in India, though, instead of finding the clarity she sought, she found only more confusion and anger—her own.

The experience of traveling across the teeming subcontinent overwhelmed Jane. Until that time, poverty had been only a word to her: "I had never seen people actually dying from starvation or a boy begging with the corpse of a little brother in his arms." The never-ending sights and smells of death and disease filled her with horror and revulsion. She couldn't understand those of her friends who had gone to India and come back singing its praises.

"I met a lot of American kids there, hippies from wealthy middle-class families in search of their individualistic metaphysical trips. They accepted that poverty. They even tried to explain it to me, saying it was because of the religion. But I said, 'To hell with that! Don't you understand that the trouble with these people stems from religion, that it's their religion that's driving them right out of existence?' All these Americans were busy rejecting the materialistic values of life, but they were unable to go one step further and relate the tragedy of the Indian people to the real cause—religion."

Conditions in India frustrated and maddened Jane the more

she journeyed through it. Not only was she shocked by her confrontation with the moral and social paralysis that religious creeds can create, she was offended by her first actual close-up view of the effects of colonialism—in this case English colonialism. Although India had been an independent nation for twenty years, two centuries of white English rule and racial exploitation had left most of the native population mired in helplessness and despair. Whereas before her knowledge of political and social oppression caused by colonialism was abstract and intellectual she now experienced it first-hand.

Her expanding sense of injustice was further inflamed by a visit to Nepal and Sikkim, where she was entertained by the king and queen. The Queen of Sikkim was the former Hope Cooke, an American who was a contemporary of Jane's. Although Jane was awestruck by the beauty and remoteness of Sikkim, she found the imperial palace to be emblematic of the corruption, inequality and injustice of life on the subcontinent. While Hope Cooke, a young woman who had come out of educational and social surroundings similar to Jane's, enjoyed all the privileges of royalty high in the mountain kingdom of her husband, she was really nothing more than a female captive. In the meantime, millions were rotting to death in the coastal lowlands of India. The five-hour return jeep trip over the narrow, rutted road between Sikkim and India was for Jane like St. Paul's journey along the road to Damascus. She knew that she would never be the same again.

Jane had promised to return to California by mid-November to engage in prerelease publicity for *They Shoot Horses, Don't They?* She departed for Los Angeles deeply depressed by her sojourn in India. But she was also fired by a growing need to do something to expiate the guilt she felt over the miserable plight of the people she had seen. She experienced another kind of revelation, reinforcing her resolve.

Arriving in Los Angeles, she checked into the Beverly Wilshire Hotel. "When I woke up in the morning," she said, "I still had in my eyes the crowds of Bombay, in my nose the smell of Bombay, in my ears the noise of Bombay. My first day back and I saw those houses of Beverly Hills, those immaculate gardens, those neat, silent streets where the rich drive their big cars and send their children to the psychoanalyst and employ exploited Mexican gardeners and black servants." The contrast was overpowering. "I'd grown up here, but I'd never looked at it in these terms before. India was urine, noise, color, misery, disease, masses of people teeming. Beverly Hills was as silent and empty and antiseptic as a church, and I kept wondering, Where is everybody?"

Jane's return to California coincided with two major events—one on each coast—that filled the newspapers and airwaves in November of 1969. The first was the Moratorium against the War, which drew huge crowds to Washington during the weekend of November 14 and 15. President Nixon responded by declaring that he would be too busy watching football on television over the weekend to take notice of the demonstration. Displaying a characteristic contempt for those of differing opinions, Nixon played straight into the hands of the organizers of the Moratorium, thus completing the polarization between the government and the ever-widening forces of dissent. Indeed, many fence-sitting members of the Establishment were so repelled by Nixon's insensitivity that they came out in support of the demonstrators.

The other event took place in San Francisco Bay when, on November 21, a group of American Indians led by Richard Oakes, a Mohawk, invaded the deserted Alcatraz Island Federal Prison and declared it Indian territory. During the previous few years the Indian community of America had quietly caught the fever of militant activism sparked by the civil rights and antiwar movements. The occupation of Alcatraz, for which the government was totally unprepared, was declared a symbolic revolutionary act by the fledgling American Indian Movement to publicize the United States government's long history of duplicity in its dealings with the rights—territorial and otherwise—of the American Indian. During the first few months after Nixon's inauguration, radical America had been fairly quiet. Now things were heating up again.

Black Panthers, White Panthers, feminists, and dozens of other minority activist groups on the receiving end of government harrassment had already become incorporated into the counterculture. With its occupation of Alcatraz, the American Indian Movement became an unwilling but full-fledged member of the organized resistance. And although such membership did not always rebound to its advantage, one immediate positive effect was that the government, suffering on all sides from poor public relations, cooled its heels for the moment on the takeover of Alcatraz.

Jane Fonda did not cool her heels, though. Fresh from the squalor of India, ensconced in the pristine luxury of Beverly Hills, and highly charged by her guilt and by the contradictions that bombarded her consciousness, she became excited by the Alcatraz story. Vaguely aware of her own forebears' role in the social and political disenfranchisement of the Mohawks and other tribes of the colonial Northeast, she was also attuned to the American Indians' struggle for self-determination as a result of her association with Marlon Brando and other Hollywood figures who had identified themselves with the Indian cause. When she heard that one of the Alcatraz leaders was a Mohawk, her curiosity was piqued.

Shirley Sutherland gave Jane a copy of *Ramparts*, a glossy liberal Catholic publication that had been transformed in the midsixties into a muckraking, left-wing political monthly. In it she read an article by a writer named Peter Collier about the Indians who had invaded Alcatraz. Sympathetic to the revelations in the piece, she decided that instead of returning to France after the opening of *They Shoot Horses*, she would remain in California for a while to learn more about the Indians' cause.

When *They Shoot Horses, Don't They?* premiered in mid-December — just in time to qualify for the Academy Awards — critical reviews varied sharply. There were those who found it unbearably depressing, but many of the more serious critics hailed it as one of the best pictures of the year. Jane was praised lavishly for giving the performance of her career, and possibly the best performance of the year by any actress. Critic Pauline Kael, theretofore only lukewarm in her assessments of Jane's acting ability, not only gave Jane's portrayal her unqualified approval but engaged in a bit of prophecy as well. "Fortunately," Kael wrote, "Gloria, who is the raw nerve of the movie, is played by Jane Fonda. Sharp-tongued Gloria . . . is the stongest role an American actress has had on the screen this year. Jane Fonda goes all the way with it, as screen actresses rarely do once they become stars. . . . And because she has the true star's gift of drawing one to her emotionally, even when the character she plays is repellent, her Gloria is one of those complex creations who live on as part of our shared experience. Jane Fonda stands a good chance of personifying American tensions and dominating our movies in the seventies. . . ."

Vadim and Vanessa joined Jane while she was still at the Beverly Wilshire. Expecting to find her mood improved after her stay in India, Vadim was disappointed to discover that she was more restless and unsettled than ever. When she told him that she intended to remain in California to do more research into the American Indian cause, he shrugged indifferently.

On December 30, 1969, Jane was given the New York Film Critics Award for her performance in *They Shoot Horses, Don't They?* She found out about it after stepping off a plane in New York, where she had arrived with Vanessa to spend the New Year's holiday at her father's house. "It's the biggest accolade I've ever been given," she said. "One tries to be blasé about things, but now that it's happened it's very nice." The Film Critics' Award was often the precursor of an Oscar. "You can't imagine what winning an Oscar does for your career. I'd love to get it. But I'm afraid to think of the Film Critics' Award as an omen. It might jinx me."

Asked about her relations with her father, Jane said they were improving—thanks mainly to the existence of Vanessa. But her father still had little tolerance for Jane's emerging political views. She recalled telling him about her trip to Russia and about how quiet and slow, how human and delightfully inefficient she had found the Russians. Then she told him how glad she was to think that her daughter was one-quarter Russian. "And my father said, 'How can you say that when you've just explained that the Russians are inefficient?' And I answered: 'But that's beautiful. Dad, you've been so brainwashed with the American idea of efficiency that, for the sake of efficiency, you forget about the human elements!' He did not understand. And this was the first time I realized the incredible gap between myself and the people who brought me up. Not only my father, but the system he represents."

On New Year's Eve, Jane gave an interview to Rex Reed for the *New York Times*, and when it was printed three weeks later, Jane again found herself the object of a heated controversy. Reed quoted her as asking, "You don't mind if I turn on, do you?" He went on to write that "She carefully rolled the tobacco out of a Winston, opened the can of a dainty snuffbox on her father's coffee table, and replaced the ordinary old stuff that only causes cancer with fine gray pot she had just brought back from—Where? India? Morocco? She couldn't remember—all she knew was that it wasn't that tacky stuff they mix with hay in Tijuana, this was the real thing." Reed studded the interview with descriptions of Jane inhaling lung-fuls of marijuana smoke, and the *Times* was blitzed by a storm of angry, denunciatory letters about her behavior.

That New Year's Eve Jane was reflective. She talked about the decade of the sixties and expressed her admiration for the political activism of the young. She described herself as being a member of the "sloth generation of the fifties, when people had been fed sleeping pills by Eisenhower." She revealed a certain envy of those who were "out participating in the life of the country and trying to improve its quality." She implied that she felt she had wasted much of her life and indicated that she was anxious to do something to make up for it. She praised Vadim, but her words had the hint of a valedictory in them. "Vadim is alive, with all the imperfections that entails. He'll make big mistakes, because he's vulnerable. He has never denied the madness in himself. . . . He's taught me how to live, and if anything happens to our marriage, he'll always be my friend." Something, it was obvious, was already happening to their marriage.

Jane returned to California early in January, settling again into her house in Malibu. While Vadim worked on another film project, she devoted most of her time to reading about Indian problems and seeking out people who could tell her more about them. Shirley and Donald Sutherland were constant visitors—Donald, actually, much more than his wife.

Jane got in touch with Peter Collier, the man who had written the article in *Ramparts*, and asked him to take her to Alcatraz for a first-hand look at the Indian occupation. When she arrived, she talked with several of the Indian leaders and was deeply impressed by their uncompromising commitment and the sad dignity of their frustration. Since the takeover two months before, which had received front-page attention, the occupation of Alcatraz had been, for the most part, forgotten by the media. The government continued to react with public indifference, thus avoiding a confrontation, and news of the "symbolic rev-olutionary act" soon became stale. The Indians remained on the island, but the press had long ago left. It was only when Jane's visit was made public that media interest was aroused again.

Jane came away from her visit with a deeper sense of guilt and outrage over the white-imposed disenfranchisement of the

American Indian. "I learned about the genocide that had taken place, that is still taking place, the infamies we had done to the Indians in the name of efficiency, in the interest of the white farmers," she bitterly told a newspaper. "And I learned that the senators who are supposed to defend the Indians haven't done a thing."

There could be no doubt that the American Indian was the most severely repressed of all minorities in North America. The history of white America's treatment of the Indians had been a long and dishonorable one, made the more shameful because it had the ongoing sanction and cooperation of the federal government. It did not take long before the fever for social and racial justice spread to the long-ignored Indian community in the 1960s. Yet their cause had remained largely ignored in the greater scheme of radical events. It was not until Alcatraz—which the small band of militant invaders vowed to defend to the last—that Indian passions made even a remote impression on white America. Once the novelty of the occupation had worn off, America forgot about the Indian cause. But not Jane. After her visit there she was ready to do something. The first thing she did was pay a visit to *Ramparts* magazine.

Ramparts was the product of a single ego, that of Warren Hinckle III. Hinckle had wrested control of the magazine from its Catholic founder, Edward Keating, and as its new editor had turned it into a high-priced radical publication aimed at the liberal Establishment in America. One of Hinckle's pet projects dealt with the question of "Who Really Killed President Kennedy." As a result, he was regularly in contact with an eccentric left-wing New York lawyer named Mark Lane. Lane had barged into the Kennedy assassination case at its very beginning in 1963 by appointing himself defense counsel for Lee Harvey Oswald, and when Oswald was killed by Jack Ruby, he became Oswald's posthumous public defender. Later, he was among a number of authors who wrote postassassination books critcizing the Warren Commission's conclusions and tendering their own theories on why and how Kennedy was "really killed."*

Hinckle and Lane were viewed by many as obsessive pub-

---

*More recently, Lane reemerged in the public spotlight because of his association with the Rev. Jim Jones, the cult leader who orchestrated the mass suicide of his followers in Guyana in 1979.

licity hounds with a common nose for the main chance and a shrewd understanding of the American public's gullibility and innate fascination with scandal and mystery. Both were champions of the left—new and old—and each involved himself in all manner of counterculture events, including the interminable trial of the Chicago Seven which, early in 1970, had dragged into its fifth month.

Lane was an overbearing but likeable bear of a man in his forties with a dry, cutting wit and a cornucopia of lawyer's gifts. He might have made millions as a Wall Street attorney if he had been so inclined. But his inclinations were diametrically opposed to representing corporate America and advancing the capitalistic system. By the late sixties he had grown out of the old-style New York socialism of his youth and was a full-fledged advocate of radical Marxist revolution in America. Those who knew Lane and had observed the progressive hardening of his political attitudes could never be sure how much of his revolutionary zeal derived from sincere conviction and how much came from his apparent need to thrust himself repeatedly into the public spotlight. In early 1970 he was a tireless campaigner for various revolutionary constituencies, and when the Indians took over Alcatraz, he was among the first white radicals to speak out on their behalf. Thus, when Jane Fonda expressed a desire to do something to help the Indian cause, he became her first mentor.

Under Lane's tutelage, the fires of reform, which had been smoldering in Jane during the previous year, suddenly began to rage. She attended meetings, parties and rallies where she met numerous exponents of various left-wing causes and soaked up chilling stories of government oppression and persecution. Only months before a peripheral member of the Hollywood drug-and-sex culture, she was transformed within weeks into a disciple of the peace-and-freedom movement.

chapter 24

FRED
GARDNER

It was only a matter of days after her return from Alcatraz that Jane found herself involved not just with the Indians but with the Black Panthers as well. Marlon Brando, the original Hollywood advocate of the Indian cause as far back as the early sixties, had identified himself more recently with the radical black separatist struggle as well. He became a Black Panther sympathizer and was attending Black Panther functions in support of their cause. Jane felt compelled to follow suit. She had no choice, really, since the militant Indian movement had gotten much of its inspiration from various black power groups that had evolved out of the early 1960s civil rights turmoil in the South.

By 1969, among all the interwoven radical groups, the tiny Black Panther Party was probably the biggest *bête noire* of federal and local law enforcement agencies. The Panthers had grown indirectly out of the Student Nonviolent Coordinating Committee (called SNCC and pronounced "Snick" three years earlier, as a result of impatience and disaffection with SNCC leader Stokely Carmichael's ideas about combatting American racism. The Black Panther Party was founded in Oakland, California, by Huey P. Newton, a former law student, and Bobby Seale, an Air Force veteran who had been a member of the Revolutionary Action Movement, a black extremist organization which, according to J. Edgar Hoover, had been providing Stokely Carmichael with much of his Marxist-Leninist, Chinese Communist ideology.

During 1969, federal and local police forces grew harsher in their campaigns against both violent white antiwar protestors and Black Panthers alike. As the police policy of harassment and provocation mounted across the country, the Black Panthers began to be shot down like skeet. Panther members and leaders in New York, New Haven, Washington, Detroit, Oakland and Chicago were killed in hails of police bullets. And in Los Angeles, on December 8, 1969, at dawn, a monumental gun battle took place between an army of local police and thirteen Black Panther members at the Panther headquarters in the south-central section of the city.

Jane Fonda saw television pictures of the Panther-police battle at the time she was learning about the Indians at Alcatraz. She had already heard about the Panthers from Shirley Sutherland and others in Hollywood's radical community. Like many whites, she was frightened by the outright violence the Panthers seemed to advocate. Moreover, she didn't understand their ideology because she had not read Marx, Lenin, Mao, Fanon and other architects of Communist revolution. Yet she had long been sympathetic to the black civil rights struggle and had been horrified by the assassination of Martin Luther King, Jr., the year before. But because of her lengthy stays in France, she felt completely out of touch with the "Black Power" and "All Power to the People" psychology that had surfaced in the black liberation movement. She possessed, nevertheless, all the credentials of what the right-wing element in American society liked to call the "bleeding-heart liberal," and like most liberals, she operated much more on emotion than intellect (as, of course, did the right-wing advocates). Thus when the Los Angeles shootout occurred, Jane's natural contempt for authority, represented in that instance by the police, immediately caused her to extend her sympathies to embrace the Panthers. And she became even more of an admirer of Shirley Sutherland, who by then was suffering FBI harassment because of her advocacy of the Panther cause.

When Jane learned from Mark Lane of the interlocking tactical connections between the Alcatraz Indians, the Panthers and the white radical movement, her curiosity was piqued even further. "I had understood that it was always the Panthers who took all the harassment, and I asked why. So, after the Indians, I decided to meet the Panthers, and when I did, I was impressed. They were not at all like I imagined. It was the first time I had met black militants with a political ideology, a political discipline, or should I say people who go right to the roots of a problem."

She heard stories from the Panthers of political and economic oppression, police persecution and provocation that outraged her. She saw pictures of police standing over the bodies of dead Panthers with the same kinds of smiles on their faces that she had seen in pictures of Nazi soldiers standing over the bodies of dead Jews. The forces of authority were fast becoming the forces of authoritarianism, as far as Jane could see, and the knowledge worked her into a fury. Her encounters with the Indians and Panthers jolted her out of her months of numbed indecision and introspection about herself. She needed a cause to which she could devote herself—a new challenge, a new ambition. What could be more fulfilling and more necessary than the cause of social justice?

Throughout her adult life, Jane's personal commitments and convictions had been sparked by the men with whom she had been intimately involved, from Tim Everett to Roger Vadim. Therefore, it was unlikely that her life would take another major turn without the corresponding catalyst of another man. Thus it seemed not coincidental that her sudden rush to right the wrongs of America came at the same time she met a powerful new personality. Not Mark Lane, for the avuncular Lane held no romantic attraction for Jane. But a man to whom she found herself responding on a visceral level. His name was Fred Gardner.

Fred Gardner, in the words of a friend, was "a brilliant, dedicated Communist who could charm the pants off Martha Mitchell." A native of San Francisco, the dynamic Gardner had come to Communism early in his life, and although he had been active in the antiwar movement from its beginning, he was a man who marched to the beat of his own drum. One of the movement's severest internal critics, he was especially outspoken about separating serious revolutionaries from the fun-and-games types who were gaining most of the headlines but contributing little to the ultimate Marxist goals of the movement. In his late twenties and married, he was a facile writer, a gifted speaker and an intrepid, tireless organizer.

In 1967, exasperated with the movement's cavalier attitude toward servicemen, many of whom in his tactical view were ripe for radicalization, Gardner began to canvas various movement groups for money and other aid to help organize GI dissent within the military. Movement leaders berated him for expecting to convert "the enemy," which in their minds every soldier was, and rejected his proposals. Thereupon he made his way to Columbia, South Carolina—the city adjacent to the huge Army base of Fort Jackson—to test his ideas. He rented a storefront on Main Street in Columbia, just down the block from the USO, called it the UFO, and opened it as the first "underground GI coffeehouse." By January 1968, soldiers from Fort Jackson—mostly draftees—were flocking to the UFO, where they got food, beverages, entertainment and clever, low-key political indoctrination.

The base had already gained national attention as the site of the court-martial of Captain Howard Levy, an Army doctor from New York who had refused to train Green Berets and was sentenced to Leavenworth Prison. In February 1968, it was the first Army post to experience a GI-staged antiwar demonstration. Because of that, Fred Gardner and his GI coffeehouse idea were suddenly hailed by the very same radical leaders who six months earlier had dismissed his ideas and refused to help him.

Gardner quickly became known as the father of the GI movement. He left the UFO in the hands of associates while he traveled to Fort Hood, Texas, Fort Leonard Wood, Missouri, and other military bases to organize additional off-post coffeehouses.

Among Gardner's many interests was writing for films. He had been hired by director Michelangelo Antonioni to work on the script for Antonioni's Hollywood production of *Zabriskie Point*. Antonioni was an Italian Communist, and *Zabriskie Point* was to be his first American film—a study of the naive, childish, self-destructive tactics of radical American youth.

While Jane Fonda was in the process of learning about the Indians and Black Panthers, she attended a party given in Hollywood for Antonioni. It was there that she first met Fred Gardner. Gardner later told me that he had gotten into a heated discussion with some of the guests about his GI coffeehouses. At one point he noticed that Jane, standing nearby, was eavesdropping and eyeing him with interest. After a while he retreated to the kitchen to escape the party's din. Within moments Jane materialized in the kitchen and struck up a conversation.

According to Gardner, the conversation soon turned into a mild argument. "She was rapping to me about how much she was learning about the movement and how she wanted to contribute. I wasn't feeling very good that night and, finally, I wasn't too impressed with all these movie people and their sudden need to identify themselves with what we were doing. I'd often tried to turn people on to things before, but I just wasn't interested in trying to turn Jane Fonda on. This was more a matter of 'Leave me alone, lady!' I said something to the effect that if she really was so eager to learn and help, what the hell was she doing sitting around Hollywood and hanging out with all the radical-chic movie people? 'If you're really interested,' I said, 'you should go out and visit these places— the military bases, the Indian reservations, the Black ghettoes.'

"I thought that would be it—not only was I condescending to her, I was being rude too. But she surprised me. 'Okay,' she said, 'I will.' Then she asked me to send her everything I'd written."

A few days later, when Gardner returned to San Francisco, he did. A few days after that, Jane appeared at his home, bursting with questions. Gardner passed her off on his wife, a left-wing feminist. "I was in the process of extricating myself from further participation in the movement," he said. "I just wasn't interested anymore in all the exploitation and backbiting that was going on. Jane rapped with my wife and some other women. We hardly talked. My main memory of her visit is making room in our refrigerator for the enormous supply of 'natural' yogurt she was traveling with."

Some friends of Jane's claim today that she was magnetized by Fred Gardner and was disappointed by his indifference to her. They suggest also that she set out to shake that indifference. During the next few months, almost everywhere she went, and to almost everyone whom she spoke, she credited Gardner as the primary influence in her conversion to radical political activism. "It got to the point," says one friend, "that everyone was sure Jane and Freddie were deep in a love affair."

They weren't, Gardner told me. Indeed, he was mystified by Jane's frequent mentions of him in the press. "We had only met twice."

A year later, Gardner was divorced. In New York for a few

weeks, he ran into Jane and at that time had a brief romance with her. Then he understood. "The first thing I asked was how come she'd been saying I had influenced her so much when in fact I hadn't. . . . I reminded her that it was obvious from all these questions she had asked that she had arrived at her viewpoint on her own. 'Why do you need to go around attributing it to a man?' I asked her.

"She started gushing about how wonderful it was that a man could say such a thing. And then she did it all over again: she said she really trusted me and would—if and when I had political advice to give her—follow it. At the time I didn't have anything but a vague warning to give her. I told her to be careful, the movement had ripped me off. I hadn't actually quit but had been driven out by the likes of Barbara Dane. Jane kept right on hobnobbing with Barbara Dane and other 'left' fakers, the heavier the better. And all the while she was telling people how she took my counsel. It finally got through my skull that her crediting me—or later, anybody else—for her actions was simply a way of minimizing her responsibility. It left a door open, and when it was time to switch she could just say, 'Well, that was really so-and-so's trip, and I'm off it now.'"

Responding to Gardner's urging that she "visit these places," in early March of 1970 Jane flew to Seattle with Mark Lane to observe an Indian demonstration that was planned for Fort Lawton. The demonstration was to be patterned after the Alcatraz invasion as a protest against the federal government's failure to keep its Indian treaty promises. Fort Lawton was a little-used, sparsely populated Army reserve base. The Indians intended to occupy it, declare it Indian territory and open a tribal cultural center on the property.

On Sunday, March 8, Jane joined Lane and about 150 Indians as they marched on Fort Lawton. They were met at the main gate by a force of military police from nearby Fort Lewis. Some of the Indians rushed the gates while others set up diversionary actions. The main force scaled a fence and managed to erect a tepee in a small clearing in some woods on the base. One of the Indian leaders read a proclamation: "We, the native Americans, reclaim this land known as Fort Lawton in the name of the American Indians by the right of discovery."

Jane was in the group with Lane at the main gate. In the ensuing struggle, nearly 100 Indians were arrested along with the ever-visible Lane, and Jane was pushed around roughly by several MPs. After a few hours under arrest, Lane was released with an expulsion order. He immediately shouted to local reporters covering the incident that MPs were beating many of the Indians still in custody. From Fort Lawton, Lane drove Jane and a group of Indians to Fort Lewis to protest the "malicious beatings." Lane, often a theatrical and shrill man, led a small caravan of cars through the main gate at Fort Lewis. The caravan was chased down by more MPs and its members, including Jane, were arrested for violating the Fort Lawton expulsion order and for trespassing. They were detained for a while, questioned, then escorted off the base.

The incident at Fort Lawton was Jane's first close-up exposure to protest-movement violence, and when she saw the burly white MPs clubbing the unarmed Indians, her blood boiled. The Indian assault on the fort, an event that otherwise would have received only passing notice in the local press, instead was splashed across the front pages of the nation's newspapers the next day because of Jane's participation and arrest. At a press conference that day, called by Mark Lane ostensibly to announce the Indians' plans to picket Fort Lawton, Jane became the focus of attention. Unwittingly she upstaged the Indians and caused a backlash of resentment in the Indian movement. Jane announced that she had decided to make a cross-country trip by car to visit Indian reservations and Army bases, and that she was joining the protest movement on behalf of the Indians and GIs. "I hear from the GIs I've been talking to that we need a GI Bill of Rights," she said, "and from the Indians that we need an Indian Bill of Rights. I always thought that the Bill of Rights applied to all people, but I've discovered differently."

Referring bitterly to her arrest at Fort Lewis, she said, "Bob Hope was greeted differently by the local branch of the military-industrial complex. But then, I did not come up here to glamorize war or to urge young men to fight." She went on to say, "I'm campaigning on behalf of human beings, whether they be Indians, GIs or whatever." But she concentrated most of her remarks on Fred Gardner's GI projects. She claimed that GIs were being deprived of their rights to the extent that they were "being put on planes at gunpoint and sent to Vietnam if they're caught dissenting." As for the military authorities, she concluded, "If they're getting that uptight about my being on an

Army base, it means they're worried about something, as well they should be."

Although the GI movement had been Fred Gardner's brain-child, he had by that time bequeathed its principal control to a left-wing political and fund-raising organization, based in New York and Cambridge, Massachusetts, called the United States Servicemen's Fund. The USSF had expanded on Gardner's idea of organizing antiwar protest within the military by subsidizing underground coffeehouses in towns near dozens of military bases around the country and staffing the coffeehouses with cadres of young organizers steeped in left-wing political creeds. Gardner had become a director of the USSF, but he grew increasingly uncomfortable with the direction the GI movement was taking under the financial aegis of the Fund and some of its other directors.

The USSF's principal activity in the Seattle-Tacoma area was its sponsorship of the Shelter Half, a coffeehouse near Fort Lewis. The Shelter Half was staffed mostly by young revolutionaries affiliated with the radical Socialist Workers Party, the Students for a Democratic Society and the Black Panthers. Its principal purpose was to promote disruption of military activities at Fort Lewis and nearby McCord Air Force Base by supplying GIs with tips on desertion, sabotage and other antimilitary acts. Such activities went beyond Fred Gardner's original concept of the GI movement. Although it was in accordance with the traditional tactics of the Marxist-Leninist revolutionary scenario, Gardner had serious misgivings about the strategy. His misgivings were based on his fear that the GIs, already victims of the military system, were in danger of being victimized also by the New Left's compulsively power-hungry and divisive revolutionary style. Nevertheless, he remained with the Servicemen's Fund and tried to temper the GI movement's new revolutionary and terrorist fervor by his insistence on maintaining the original concept of the GI projects—the protection of servicemen's civil rights from the unconstitutional excesses of military law.

Mark Lane was older than Gardner, but he had considerably more energy when it came to drawing attention to himself. Once involved in the GI movement, he exhibited some of the political opportunism and egomania Gardner had begun to criticize. Nevertheless, Lane was a national celebrity of sorts, had a certain amount of clout with the press, and was, in his flamboyant way, an effective radical lawyer. As Jane watched Lane operate, she became further sold on lending her name, her presence, and her money to the movement.

Howard Levy was another kind of national celebrity and one of the many movement leaders Jane met in the early days of her commitment. Levy was the young Army doctor who had been sent to prison for more than two years for his refusal to train Green Berets as medics for Vietnam, and in whose case the GI movement had originally found much of its inspiration when Fred Gardner set up the first coffeehouse at Fort Jackson in 1967. Levy had been released on parole the summer before by order of Supreme Court Justice William O. Douglas. He immediately joined the USSF, becoming a manager of the Fund's New York office.

"When I first encountered Jane," Levy recalled, "I couldn't have been more impressed. She was full of energy and a sense of commitment and she had been going to school on all the people she'd been talking to. I'd say that by the time I met her, she was very knowledgeable on many of the objectives of the GI projects."

"I first met Jane at a meeting with Freddy Gardner—I think it was at the Essex House hotel," Levy told me. "There were a few others there, some people connected with the Fund, a lawyer and so on. Jane questioned me intensively, and we had a really good discussion. She was open, curious, absolutely without any kind of rhetoric—just very nice and very warm. For a while I was taken aback by being in the presence of this big movie star, but she quickly dispelled any feelings of awe I might have had. She was down-to-earth and completely open, just one of the guys, and pretty soon I forgot the movie-star business and concentrated on her as a person. And as a person, she was terrific."

Jane had traveled to New York shortly after her Seattle arrest to meet with the USSF, to appear on the *Dick Cavett Show*, and to welcome her French friend Elisabeth Vailland, who was arriving from France at Jane's invitation to accompany her on a cross-country automobile trip.

Elisabeth Vailland was astonished at the changes she perceived in Jane when Jane picked her up at Kennedy Airport during the second week of March. "It was my first trip to America," she recalled, "but on the ride in from the airport I noticed nothing, so intent was I on the voice of my young friend as she spoke of her commitment, her preoccupation with the political conscience that was in the process of being born."

Jane took Elisabeth Vailland to a meeting with Gardner, Levy and other USSF representatives within hours of her arrival. The next day they were joined by La Nada Means, a young Indian woman Jane had met at Alcatraz and brought to New York to appear with her on the *Dick Cavett Show*. That evening, leaving the theater where the show was taped, Jane, who had spoken passionately but inexpertly about the injustices the Indians had suffered, was spat upon by a man from the audience.

On March 15 she and Elisabeth Vailland flew back to Seattle, where they were met by Mark Lane. Lane had persuaded Jane to sue the Army for her arrest. While she was in New York, he had been occupied with a group of young, radical Seattle lawyers in drawing up the papers. Jane remained in Seattle for an intensely busy day, first visiting the Shelter Half coffeehouse to give the staff a pep talk, then filing her lawsuit in the local federal court with Lane along as her lawyer, and finally picketing and meeting with the Fort Lawton Indians.

There was considerable tension among the Indian leaders over Jane's presence. At a meeting, she was accused by one of using the Indian movement for personal publicity. The Indians trusted no white people, not even self-appointed white advocates, and several of them felt that Jane's appearance on the *Cavett Show* had hurt their cause because they were now identified with a Hollywood celebrity suspected of publicity seeking.

Jane took the rebuke calmly, claiming that she was interested only in helping and had no desire for personal gain. She found it difficult to understand the hostile attitude, however, until it was analyzed for her at another meeting by a more sympathetic leader. He explained that, from their point of view, she had performed poorly on the *Cavett Show*. He told Jane that she could help them only by joining with them in their demonstrations, not by trying to be their spokeswoman. It was one thing to identify publicly with the justice of the Indian cause, another to attempt to represent the Indians in the court of public opinion. Jane simply did not know enough about the long history of white oppression to be an effective advocate. Jane, chastened, was all the more eager to start her journey among the Indian reservations.

The next day she and Elisabeth Vailland flew to Los Angeles, where Vailland met Henry Fonda for the first time. Jane was now intent on getting her father to share her outrage over the things she had been told by Fred Gardner, Mark Lane and others about American atrocities in Vietnam. "When My Lai broke, it was no surprise to me," she later recalled. "The soldiers I had talked to had already told me too much—about the generals who give transistor radios as awards for the cut genitals or the cut ears of the Vietcong, or about the way they throw Vietcong out of helicopters."

Jane said she had been brought up to believe in America's moral perfection and had clung to her beliefs despite the growing evidence to the contrary, even in the face of the critical cynicism of her left-wing friends in France. Now, horrified by the stories she had heard and pictures she had seen, her feelings against the military had hardened into outrage. "I told my father all the things I'd learned. He exploded, 'You don't know what you're talking about! We don't do that. We're Americans. And even if the soldiers did do it, they wouldn't talk about it.' So I explained to my father that when they start talking, you can't stop them. And he said, 'If you can prove that it's true, I will lead a march to Nixon and confront him.'"

Jane invited Donald Duncan, a former Green Beret sergeant she had met through Mark Lane, and another Vietnam veteran, a former officer, to her father's house in Bel Air to talk to him. "They told him about the massacres, the tortures, everything. My father sat and listened very quietly, obviously moved. But he never went to Nixon and confronted him. He said sadly, 'I don't see what I can do besides what I'm already doing—that is, campaigning for the peace candidates.'"

Henry Fonda, like almost every other American liberal, finally had turned against the war. But like most liberals he continued to defend the American system, and he clung instinctively to the belief that the cure for the country's problems did not lie in action based on alien and absolutist radical theories.

chapter 25

A CROSS-COUNTRY ODYSSEY

Henry Fonda was too rational a man to yield to the kind of simplistic, undiscriminating sloganeering that he saw Jane succumb to. Yet he failed to realize that each time in his life he had rejected Jane's attempts to get him to approve of her enthusiasms, his rejection had sent her off on a new vector of rebellion that eventually came back to haunt him. He tried, in his way, to reason with her on "this protest business she was getting caught up in." But as before, the more they argued, the more they forced one another into contrary ideological positions.

During the next week, while preparing to embark on her cross-country automobile trip with Elisabeth Vailland, Jane engaged in a frantic round of meetings and rallies on behalf of Black Panthers, Indians and servicemen. On March 20, she attended a meeting with Black Communist Angela Davis, French playwright Jean Genet and Panther lawyer Luke McKissick to discuss raising bail money for the Panthers who had been arrested in the shoot-out three months before. Also at the meeting were Shirley and Donald Sutherland, along with Roger Vadim.

Jane and Vadim were still living together at the Malibu beach house, although Jane was growing more and more distant from him. When asked about Vadim's attitude toward her new activities, Jane said, "Well, he approves of what I'm doing, though he doesn't agree with it all. It's very difficult for a Frenchman. . . . For example, I'll talk to him about the fact that a Black Panther's bail will be a hundred thousand dollars, and he'll say, 'What are you talking about? In France, nobody has bail.' And I'll talk about a no-knock warrant, and he'll say, 'You never have to knock to come into a home in France.' So it's very hard to explain these things to him. . . . What I'm doing concerns him a great deal, but he knows that he can't stop me from doing it." One could imagine the ironic tableau of Henry Fonda and Roger Vadim commiserating with each other over what they considered to be Jane's ultimate folly.

On March 22 Jane visited Black Panther headquarters in Los Angeles—the scene of the recent shoot-out—where she talked to some of the Panthers who had been in prison. They told her stories about how, at the Los Angeles County Jail, blacks and especially Panthers were constantly provoked and tormented in the hope that they would fight back and thus cause their bail to be increased. Then, with a survivor of the Panther-police battle who had been the first of the prisoners to be released on bail, Jane traveled to San Diego to visit the Green Machine, another GI coffeehouse—this one set up for Marines stationed at nearby Camp Pendleton. There she sat through more political indoctrination meetings in which the solidarity of oppressed servicemen, Blacks and Indians was hailed. She was becoming increasingly impressed by the Panthers and the quiet, cool way they handled themselves, and she resolved to do more on their behalf.

March 23 found Jane back in Los Angeles, where she spent most of the day touring the movie studios trying to raise Panther bail money, then meeting with Angela Davis, who had just lost her University of California professorship for being a Communist. She also met with Donald Duncan, the former Green Beret sergeant, at his house in the San Fernando Valley. They discussed her forthcoming trip, and he gave her an itinerary of Army bases to visit.

Two evenings later Jane and Elisabeth Vailland stood in the driveway of her father's house, ready to embark on their trip. Jane had acquired a large Mercury station wagon for the journey, and as she and Vailland finished loading their traveling gear and Henry Fonda took pictures, one-and-a-half-year-old Vanessa scurried around saying, "Bye. . . ." By 6 P.M. they were on their way, with Jane at the wheel.

Their first extended stop was the Pyramid Lake Indian reservation in northern Nevada. Pyramid Lake had been a longstanding bone of contention between the Indians and the government. Angry groups of Indians were protesting the United States Bureau of Reclamation's diversion of the waters of the Truckee River to a non-Indian irrigation project. The Truckee was the only major source of water for the lake. Pyramid Lake covered practically the entire reservation, and its fish had been the main source of livelihood for the local Paiute tribe. Now, with the waters of the lake drying up, the fishing industry was dying. The Indians saw in this a signal example of how the federal government, serving the interests of white farmers, was still intent on abrogating its treaties and further destroying Indian culture.

Pryamid Lake was not the only case of white America's blatant usurpation of Indian resources. Indians elsewhere were inflamed by strip-mining and power plant developments on the Hopi's sacred Black Mesa in Arizona, on Navaho lands in Arizona and New Mexico, and on the Crow and Northern Cheyenne reservations in Montana. Still others were fighting white real estate developments on a number of Southwestern reservations. These and other white incursions of Indian territory were accompanied, moreover, by frictions that made them worse. Indian water rights had been taken away from tribes through fraud and deceit, leases had been signed with grossly unfair terms, and even those terms were not being lived up to or enforced.

The ways in which leases for Indian-owned resources were approved and signed was another source of Indian anger. Prior to their conquest by white America, Indians employed ages-old methods of governing themselves, some by councils of wise and respected elected chiefs, others by hereditary religious or clan leaders. But in 1934, the federal government imposed on almost every tribe a uniform system of tribal government—styled in the white man's fashion—that appointed the top tribal officers. Council members were supposed to be elected democratically by the people, but in practice the new system was so alien to large numbers of Indians that majorities of them on many reservations consistently refused to vote in tribal elections and continued to regard the new-style councils as imposed institutions of the white man rather than of their own people. Many Indians felt that the modern tribal councils were responsible for permitting white exploitation of their resources and that in many cases they cooperated in it—a charge not far from the truth. Thus, many Indians not only were angry with the whites, they were also divided sharply among themselves. The most militant of them had formed the American Indian Movement to reestablish the traditional Indian methods of government, to restore tribal customs and religions, and to effect Indian autonomy over their own affairs.

Jane was aware of all this when she and Elisabeth Vailland stopped at Pyramid Lake, but she was not prepared for what she found. Some of the Indians she had met at Alcatraz arrived at Pyramid Lake to conduct a demonstration on behalf of the local Paiutes. According to Elisabeth Vailland, she and Jane were astonished at the difference between the Alcatraz militants and the inhabitants of the reservation. The Alcatraz group was dynamic, fired-up, united, whereas the Paiutes were indifferent and melancholy, led by a grossly overweight council leader. Jane was depressed by the poverty of the Indian settlement and by the incongruous fact that many of the Indians who lived there were repugnantly obese.

It was the Indians' obesity that remained the dominant image in Jane's mind as she and Vailland resumed their trip. Their next stop was the reservation at Blackfoot, Idaho, where they were to meet up with La Nada Means, the Alcatraz girl whose brother, Russell Means, was one of the more violent leaders of the Indian movement. "On all the reservations we went to," Elisabeth Vailland said, "the Indians were almost without exception grossly fat, the result of all the beer they drank. They drank beer without stop. At first, Jane thought it was due to malnutrition, but she finally agreed that it was the beer." Any illusion Jane might have had, based on her Alcatraz visit or on movies she had seen as a child, of the Indians as sleek, stealthy warriors was shattered.

Another source of disappointment was the fact that the Indians—especially the Indians of the militant movement—insisted that in order to reunify themselves, they had to revive their ancestral religion. One of their cardinal principles was that white Christianity, to which so many Indians had been converted through the years, had kept them locked into their serfdom. The only way to combat this was to throw off the hold of the white man's religion and reestablish their traditional beliefs and rituals. To Jane, by then an avowed atheist, this was "negative, antiprogressive and antirevolutionary," and she argued heatedly with some of her Indian friends about it.

From Blackfoot, Jane and Vailland drove to Salt Lake City. As expected, Jane had been nominated for an Academy Award for *They Shoot Horses, Don't They?*, and she had decided to fly back to Los Angeles for the ceremonies. When she arrived, she found that the publicity over her arrest in Seattle and her other activities during the past two months had made her a *cause célèbre* in the film industry. Speculation ran high about whether she had jeopardized her chances for the Oscar, which almost everyone agreed she deserved. When she showed up at the Santa Monica Auditorium on Oscar night, she was greeted by the usual crowd of movie fans packed in banks of bleachers opposite the entrance. When they spotted her, many cried out radical slogans, waving their hands in the V sign or raising their fists in the Black Panther salute. Jane stopped for a moment, looked at them, smiled, and raised her fist in return.

She didn't win an Oscar, and although she took her defeat calmly, many of her friends were incensed. "A pure case of political prejudice," said one. "The whole country knew that Jane should have had it," said another. "It was no contest. They kept it from her because they were afraid she'd get up and make a political speech." Jane shrugged. Three months before, the Oscar had been important. Now it was irrelevant except in one sense. It increased her contempt for the institutions of the Establishment.

Jane flew back to Salt Lake City with Elisabeth Vailland to retrieve her car and continue their trip. From Salt Lake City they drove to Denver, where they took part in a thirty-six hour Fast for Peace organized by various Denver antiwar groups. The small crowd of fasters, which included Dr. Benjamin Spock, Jane and several local Black Panthers, camped out on a small traffic island at a busy downtown Denver intersection. Jane gave television and press interviews praising the revolutionary spirit in America and expressing solidarity with the peace movement. By the end of the fast, she was overflowing with radical ardor.

Her next stop was Colorado Springs, the site of Fort Carson, where she had agreed to participate in an antiwar demonstration organized by the staff of the local coffeehouse, the Home Front. Everywhere she went in the Denver area she was trailed by reporters, photographers and television crews. It was not long before it became apparent that as far as the news media were concerned, Jane Fonda was the biggest thing to hit the movement since the Yippies and Crazies of Abbie Hoffman and Jerry Rubin in 1968.

Jane took two days off and flew incognito from Denver to New York, where she held strategy sessions with Howard Levy and other Servicemen's Fund representatives. Then she flew back to Los Angeles for meetings with Donald Duncan. During her visit to Fort Carson, she had demanded to see the stockade, where three black servicemen with Black Panther sympathies were under arrest. Now she wanted to return to Carson and mount a demonstration for the prisoners, who she believed were imprisoned primarily because of their Black Panther connections. Duncan advised her on how to go about making an effective protest at the fort and helped her write a speech. Later she went out to Malibu to visit with Vanessa, then dropped in on a fund-raising party at the Sutherlands'.

Political activism had intensified in Hollywood on the heels of Jane's failure to win the Oscar. The journey from the hippie exhibitionism of the sixties to a more sober political consciousness was complete, and all sorts of actors, writers, directors and producers both young and old, were in the process of making the fashionable switch. With Marlon Brando diverted by personal concerns, Jane became the focus of the new activism. And once everyone realized that she was in it for real, they flocked to join the bandwagon.

Howard Levy says, "When Jane came to New York and asked about what she could do, she was still confused about her identity. She kept saying, 'I don't just want to be known as Jane Fonda the actress. I want to be something more than that.' She was really champing at the bit to get more heavily into the movement. So I said, 'Now, wait a minute, Jane, you are an actress. I'm a doctor, and one of the things I'm trying to do is organize the medical profession—you know, get doctors to give money and support to the movement. If you were a lawyer, I'd tell you to get out and organize the legal profession. But you're an actress. Organizing is what the movement is all about. So go back to Hollywood and start organizing the film industry.' She agreed, and that's what she started doing. She hated going around asking people for money or calling up strangers on the phone. But she gritted her teeth and did it. It was quite remarkable, the way she blasted right in. Of course, she was very close to Freddie Gardner then. He was a pretty demanding guy, so I suppose a lot of her drive came about as a result of her trying to please him. But she really went at it."

Jane returned to Denver on April 20 loaded with political books for the prisoners at Fort Carson. When as expected she was refused reentry to the base, she went back to the GI coffeehouse and devised a plan to enter illegally with the help of a few dissident soldiers. Wearing a disguise, she got through the main gate in a soldier's car and drove to an enlisted men's service club. Once inside, Jane removed her disguise and started lecturing the crowd of GIs and passing out the books she had brought from Los Angeles. The astonished GIs flocked around her, and when they realized who she was, pandemonium broke out.

The military police were called. As Jane tried to drive off the post, she was stopped and arrested. After being detained for a short time at the guardhouse, she was released on orders of the commanding general. "He no doubt chose to avoid a scandal," said Elisabeth Vailland, who was detained along with Jane. "The young soldiers who were with us were disillusioned. They dreamed of being arrested."

From Colorado Springs, Jane and Vailland drove south to visit a Navaho reservation in New Mexico. They spent the next week traveling through the Southwest, visiting other reservations. They arrived in Santa Fe on April 30, a few minutes before President Nixon announced over television that he had ordered the American invasion of Cambodia.

To the antiwar movement, the invasion of Cambodia was the grossest betrayal yet of Nixon's election promise to end the war. It discredited him forever and marked the beginning of a new wave of mass protest and violence throughout the country. At first, Jane was stunned and dispirited. The leaders of the movement had been boasting that their years of sacrifice had finally begun to pay off, that the United States would never dare escalate the war again. When their claims proved empty, a pall of despair swept over the movement, followed by a new outburst of violent reaction.

Jane met her brother in Santa Fe on the evening of Nixon's announcement—he was there filming scenes for his new movie, *The Hired Hand*—and they brooded together over the turn of events. On May 1, Jane gave a televised interview to the press. She spoke coldly and cynically of Nixon and condemned the

American invasion of Cambodia as an unforgivable breach of faith on the part of his administration. Even Elisabeth Vailland was surprised by Jane's bitter, despairing tone. "I had never seen Jane speak like that before. Her sense of tragedy and outrage was overwhelming. She was crushed by what Nixon had done, she felt betrayed and was very angry, yet her analysis was clear and to the point."

Jane and Vailland spent the next two days in the Taos area, bringing news of the Cambodian invasion to isolated hippie communes. Then they drove to Albuquerque, to the campus of the University of New Mexico, which was in the midst of a frenzied, student demonstration over Cambodia and the killing of four students at Ohio's Kent State University by the National Guard. Jane was invited to speak at a rally. It was the first time she had ever addressed a throng of such magnitude. The mood of the crowd was white-hot with rage and anarchy. Previous speakers had incited it further. When it was her turn to speak, Jane announced in a cold, hard voice that she was not there as an actress but as a participant in a political action in order to bring everyone together to join the struggle against the ignominy of America. After receiving a rousing ovation, Jane joined a march on the residence of the university president, where the massed students demanded the closing of the university as a symbol of protest against Cambodia and the Kent State killings.

She flew back to Los Angeles the next day to attend a press conference announcing plans for mass demonstrations against the Cambodia escalation. Jane was now completely committed to the movement and offered to exploit her publicity value anytime, anywhere, to draw media attention to it. Donald Duncan presided over the press conference. He announced a series of demonstrations for May 16, Armed Forces Day, at military installations across the country, and the formation of the Cambodia Crisis Coalition, a group of sixty antiwar organizations. The reporters bombarded Jane with a barrage of questions about her activities in Colorado and New Mexico. "The reporters were sarcastic and aggressive," Elisabeth Vailland said. "They kept trying to make Jane contradict herself, and the atmosphere became very tense. The conference ended up with everyone in a bad mood. It didn't go well."

Jane spent the night at Malibu with her daughter and had a long dinner with Donald Sutherland, who told her that his wife

Shirley had left him. The next day she was on her way back
to the University of New Mexico, where she had promised to
return to take part in further demonstrations. When she arrived,
she found the campus ringed by state police, and the Albuquerque newspapers full of references to her as "a dangerous
agitator." In Jane's brief absence there had been riots between
radical and conservative students, and the university had been
ordered closed. With nothing further to accomplish there, she
and Vailland set off for Killeen, Texas, where they planned to
visit the Oleo Strut, the off-base GI coffeehouse that Fred
Gardner had organized in 1968.

The Oleo Strut had been set up originally as a Gardner
indoctrination center on rights, but it had been transformed by
1970 into a busy cell of political revolutionaries. Managed by
a young radical named Joshua Gould, its staff was riddled with
dissension over the correct approach to radicalizing GIs. The
more moderate followers of Gardner sought to keep the focus
on legal rights and the avoidance of Vietnam duty, whereas
the extreme Trotskyites, as they were called, encouraged Fort
Hood enlisted personnel to carry out acts of sabotage and
terrorism. Gould had been hauled into a local court on a variety
of charges, including marijuana possession. When Jane arrived,
on May 7, he was out on bail and was hurriedly trying to
organize an Armed Forces Day demonstration within Fort Hood.

No sooner had Jane arrived then she received a call from
Donald Duncan to fly to Washington the next day to give a
speech at a huge protest rally and march on the White House.
Jane and Vailland left for Washington by plane and found the
capital swollen with protesters, police and troops. At the rally,
Jane opened her speech by crying "Greetings, fellow bums!"—
a parody of President Nixon's characterization of the protesters
a few nights before. Then, with dozens of other celebrities,
including Shirley MacLaine, she joined the head of the march,
her fist raised in the Black Panther salute.

Jane flew back to Fort Hood that night. The next day, she
joined the staff of the Oleo Strut in a round of meetings and
discussions. At the time the GI movement was suffering an
intense dispute over the role of women as well as other forms
of internecine strife. Many of the movement's young female
radicals resented the ways in which they were used—being
assigned mostly to traditional women's tasks—and they were
lobbying furiously within the movement for more voice in

policymaking and strategy. Everywhere Jane stopped on her tour, she was forced to listen to complaints about how the male leadership of the movement accepted women's inferior status while trying to revolutionize everything else. The complaints of the young women at the Oleo Strut were especially bitter. Jane agreed with them and promised to work on their behalf.

The next day she drove to Fort Hood to distribute leaflets to GIs, inviting them to the Armed Forces Day demonstration. The Oleo Strut staff had been barred from the base for engaging in such activities, so Jane went in accompanied only by Elisabeth Vailland. They were stopped immediately by the military police and taken to MP headquarters. There an officer read the military regulations that prohibited the distribution of leaflets and other materials. Jane argued that she was within her rights to be on the base, so the officer placed her under arrest. She was mugged and fingerprinted and, three hours later, escorted off the post. She returned to the Oleo Strut, where local newspaper and TV crews had gathered, and gave what had by then become her customary outraged interview attacking the military establishment for violating the rights of servicemen.

Jane and Vailland left Texas on May 12 for Fayetteville, North Carolina, to meet Mark Lane and take part in the Armed Forces Day demonstration at Fort Bragg. As they made the long drive during the next two days across the South, they had time to reflect on their achievements and their plans.

Elisabeth Vailland was an experienced, well-read Marxist. Jane was still a novice insofar as her knowledge and theoretical education were concerned, and she was eager to learn more about the history of Socialism and Communism. They discussed the various manifestations of Communism throughout the world and argued their relative virtues and defects. Vailland was a traditionalist; she believed that revolution could be achieved only through the political transformation of the working classes, particularly the blue-collar workers, and it was to this end she had devoted almost her whole life. Jane was less traditional; she had learned to abhor nationalism and was much less an admirer of Russian Communism than Vailland. Nevertheless, the Russians had started it all, Vailland convinced Jane. Even if they had failed to achieve the pure Marxist ideal, they had at least made it a possibility.

On the way to Fort Bragg, Jane and Vailland stopped at

Columbia, South Carolina, where they immediately became embroiled in a student demonstration at the University of South Carolina. Jane experienced her first bitter taste of tear gas as police dispersed protesting students. They took refuge at the home of the aging liberal aunt of one of the staff workers at the GI coffeehouse in Jackson. Later, when the aunt learned that her niece had been arrested in the demonstrations, she blamed Jane and Vailland for encouraging violence and exposing the young girl to danger. She ordered them to leave her house. Jane thanked her for her hospitality, then transferred with Vailland to a motel. The next day, driving from Jackson to Fayetteville, Jane was contemptuous of the elderly woman, claiming that such an attitude was typical of the hypocrisy of American liberals. "They talk and talk about supporting progressive causes," Vailland remembered Jane saying. "But when the chips are down, when their tight and comfortable little worlds are threatened, they completely fold up."

Jane and Vailland met Mark Lane at the Quaker House in Fayetteville. Lane had arrived the night before with Rennie Davis, a radical leader and one of the defendants in the Chicago conspiracy trial, and the two planned the day's activities. "Power to the People" was to be the cry of the day. The demonstration began at a local park under a scorching noonday sun, with speaker after speaker issuing the cry and thousands of sweltering demonstrators repeating it. Then the demonstration moved to Fort Bragg itself. Jane, Vailland, Lane and other activists drove through the gates and started passing out pamphlets on GI rights.

They were quickly arrested. With Lane loudly protesting that he was a lawyer and knew his rights, they were driven off to be photographed and fingerprinted. Singing peace songs and clapping their hands to revolutionary chants, each of the arrested group raised a fist when the Army photographer took mug shots. They were then escorted off the base.

After stopping for a few days in Washington to call on Congressmen sympathetic to the peace movement, the foursome drove to the University of Maryland campus, just outside Washington, where Lane had agreed to speak at a student rally. Waiting for them was a crowd of about 2,000, many of them sitting quietly on the grass in the sun and smoking marijuana. Jane stood in a tight cluster of people behind the mike while Mark Lane held forth about Vietnam. As his speech dragged on, an undercurrent of chatter rose and students began pushing closer to gawk at Jane. People kept trying to talk to her, but her replies were chilly and abrupt; she was concentrating on Lane's words. At last she was introduced and her voice, at first nervous and hesitant, then strident with passion, stilled the talkers and halted the wanderers.

"Who's getting rich off this war?" she exclaimed through the microphone. "When World War II ended, the Defense Department had a hundred and sixty billion dollars worth of property. It's doubled since then. . . ." This was to be a central part of Jane's modus operandi as she became a public advocate of the radical movement—the recital of statistics. The use of statistics has always been an effective oratorical technique, and Jane was learning to reel them off, like a veteran politician. More than occasionally, though, her use of statistics would backfire on her, causing her acute embarrassment. But that day she pressed on.

"Some of you people are just here to get a suntan and have some fun, and this weekend you'll probably go to the beach and lap up beer," she chided. The crowd blinked and grinned. The GI movement—the attempt to turn soldiers themselves against the war—struck at the cutting edge of military policy, she told the crowd. "The Army builds a tolerance for violence. I find that intolerable. They think it's normal to throw prisoners out of helicopters because it's the only way they can make them talk. I find that tragic." It was vital, she went on, to get soldiers into the peace movement. And it was vital to support them because it was more of a sacrifice for a soldier to wear a peace button—the risk being court-martial—than for a student to demonstrate. She urged the Maryland students to show their support for the GI movement by distributing antiwar leaflets at Army bases, subscribing to GI newspapers, inviting servicemen to speak at rallies, and contributing to their legal defense funds.

When Jane was finished, a large group of students gathered around to ask her questions. A young man, a drama student, asked her why she was still acting, still taking part in Establishment activities. "I'm not questioning your motives, of course," he said.

"Well, you are, that's just what you're doing," Jane snapped. Lane broke in: "You think Jane, as an actress, is any more a part of the Establishment than you are as a student?"

"Tell me," said another man with short hair, not so young. "What are you doing this for? For the publicity? Is this helping your movies?"

"Publicity?" Jane shot back. "What do you mean; I don't get it?"

"Well, you must be getting something out of this."

She glared at him. "You think this is fun? Standing in this heat talking to a bunch of lethargic students? I could be lying by a pool in Beverly Hills getting a tan. You think this is for kicks?"

The man drifted off, and another appeared to ask what she would be doing next. Jane growled: "Doing? What are you doing? Everyone always asks what we're doing. Why don't you stop worrying about us and start doing something yourself?" This was another tactic she had picked up from Mark Lane—to turn hostile questions around and throw them back so that they reflected on the people asking them rather than on her. It was an old debater's ploy, and Lane was a skilled debater. For Jane, the execution of it came hard, but she was learning.

From the Maryland campus the group, trailed by a caravan of press cars and students, proceeded to nearby Fort Meade to make another test of the Army's regulations against distributing antiwar leaflets and petitions. The press entourage arrived at the sprawling Fort Meade PX just in time to see Jane, Lane and Elisabeth Vailland stuffed briskly into military police jeeps. "We haven't even been able to ask anyone to sign our petitions!" Jane shouted across the parking lot as the jeeps pulled away from the arriving reporters. Expressionless MPs moved swiftly on the dozen students who trickled into the lot.

Jane, Lane and Vailland were taken to the Fort Meade provost marshal's office. According to Vailland, "For the first time in our three months of visiting Army bases, we experienced brutality on the part of the military police." They were pushed, shoved and bullied. Mark Lane was recording it all on his tape recorder, and when one of the MPs grappled it out of his hands and smashed it against the wall, Lane began to scream in protest, identifying himself as Jane's lawyer. Jane and Vailland were separated from him, locked in a room and searched by two female MPs. When Jane saw reporters gathered outside the small window, she rushed over and started shouting at them about the brutal treatment the three were receiving.

When they were all released an hour later, they adjourned to a snack bar along the highway next to the base, where Jane proudly displayed her bruises to news photographers. Fort Meade had been, she reminded the reporters, her fourth arrest "in the cause of peace."

Jane planned to stop in Baltimore before winding up her cross-country trip in New York. She called her father in Los Angeles just after her arrest at Fort Meade to ask him if she and her friends could stay at his house on Seventy-fourth Street. Henry Fonda was just about to sit down for an interview with Guy Flatley of the *New York Times* when he received the call. "Sorry I'm late," he said to Flatley, "but I was on a long-distance call to Washington, talking with my—how should I say it?—with my erstwhile, with my alleged daughter. . . . She asked me if she could go to my house in New York and bring her whole entourage with her—for a week! Gee, I would love to have been able to say, 'I'm sorry, but the house is all filled up,' but I just couldn't do it."

How many were in her entourage? Flatley asked.

"Oh, it's not how many," Fonda replied wearily. "It's how unattractive they all are."

chapter 26

KLUTE

Jane spent the summer of 1970 crisscrossing the county by plane—attending rallies and demonstrations, giving speeches, raising money and donating personal funds to various radical organizations as her affiliations spread. When asked if she knew that several of the groups she was representing were avowedly Communist, she shrugged. "Any organization interested in getting us out of Southeast Asia, I'm speaking for," she responded. Then she announced that she was leaving her husband. She had no choice, she said—she could no longer abide Roger Vadim's unalloyed male chauvinism.

What few people knew was that Jane had started an affair with Donald Sutherland. But as several friends agreed later, and as one put it, "Jane didn't really love Don. But she did trust him. It was her way of breaking out of her marriage sexually without running off with some stranger. It was like keeping it all in the family. She even had Shirley's [his estranged wife] approval."

When Jane was asked if Vadim understood her leaving him, Jane said that at first he didn't. "But I think he's beginning to understand now. He's an intelligent man, he respects people, but he wasn't prepared for what happened. He would better understand a woman who leaves him for another man than a woman who leaves him for herself." She claimed that her whole idea of love had changed, that her love for people, especially oppressed people, had made it impossible for her to devote herself to the kind of selfish love that exists between a man and a woman. The only specific love she felt was for her daughter. "I couldn't live without her. I never knew a child could be such a joy."

When Vadim was asked about Jane's activities, he sighed and made a pained reference to Joan of Arc. Then he started being seen in public with a succession of Hollywood starlets. Vadim stayed at the beach house in Malibu and Jane rented a $1,000-a-month house for herself and Vanessa in Los Angeles. But since Jane was traveling almost continually, Vanessa spent most of her time with her father. "The fear that threatened Vadim the most," Jane said, "was that we would no longer be friends and that I would take Vanessa away from him. But now he knows I would never do that. . . ."

In July 1970, Jane kept busy with Donald Duncan and Mark Lane raising money for the Servicemen's Fund. They also made plans to open an office in Washington, to be staffed by Duncan and Marilyn Morehead, the woman he lived with, to gather data on the military persecution of servicemen and to lobby on Capitol Hill for fairer treatment of GIs.

In August it was the Black Panthers who occupied most of Jane's time and attention. Huey Newton, accused of murder, had been released from prison on $50,000 bail pending a new trial. When Jane encountered him, she was overcome with emotion. "Huey Newton is a great, great, gentle man," she told a reporter. "He's the only man I've ever met who approaches sainthood."

Asked whether she was giving up her acting career, Jane said no but insisted that she was interested only in doing films of social and political importance and was not going to play "any more roles that perpetuate the sexist exploitation of women." She had started reading movie scripts again, and in June she agreed to star with Sutherland in a film to be produced by Alan Pakula for Warner Brothers called *Klute*. In it she would play a stylish, cynical New York call girl who becomes romantically involved with an out-of-town policeman who arrives in New York to find a missing man suspected of having employed her services. It was not exactly a film of political or social interest—indeed, it was an ordinary crime thriller—but Jane managed to give it that interpretation when she said, "The movie is about a prostitute. Prostitutes are the inevitable product of a society that places ultimate importance on money, possessions and competition."

Filming of *Klute* was to start in New York late in the summer and last into the fall, so in August Jane rented a furnished East Side penthouse not far from her father's place and immediately turned it into the local headquarters of the various groups she was involved with. After returning from Washington early in August, where she, Lane and Duncan held a press conference to announce the opening of their GI Office, she settled into the penthouse with Sutherland, Vanessa, and a nursemaid and began to prepare for *Klute*.

The summer of 1970 had been an apocalyptic one for Jane. She roamed far and wide in the service of the radical movement, and by August she was more passionately dedicated than ever to changing America. "Once you've had a vision . . ." she started to say in an interview shortly after moving into the New York penthouse. "People want to love, people want to be loved. Why not allow people to reap truly the benefits of their labors, to enjoy themselves, to expand as human beings, to relate to each other? But in the system we have in this country today, it is impossible to be anything but greedy and avaricious and competitive. The system pits people against each other."

What was the solution? A true revolution, she said, indicating that she fully intended to be in its vanguard. "As long as there's exploitation, as long as there's oppression, as long as there's investment, as long as there's efficiency—I will try to change it. Because this is the kind of system we live in! It doesn't respect human life, it makes you a slave, and it's wrong! Look what it does to women. Just look at the television sets. . . . It pits women against each other. It's like a disease, a cancer. Ninety-five percent of the women in this country are totally brainwashed by this. They truly believe they only exist as a function of how they look, of how they dress, of the kind of man they're with. The system does terrible things to women."

Like most people caught up in revolutionary fervor, Jane was unwittingly beginning to be infected by the same totalitarian psychology she professed to despise. It was this that would turn out to be the ultimate irony of her life as an activist. It is a cardinal axiom of history that in any revolutionary situation, the oppressed tend to become the oppressors. Indeed, the history of revolution would seem to indicate that the hunger for power is the real demiurge of the revolutionary spirit, not justice. Jane had acquired a reasonably good grounding in the defects of the American system, but her sense of history and her knowledge of the political, social and economic evolution of mankind remained superficial and one-sided, grounded as she was much more in idealism than experience. And like many idealists, her responses to her perceptions were almost entirely emotional and without the leavening influence of a deeply knowledge-refined logic which enables a perception of history as a process rather than a series of radical leaps from ideal to ideal. Of course, emotion and conscience are the wellsprings of altriusm, and they have a unique logic of their own. But history shows that these do not, cannot, operate in a vacuum.

Although Jane was intelligent and well-spoken, she constantly betrayed her lack of understanding of the balance of forces that had operated throughout history to make the world what it was in 1970. Her radicalism was well-meaning but undiscriminating. Thus she had become trapped in her non-discreet, uncompromising emotional logic and an unwitting disciple of the totalitarian point of view that insists there is only one way for a society to exist.

By that time Jane had broadcast her radicalism far and wide. As a result, she had rapidly earned the hatred of almost everyone in the country who was not committed to her passions. It was not just conservative America that despised her, though; she also made bitter enemies within the radical movement itself, especially among the more intellectually sophisticated. She unfortunately too often made known her lack of historical perspective and political sophistication in the most public of places, and more than one hardened movement leader cringed when she went on the *Dick Cavett Show*—her favorite commerical forum—and plainly revealed her ignorance in front of millions.

It was there that she was caught by an opposing debater on the Vietnam War who asked her if, after all, the American colonies hadn't sought foreign support in their Revolution against the British. "Not that I know of," she answered with high-strung defensiveness. Later, after her opponent had thoroughly embarrassed her, she confessed, "My analogy was beautifully clear in my head, but I completely forgot about Lafayette and the French and all that. I didn't try to cover up, I just said, 'Well, I made a mistake.' Of course, everybody jumped on me: 'How dare she go on a talk show without—you know, she doesn't even know anything about the American Revolution!'

"Plenty of people laughed at me," Jane admitted. She was envious of "those guys who've thought everything out," and she declared, "I've got complexes about my lack of political sophistication." And as she rushed to fill in the gaps in her education, she took her information unfiltered out of a single reservoir—the reservoir of New Left pamphlet literature.

No one who knew Jane well ever doubted the sincerity of her radical commitment or even disliked her for it. Personally she was easy to like. She had a way of establishing instant, warm, direct contact with people. She treated everyone alike, created an immediate feeling of sincerity, candor and unaffectedness, and projected an energy and selflessness that were, to many, awesome. In private, even after her radicalization, she always remained friendly and considerate toward people with whom she did not agree.

But as her ideas became more uncompromising, her public style grew more petulant. One suspected, knowing Jane, that her increasingly inflammatory statements were an effort on her part to gain acceptance among those in the movement who doubted her value to it, an overcompensation for her lack of expertise. She might have been more effective in getting her message across had she not so assiduously shattered the image people had of her. Had she continued, at least publicly, to be the Jane Fonda everyone was comfortable with and then quietly recited the horrors she had perceived in the American system— the effect would have been that much more stunning. As an experienced actress, she should have sensed this.

She chose to follow a different course, however. Because she felt militant, she felt that she had to act like a militant. And when she did, using as her models the many rhetoricians she had met in her travels along the radical trail, she lost much of her potential effectiveness. Naturally she had to be true to herself. But in doing so, paradoxically she compromised her impact as a spokeswoman for the movement. And when she was caught in errors of fact or statistics (the more she used the statistics supplied to her, the more she found herself successfully challenged), the less credible her militant posture became.

Many of the people who were involved with Jane in her early days of activism still criticize her for this tactical mistake.

There are even those, no matter how much they admired her personally, who insist she did the movement in general—especially the antimilitary phases of it—considerably more harm in terms of defective public relations than good in terms of fund raising. Perhaps she received wise public relations advice and failed to heed it. Then again, perhaps she received poor advice and accepted it. Many experienced activists who were involved with Jane insist that it was the latter, particularly Fred Gardner and Howard Levy.

On August 22 Huey Newton, fresh from San Quentin, flew from California to New York. Jane, Donald Sutherland and Mark Lane went to Kennedy Airport to greet him publicly and bring him back to Jane's penthouse apartment for a press conference. Somehow the whole production seemed incongruous, a fact hardly a reporter present did not fail to mention in his coverage. The sight of Huey Newton, the Black Panther desperado (which is how most people thought of him), sitting in the opulent, gilded, baroque East Side apartment that was a symbol of the racist system he was vowing to overthrow, put a comic cutting edge on the entire affair and made both Jane and Newton seem like play-acting revolutionaries. And the shouts of "Right on!" and "Power to the People!" from numerous white and black supporters jammed into the genteel, expensively furnished living room exposed the whole event to ridicule.

Jane, dressed in sweater and jeans, took no part in the press conference other than to answer the door, hold the television equipment for overburdened camera crews, get newsmen cold drinks, and occasionally toss in a "Right on!" Yet long after Newton left, she suffered ugly repercussions from the news conference. Not only was the bizarre scene made light of by the press, particularly by some of New York's acerbic local newscasters and columnists, but one of the apartment's telephone numbers, as well as its address, was printed. As a result, she was harassed by obscene and threatening telephone calls and was inundated by anonymous threatening letters.

The filming of *Klute* ran through September and October. In order to get a good grip on her part as the call girl, Jane accompanied a real prostitute on the rounds of pickup bars to observe the action firsthand. According to stories from insiders connected with the picture, she even paid a visit or two for a few nights actually working as a dispenser of sex to one of the city's high-priced brothels in order to be able to lend further realism to her characterization of Bree Daniels.

The shooting of the film somewhat limited the scope of Jane's radical activities, but she still found time to attend Black Panther rallies, raise money by telephone for the GI Office in Washington and even espouse a new cause—the Young Lords, a Puerto Rican Black Panther-type organization. "A year ago, for me to pick up the phone and call practically anyone except the people I was really intimate with was a trauma," she said one day in October. "I hated the telephone. I never answered the phone, Vadim always answered. And if there was any way I could get him to make a telephone call for me, I would do it. Sometimes I would break out in perspiration when I had to make a call to a stranger. Now, I must make forty calls a day to people I don't even know . . . asking them all for favors, for money. I sometimes think: 'What am I doing?' It's impossible that someone has changed this much! When Vadim was here the weekend before last and he saw me making all these calls, he sat there and he said, 'I do not believe it. I do not. I just cannot encompass the change in you!'"

Much as she did with Gloria in *They Shoot Horses, Don't They*, Jane infused Bree Daniel with all of her own hard-edged private tension. She had already proved that she performed best in roles that mirrored a troubled world, and because she sincerely believed that *Klute* could make a statement "about the breakdown and decaying of our society," she attacked the part of Bree with slavish dedication. She positioned Bree on the crest of her own churning emotions and carried her there like an alter ego for two months. By the end of the filming, the Bree Daniels that was captured on celluloid possessed every bit of Jane's alert intelligence, droll sense of humor and appealing vulnerability beneath, as written, the character's layer of cool cynicism. In exchange, the Jane Fonda of real life grafted some of the tough, hard-bitten Bree Daniels' invulnerability onto her own character and personality. Jane's portrayal was not so much a performance as it was an extension and expansion of herself into another person. Afterward she carried Bree around inside her for months, the way she had Gloria the marathon dancer the year before.

Once *Klute* was completed, it was back on the speaking and fund-raising road for Jane. There she would undergo an experience that would abruptly complete her radicalization and explode whatever hopes her more moderate friends and her family had that her political activism was just another passing phase.

chapter 27

CLEVELAND

While filming *Klute*, Jane added the Vietnam Veterans Against the War (VVAW) to the growing number of radical organizations she supported. The VVAW was a coalition of antiwar veterans groups that had surfaced during the late sixties and been incorporated into the radical movement in 1970. After the story of the My Lai massacre broke in the newspapers, confirming many of the things Donald Duncan and other dissident veterans had been claiming about the cruel excesses and atrocities of the American military forces in Vietnam, the VVAW's stock and credibility rose meteorically.

To bring further knowledge of military atrocities home to the American public, the VVAW hit on a plan to put together a series of public hearings at which veterans would testify to the atrocities they had either committed or witnessed. To exploit the hearings' public relations potential, their sponsors called them the Winter Soldier Investigation—an ironic title that derived its inspiration from the famous saying of Thomas Paine during the American Revolution: "These are the times that try men's souls. The summer soldier and the sunshine patriot will in this crisis shrink from the service of his country; but he that stands it now deserves the love and thanks of man and woman." The true patriots of the American Revolution, then, were the winter soldiers. Thus the Vietnam Veterans Against the War

chose that designation for themselves to underline their patriotic
motives.

The hearings were scheduled for Detroit the following January and February. The reason Detroit was chosen was its
proximity to Windsor, Canada, where the VVAW hoped to
have American military deserters and Vietnamese civilians testify on a closed-circuit television. As always with any major
antiwar endeavor, a large sum of money was needed to fund
the Winter Soldier Investigation. Jane, instantly enthusiastic
about the hearings, volunteered to tour the country to help raise
funds. She started out as soon as she finished *Klute*.

A few minutes after midnight on Tuesday, November 3,
1970—a national election day—an Air Canada jet carrying
Jane from a speaking engagement at Fanshaw College in Canada to another at Bowling Green University in Ohio touched
down at Cleveland's Hopkins International Airport. Jane, traveling alone, was in a state of deep fatigue from her practically
nonstop solo tour of college campuses. She planned to spend
the night at a motel near the airport before flying the next day
to Toledo and Bowling Green. Wearily she disembarked from
the plane and followed the sixteen other passengers to the
United States Customs hall.

Jane was stamped through Immigration and directed to the
baggage inspection counter at the opposite end of the hall. She
placed her suitcase on the counter and waited her turn in line.
She said later that when her turn came, the Customs inspector—
Lawrence Troiano—immediately ordered her to sit in a chair
while he called a superior in Cleveland. It was 12:15 A.M.

Jane said that she was so tired that at first she sat in the
chair and paid no particular attention to the strange order. Then
she realized that something was up—the inspector had not yet
opened her bag. She rose and asked Troiano why he had ordered
her out of line. According to Jane, he told her to shut up. When
he finally opened her bag, he confiscated her address book.

Also crammed into the suitcase were 102 vials of organic
vitamin pills. Jane seldom ate regular meals anymore; most of
her nourishment was in the form of vitamins. The top of each
vial was marked with the letter B, L, or D, which stood for
breakfast, lunch and dinner. When Inspector Troiano saw these,
according to Jane, his eyes lit up. She told him what the letters
meant—that the pills were vitamins, not LSD-type drugs—
but the inspector replied that she would have to remain in

JANE FONDA: HEROINE FOR OUR TIME

detention until his superior arrived from Cleveland. He then called a Cleveland city policeman into the hall and asked him to guard the exit.

Troiano's superior was Special Agent Edward Matuszak. He arrived at the airport in response to Troiano's telephone call at 12:45 A.M. When he entered the Customs hall, he found Jane in a phone booth speaking on the telephone. She had called Mark Lane, who was in Boston, to tell him what was happening. Matuszak ordered her to hang up and accompany him to the baggage inspection counter.

Jane complied with the order. Then, as she later told it, she was further ordered by Matuszak into the Customs office, where she was instructed to remain while he consulted by telephone with *his* superior in the Cleveland branch of the Customs Service. Jane was having her monthly period and was experiencing considerable discomfort. She told Matuszak that she had to use the restroom. Matuszak denied the request and told her that she wouldn't be able to use the bathroom until two Cleveland police matrons arrived to search her. This infuriated Jane. She repeated her request. Matuszak again refused, claiming later that he did so because he suspected that her intent was "to destroy possible evidence of contraband drugs she might possess on her person."

Meanwhile Mark Lane, having heard from Jane on the phone that she'd been ordered to hang up, called a lawyer he knew in Cleveland. He roused attorney Irwin Barnett out of bed and explained what was happening at the airport. Barnett, who had never met Jane, immediately got on the phone to Cleveland airport.

At about 1:35 A.M., Special Agent Matuszak called the Cleveland policeman guarding the Customs exit over to the office where Jane was being detained. He told the policeman to keep an eye on her while he went to the adjoining Immigration office to use a telephone. While he was on the phone, he saw Jane leave the Customs office with the policeman behind her. He shouted to the officer, "Where's she going?" When he saw Jane heading for the bathroom, he rushed out of the Immigration office and blocked her way. Jane pleaded that she desperately needed to use the bathroom. Matuszak ordered her back to the Customs office, telling her once more that she was not permitted to use the facilities until the police matrons arrived to search her. Jane responded, according to Matuszak, by angrily shouting, "What do you want me to do, pee all over your foot?"

They argued for a moment. Then, Matuszak said, Jane tried to throw a punch at him. He blocked the blow and immediately announced that she was "under arrest for striking a federal officer."

"I didn't hit you," Jane said.

Matuszak turned to Inspector Troiano and the policeman and said, "Did you see it?" They nodded in agreement.

Jane started shouting and cursing. By this time two more police officers, having heard that Jane Fonda was being detained, were on the scene. As she struggled to get by Matuszak and reach the rest room door, one of the officers, Robert Peiper, made a grab for her. She spun around and kicked out at him. The combined force of Customs agents and policemen finally subdued Jane. They guided her back to the Customs Office, where she was shoved in a chair, handcuffed and advised of her rights. She now had an additional charge lodged against her—assaulting Peiper, the Cleveland policeman.

In the meantime, Irwin Barnett had reached the Customs hall by phone, identified himself as Jane's attorney, and asked to speak to his client. Matuszak refused to let Barnett talk to Jane until she was searched by the police matrons, who, he said, had just arrived. He told Barnett to hang on for a while and put the open phone down on the desk. Jane claimed that Matuszak denied her the right to speak to her lawyer. Believing that it was Mark Lane waiting on the open phone, she started to sing the French national anthem to let him know she was being prevented from talking to him. Lane didn't hear her, but Barnett did.

According to Jane, it was another twenty minutes before the police matrons searched her. Later she said, "A policewoman finally arrived with a sanitary pad. Then she stripped me and searched my handbag and found some tranquilizers, plus an old bottle with a few Dexedrine pills. Dexedrine is not a drug; it's a medicine to help you stay awake when you haven't slept for two nights. I had bought it in the States with a prescription."

After Jane was searched and the pills discovered by the policewoman were turned over to Matuszak, he applied to her arrest sheet an additional federal charge: "Fraudulently bringing merchandise into the country contrary to law." Matuszak picked up the phone and told attorney Barnett, still waiting to talk to Jane, that he was taking her into Cleveland to book her on a warrant charging her with assault and the illegal importation of drugs. Although he was obliged by law to ask Jane whether she had prescriptions for the pills, which were clearly labeled, he failed to do so.

The Cuyahoga County Jail, a tall red-brick building, rises several stories over the adjoining Cleveland Central Police Station in a ramshackle section of the city just east of the business district. Jane was brought to the police station at about 3 A.M. and booked. She was then remanded to the county jail pending a hearing and the possible granting of bail the next day. Through an agreement with the federal government, the Cuyahoga County Sheriff's Office, which administered the county jail, also looked after federal prisoners. Jane was considered primarily a federal prisoner, although she also faced charges of assaulting the Cleveland policeman.

Jane spent a sleepless night in the women's pen of the county jail. When she was brought in and her handcuffs were removed, she found an audience of a dozen or so female prisoners awaiting her. Two were black women accused of murdering a man and distributing various parts of his body around the city. Another was a young white girl by the name of Barbara Cahn. She called herself a Maoist and had been arrested on several occasions, most recently for assaulting a police officer in a melee between antiwar militants and hard hats. The three prisoners immediately elicited Jane's promise to announce to the world that they had been beaten repeatedly by jail guards.

Irwin Barnett arrived at seven the next morning, according to Deputy Sheriff Albert Brockhurst, the jail's administrator. The deputy was a big, gruff cop, a veteran police official who had the air of a man who had seen everything and was surprised by nothing. "As soon as I was notified that Jane Fonda was a prisoner," he told me, "I got over to the jail from my house. I was told that when she was brought in, she was really charged up, cursing and swearing, calling everybody pigs and the like. Now remember, my job was not to judge whether her jailing was right or wrong, it was only to make sure she was secure like any other prisoner and that the jail's routine was kept in order. Anyway, Mr. Barnett showed up around seven. He was a quiet spoken man, very lawyerlike. He explained the situation to me, that he wasn't able to talk to her at the airport, so I so I made a deal with him. I told him if he would see to it that his client calmed down and stopped raising such a ruckus, I'd let him go upstairs and see her. I didn't have to do it, I could've kept her up there until regular visiting hours. But Mr. Barnett said he would try to calm her down, so I let him go up."

By then the word was out that Jane had been arrested. Reporters and photographers from the Cleveland papers were crowded into the jail's reception room near the ground-floor entrance. Brockhurst recalled that Barnett came down from his talk with Jane and assured him that Jane would behave. "He told me that this character Lane would be coming to see Jane Fonda. But he didn't let me know what I was in for."

Mark Lane arrived from Boston later that morning while Jane was still in the women's pen. Heavily bearded, he stormed into the jail in a fury. He was told that Jane was to appear before U.S. Commissioner Clifford Bruce at 1 P.M. for a preliminary hearing. Lane insisted loudly on seeing Jane, even though he had no license to practice law in Ohio and Barnett was her lawyer of record. Brockhurst said that at Barnett's urging, he assented to Lane's demand and arranged for Lane to meet with Jane in his office. "She came in," Brockhurt recalled, "and as soon as she saw Lane there, the two started shouting about brutality and terrorism. She used a lot of filthy language and was going on about how she was going to sue everybody in Cleveland, including myself, for the conditions of the jail and the alleged beatings of the prisoners. If you ask me, this Lane fellow seemed to incite Jane Fonda. Anyway, I let them have their say. Then I had her hustled back to the women's area."

Immediately Lane went to the reception room and held an impromptu press conference. He repeated Jane's charges about the conditions in the jail and the beatings of female prisoners and claimed that Jane's arrest had been illegal, the result of the government's program of harassment of antiwar activists. "Her arrest was an act of terror, pure and simple!" he cried. "An act of violence. . . . This is the Nixon-Agnew terror!"

Lane had never been known for understatement, so no one was overly impressed by his charge. Yet as subsequent events were to show, the charge, at least the essence of it, was correct. Jane's detention and arrest at the airport appeared indeed a form of government intimidation and harassment. The Nixon administration had been accused in many quarters of promoting a police-state mentality in the United States and of using federal law enforcement agencies to exercise its political muscle. The Jane Fonda case turned out to be eloquent testimony to the truth of the accusation.

Any doubts about whether Jane was singled out by the Nixon administration to be persecuted for her political beliefs were later demolished by some of the revelations produced by the Senate Watergate investigation. America learned that like many other celebrated Americans, Jane Fonda was considered an "enemy" of the administration and was included in a secret White House list of people to be harassed and intimidated. Capricious Customs and Immigration Service detention was just one of the methods the administration used to carry out its program of political repression. Among others were phone bugging, personal surveillance, mail interception, entrapment tactics and special tax audits. Jane later claimed to have been a victim of most of these. Knowing what we do today about the administration's "national security" program, there was little reason to doubt her.

Jane was taken in handcuffs before Commissioner Clifford Bruce at Cleveland's federal district court ten hours after being put in jail. He released her on $5,000 bail and scheduled a probable-cause hearing for November 9, the following Monday. A probable-cause hearing is a procedure designed to determine whether there is enough evidence of a crime to send a case to a grand jury for possible indictment and then on to trial. If there's not, the case is dismissed. If there is, it is bound over to a federal grand jury for further investigation and, most likely, prosecution. On the combined federal charges against her, Jane faced, if found guilty, a possible maximum prison term of more than ten years and more than $10,000 in fines.

After her release, Jane and Mark Lane held another press conference. Lane continued to harp on the political character of her arrest. He declared that Jane's name was on a special Customs list requiring that she be stopped, detained and searched every time she entered the country. He also claimed that her personal property—her address book, tapes, lecture notes and pamphlets, which had no bearing on the charges against her— had been confiscated by the federal authorities and were at that moment being photographed by the FBI.

Jane gave her version of the incident. "I am not a smuggler," she said. "I am a health-food freak, and the pills they found in my luggage were vitamins you can buy in any health-food store." The tranquilizers, she said, were the same type she had been taking on her travels for the past six years. "I was never hassled until I started talking against the war. . . . It was a political arrest." As for the assault charge, she claimed that she did not strike Matuszak or Peiper. She said she had been held incommunicado at the airport for almost three hours, searched and humiliated, and had "pushed" Matuszak only after he blocked her way to a rest room. About her night in jail, she quipped defiantly, "When you think of some of the people in this country who are now in jail, I didn't mind it at all."

The next day's papers headlined her Cleveland adventure: "JANE FONDA ARRESTED: ACCUSED OF SMUGGLING DRUGS, ASSAULTING OFFICER." That morning she was brought to the grimy police court at the Central Police Station, where she was arraigned on the charge of assaulting Officer Peiper. With her arrest all over the front pages of the Cleveland press, the courtroom was jammed with curious onlookers. It was the biggest local show in recent history, and scores of people had stood all night in the cold, biting wind off Lake Erie to assure themselves a glimpse of the controversial movie star. "I saw her in *Playboy* a couple of years ago," said Fred Jurek, a local lawyer who paused to watch the proceedings. "So last night I took the magazine out again to check what she really looked like. Now she's mixing with all those hippies and she doesn't look so good anymore."

A furious but controlled Jane pleaded not guilty to the Peiper assault charge and requested a jury trial. Municipal Judge Edward Coleman obliged by setting a court date for the following January 6. She was intent on vindicating herself and would accept nothing less than the forum of a public trial.

The show then moved to the Cuyahoga County Courthouse, where Jane and Mark Lane filed a formal complaint alleging that Barbara Cahn, the Maoist, had been systematically beaten by guards at the county jail. As Jane left the courthouse, she encountered the battery of reporters that was now part of her Cleveland retinue. She described Cahn's bruises and promised to follow through on the case until the brutality in the county jail was exposed for all to see. A deputy sheriff—not Brockhurst—raised his arm in a mock Panther salute and shouted, "Right on, doll!" Strapped to his wrist, one observer noted, was a Spiro Agnew watch.

Jane left Cleveland that afternoon to give a speech at Central Michigan University for the GI movement and the Winter Soldier Investigation. As she was about to get on a plane at the Cleveland airport, she was served with a summons announcing a $100,000 personal injury suit against her by none other than policeman Peiper. At first irritated by this additional harrassment, she would later be immensely glad of it, for it would enable her laywers to destroy the government's entire smuggling case against her. After her talk at Central Michigan she returned to Cleveland, where she spent the next few days with Barnett and Lane preparing for the probable-cause hearing the following Monday.

Although Barnett was Jane's lawyer of record and did most of the legal research in preparing her defense, Lane was intent on being her lawyer of fact in the courtroom. The hearing started at 10:40 A.M. on November 9. Docket No. 8, Case No. 3684, it was officially entitled "United States of America, Plaintiff, vs. Jane Fonda, Defendant. Commissioner Clifford E. Brown, Presiding." Assistant United States Attorney Edward F. Marek represented the government with the help of two other assistant prosecutors. Lane and Barnett represented Jane, who sat at the defense table dressed in one of her colorful Bree Daniel call girl outfits.

The hearing lasted for more than three hours, with most of its early stages consumed by a heated dispute between the outraged Lane and the phlegmatic Marek on whether Lane had a right to represent Jane in view of the fact that Lane was not admitted to practice in Ohio. During the protracted debate, Jane heaved a disgusted sigh and turned her chair so that her back was to the bench. She remained in that position, she said later, as a symbol of protest against the government's attempt to deny her "the right of the lawyer of my choice."

Once the argument was settled in Jane's favor and Lane had gained the right to cross-examine witnesses, it was the last point the defense won. Barnett moved for immediate dismissal of the charges on the ground that they did not indicate the commission of any crimes. Bruce summarily denied the motions, and from that point on he conducted the hearing within the strictest bounds of courtroom procedure. He allowed Lane, who quickly took over the defense, no leeway in the more subtle aspects of cross-examination. Often he overruled one of Lane's questions even before prosecutor Marek had a chance to object to it. To Jane, the hearing was remindful of the Chicago conspiracy trial of the year before, with the presiding judge constantly protecting the prosecution and stifling defense efforts to show that the government's charges were politically inspired.

Edward Matuszak, the Customs agent who had first arrested Jane, was the government's only witness. Lane pounced on Matuszak, using every courtroom tactic he knew to shake the agent's testimony and elicit an admission of government wrongdoing. But each time he ventured onto sensitive turf—sensitive from the government's point of view—Marek objected, and Bruce upheld him on the ground that Lane was wandering beyond terrain relating to the government's simple charges. Lane countered that he had a right to show that Jane's detention had been a premeditated act of political intimidation—that the actions leading to her assault arrest were encouraged by the Customs agents' illegal detention, that the pills Jane was supposed to have fraudulently brought into the country had been properly prescribed and were her personal property (which would have exploded the charge of fraudulence), and that her arrest on the smuggling charge was illegal on its face because Matuszak had failed to ask her if she had the prescriptions for the pills found in her handbag.

As the hearing progressed and Lane got nowhere with the magistrate, Jane grew more furious at Bruce's progovernment favoritism. She punctuated his frequent antidefense rulings with cries of disgust, and every time she did she drew an appreciative response from the spectators crowded into the courtroom.

Finally, faced with procedural dead ends on every side, the exasperated Lane took a new tack. The commissioner repeatedly forbade him to introduce questions on matters that had not been raised in prosecutor Marek's direct examination of Matuszak. But Lane finally prodded Matuszak into admitting he had made a telephone call to Washington shortly after Jane's arrest. And before the judge had a chance to stop him, Lane managed to get into the official record the suggestion that the local U.S. Attorney's Office was pressing the case against Jane on orders from someone in the Nixon administration. Marek erupted with a flurry of objections.

Lane knew he had touched an exposed nerve in the government's case. He was attempting to lead Matuszak into the admission that Jane had been detained in the first place because she was on a secret government harassment list. Such an admission not only would have wrecked the government's case; it would have been a significant public relations coup for Jane in view of its potential for exposing the then little-known fact that the Nixon administration was using its law enforcement powers to harass and intimidate political opponents and dissidents.

Although the ploy failed, the fury of Marek's objections provided Barnett and Lane with the key to their later strategy. After three hours of Lane's pyrotechnics, Commissioner Bruce, still holding to his narrow interpretation of evidentiary procedure, affirmed the two counts against Jane and bound her over to a federal grand jury.

After the hearing, Jane was released on the initial $5,000 bail. That evening she attended a fund-raising cocktail party at the the home of a prominent local merchant. The following day she traveled to nearby Case Western Reserve University to give an antiwar speech at a student rally. A conservative newspaper reported that the speech was received with apathy by a small crowd and that she was booed and jeered by most of the students. A lawyer who was there, however, denied it: "It was a large crowd—maybe six hundred students and teachers. There was a handful of ultraradicals camped up front, and at first they heckled Jane for being too conservative, but I'd say she won them over very quickly. And the crowd was far from apathetic. They were damned enthusiastic."

It was the beginning of an expanding pattern of negative press, though. As Jane stumped the country during the next few months, the drug-smuggling charge remained fresh in the public's mind. Newspapers, especially conservative and even a few liberal ones, distorted reports about her activities and belittled her in editorials. Dozens of TV newscasters had difficulty concealing their smirks of contempt as they reported her latest antiwar or pro-Black Panther utterance. And not a single Establishment media outlet took more than passing note of the fact that both the state and federal assault charges, as well as the drug-smuggling charge, were eventually dismissed.

The dismissals were due mainly to the legal expertise of Irwin Barnett. When Jane was served with the personal-injury summons by Robert Peiper, she was profoundly angered and depressed by what she saw as the cop's hypocritical attempt to gain personally from the misfortune he had helped create for her. But when U.S. Attorney Marek learned of the suit, he was even more dismayed. Barnett, on the other hand, couldn't have been happier. When he explained the reason for his pleasure to Jane, her mood brightened considerably.

One of the traditional procedural rules of criminal prosecution is that a defendant does not have the right to learn before trial what the prosecution—in Jane's case the government—possesses in the way of evidence. But what is known in legal circles as "discovery" always operates in a civil action. Thus, a defendant in a civil suit has the right to discover prior to trial all facets of the plaintiff's evidence against him. And when a civil action becomes part of a criminal case, discovery automatically extends to the evidence in the criminal case. The prosecution is therefore required to disclose its evidence in the criminal case. It was upon this technical detail that the government's case against Jane turned sour. When Peiper filed his civil injury suit, he unwittingly opened up the government's criminal case to discovery and, ironically, eventually brought about the downfall of his own civil suit.

Once Jane possessed the right of discovery, Barnett went to work on the government's position. His intention was to force the government into disclosing its evidence for having originally detained Jane at the airport. To supply this information, the government would have to provide answers as to how and why Jane was on Customs' special automatic-detention list—the reasons why any U.S. citizen was on the list, for that matter. It would also require a public admission on the part of the government that the list existed. Barnett's hunch was that the government would sooner request dismissal of its case—which was at best fragile, than release such information. He was right. After six months of legal wrangling in which the government kept moving for postponements of the disclosure of its evidence, it finally made a motion to dismiss the charges against Jane. The complaint was dismissed on May 28, 1971.

Barnett dealt with the State of Ohio's criminal assault charge with equal dispatch but by a different legal technique. Through Jane's right of discovery, he soon learned that officer Peiper had actually been moonlighting on the morning of November 3. There had been a bomb scare at the Cleveland airport, and Peiper had been hired by one of the airlines to stand private guard duty. Thus, he was not on official police duty when he assisted Customs Agent Matuszak in restraining Jane from using the rest room.

But Barnett didn't really require that information to defeat the state's assault charge. There were innumerable legal precedents in the law to show that Peiper, even if he had been on official duty, lacked the power to arrest Jane under the circumstances. Peiper was an officer of Cleveland's municipal police department, which was responsible for law enforcement at the Cleveland airport. But the Customs hall at the airport was the property of the federal government, therefore federal territory. By virtue of the precedents in law, Peiper had neither authority nor jurisdiction within the Customs hall.

Barnett presented a motion to this effect to the Cleveland Police Court. On June 25, 1971, Municipal Judge Edward Feighan ordered the state charge against Jane dismissed. Soon afterward, Policeman Robert Peiper's personal injury suit against Jane was dropped.

chapter 28

FTA

The Cleveland experience left Jane supercharged with both outrage and satisfaction. Her outrage came as a result of her first-hand experience with official government repression. Her satisfaction derived from the sense of achievement her unexpected arrest gave her. Although she had at first been frightened by being detained by the Customs people, once arrested she saw the positive side of it. It was a perfect opportunity to heighten the level of her acceptance within the radical movement and let everyone know—radical, middle-of-the-roader and reactionary alike—that Jane Fonda wasn't playing games.

Money was becoming a problem though. Jane had been spending personal funds lavishly on her travels and in support of various organizations—especially the GI Office in Washington, whose operating expenses she had guaranteed for a year. Most of the money she had earned from *Klute* was already spent, and she began to divest herself of possessions and personal property, including her beloved farm in France, in order to raise more capital. Parting with the farm at any other time would have been heartbreaking, but now she regarded its sale with unsentimental pragmatism. Besides, she said, "I have no desire to live in France anymore. The fight is here, and this is where I belong."

Jane also gave up the expensive house she was renting and

acquired a smaller one in a run-down, low-rent neighborhood hard by the Hollywood Freeway. She furnished it in early Salvation Army style, with mattresses on the floor instead of beds, and turned it into a combination working headquarters and crash pad for radical friends. "As you can see," she told a visitor, "this place is nothing. Everything I have or earn goes to my various causes." The only personal luxury she continued to indulge in was a nursemaid for Vanessa.

Being "poor" didn't bother Jane much; in fact, it gave her a sense of pride. "All I need for my current life is a plane ticket, two pairs of jeans and two sweaters." With her passion fired brighter than ever by the events in Cleveland, she was back on the road immediately, jetting from city to city to speak at antiwar rallies, to demonstrate for Indians, Black Panthers, migrant workers and welfare mothers and, most important, to raise money for the Winter Soldier Investigation and the GI Office.

She claimed the pace was necessary because "I still have so much catching up to do, so much guilt to work off. I still need to educate myself. Involving myself in as many causes as I can is a big part of that education. As they say, if you're not part of the solution, you're part of the problem. I'd rather be part of the solution."

And what was the solution? "All I can say is that through the people I've met, the experiences I've had, the reading I've done, I realize the American system must be changed. I see an alternative to the usual way of living and relating to people. And this alternative is a total change of our structures and institutions—through socialism. Of course I am a Socialist. But without a theory, without an ideology."

If she had no theory or ideology, what did she mean by socialism? "I mean a way of living where nobody can exploit the others and where the leaders are concerned about people and where there is no competition." Jane admitted that her ideas were utopian, but she still insisted that radical changes could be made, must be made. When asked if she used the Russian form of socialism as her model, she said, "No . . . Russia is just as bad as the United States." But she was impressed with what she had heard about China. "You know, the delegation that just came back from China, they all said to me, 'It's very difficult to talk about because it seems like we're naive. We were really trying to find the faults. . . .' And then they said, 'We couldn't find any faults. Everyone has enough to eat, everyone has a place to live, everyone has clothes, everyone has a pair of shoes!' They talked about a feeling of everyone being involved, everyone working together. And the most incredible lack of coercion . . . about how everyone dressed alike. Which I think is extraordinary, the leaders wearing the same clothes as the peasants. There are no differences, no class distinctions. . . ."

It was clear that Jane's idealism was racing far ahead of her common sense and that her limited sense of history was growing increasingly overbalanced by the heat of her emotional rhetoric. Nevertheless, after her Cleveland arrest there was no stopping her. And as she grew more vocal, public criticism and scorn intensified. She expected it surely from her enemies, who were becoming legion, but she did not expect it from some of the people she thought she was representing.

Her passionate activism on behalf of the Indians had cooled somewhat, especially after she showed up on a television show to talk about their mistreatment and an Indian leader in the audience rose and invited her to "butt out of Indian affairs." Indian folk singer and activist Buffy Ste. Marie announced to the press that Jane was "sincerely trying to tell other people what's going on, but she has unintentionally blown a couple of our most important issues by not really understanding our problems."

Despite her Cleveland adventure, many experienced radical leaders still thought she was doing the antiwar movement more harm than good through her naive representations of what the movement was trying to accomplish. "A hitchhiker on the highway of causes," Saul Alinsky, the veteran radical activist, called her shortly before he died. "I'm sick unto death of these young revolutionaries who think they've been the first to discover the 'answer.' They talk about revolution the way Billy Graham talks about the Bible. You know, 'Come over to Jesus and you'll all be saved.' It's all bullshit. They're just the new evangelists with a new shaman, hung up on their neurotic-romantic delusions. They know no more about organizing a revolution than I do about making a baked Alaska. They've set real social and political reform in this country back fifty years with their shenanigans and their constant shouting about right-on revolutionary acts. They wouldn't know a revolutionary act if they tripped over it."

Alinsky's tirade reflected the deep divisions that existed within the radical movement by the time Jane came into it. It was not just a case of sour grapes on the part of the older, more experienced activists; there were definite sharp differences over strategy and tactics. The differences did not exist merely between the young and the old, either; they existed basically between the politically sophisticated and the politically naive, no matter their age. The patient, selfless organizers were pitted against the impatient champions of action.

With her relative lack of political sophistication, and with her emotions racing at full speed after the Cleveland incident Jane was in the action camp. Originally influenced by Fred Gardner, she began to grow impatient with his brand of revolutionism, which believed that the slow, tedious business of organizing society's economically exploited factions was the only way to effect change. Jane, to reinforce her revolutionary fervor, needed more immediate results. She therefore parted ways with Gardner over this issue. As she did, the romantic aspect of their relationship died. She said later, "I was in love, but I had to cut if off because I did not understand him. And having the same political views with a man is now so important to me."

With her need to go where the action was, Jane's militancy became more visible and elicited ever-growing derision from the public. This she was prepared for—she even welcomed it because it reinforced her sense of mission and further legitimized the absolute rectitude she felt about what she was doing. But if the sniping she received from the Establishment counterbalanced the criticism she was getting from within the movement, there was one source of criticism that continued to leave her hurt and angry.

She seemed indifferent to the renewal of her father's complaints. "I never got hate mail until Jane took off on this revolutionary kick," Henry Fonda bitterly told a reporter. "She's a bright girl, but she doesn't think for herself. She hears a second or a third-hand opinion about some injustice, and the next thing you know she's screaming revolution. The trouble is that because I'm her father, other people think I agree with her. . . . I get letters calling me a Commie because my name is Fonda."

"I think she makes a lot of mistakes," he said on another occasion. "I think she hurts her causes more than she helps them. She turns people off that she shouldn't turn off. She should turn them on! She is only turning on the people who are already revolutionaries. She doesn't persuade people that *should* be persuaded."

Although her father's public remarks often bothered her, Jane usually shrugged them off with a wisecrack. But when her brother began releasing sarcastic quotes to the press, her hackles rose. "It hurt when he told a reporter that I get involved in causes without really understanding them," she said. "Why, Peter was the one who really turned me on to thinking about others in the first place. Now he goes around telling everyone that I need to grow up and broaden my outlook."

Jane's most pressing project immediately after leaving Cleveland was on behalf of the Black Panthers. As a result of her activities, she found herself on the receiving end of further criticism within the movement. She went to New Orleans late in November to demonstrate her support for a group of local Panthers who had been occupying a housing project for the previous six weeks while police tried to flush them out. The confrontation had turned into a standoff. In the meantime, the national Black Panther Party had called a "convention to rewrite the Constitution of the United States" in Washington, D.C., for November 28. In order to enable the New Orleans Panthers to escape from the housing project and attend the convention, Jane rented four cars in her name and had them taken to the site of the project. On November 25, as the Panthers left the project in the cars—secretly, they thought—they were stopped at a police roadblock and arrested on various charges related to the housing-project takeover. New Orleans Police Chief Clarence Giarusso told a news conference the next day that it was "thanks to Jane Fonda that we knew the militants were going to try to make a break." Giarusso said that Jane, by renting the four cars while she was in New Orleans the previous day, had unwittingly supplied the police with the intelligence information they needed to make the capture. "She probably doesn't know yet that she helped us," Giarusso said. "But I want her to know that she has our thanks."

After attending the Panther convention, Jane flew from Washington to Detroit, then to Atlanta, Chicago, New York, Texas and North Carolina to appear at rallies and meetings— all within a few days. She spent most of December in southern California, where she gave speeches and raised funds for the forthcoming Winter Soldier Investigation. She also visited with Vanessa, who had remained with her father at Malibu while Jane was on the road. Vadim was living with Hollywood starlet Gwen Welles by that time. Friends of Jane say she was perfectly amenable to the arrangement.

The Winter Soldier Investigation convened during the first week of February 1971, but it passed generally unnoticed except by the radical underground press. Moderated by Donald Duncan and others, the investigation consisted of Vietnam veterans rising to tell of their guilt for having participated in atrocities against Vietnamese civilians and prisoners. It was a moving four-day litany of horror stories that brought chilling insights into the officially condoned practices of military leaders in Vietnam. The point of the hearings was to prove that the responsibility for war crimes rested in the highest councils of the government, but these conclusions went largely unnoticed too.

America was tired of the war, as well as of the antiwar movement. After the Winter Soldier Investigation, the movement in general went into a state of sharp decline as President Nixon began withdrawing troops from Vietnam in wholesale numbers, thus lulling the public into an anticipation of impending peace. There was to be no letup for Jane, however. The war was no longer the main issue, as far as she was concerned. "As a revolutionary woman," she announced, "I am ready to support all struggles that are radical."

With Donald Sutherland in almost constant attendance, Jane, now thirty-three, began 1971 full of impatient revolutionary plans and a brand new cause—feminism. Her first major announcement was that she intended to organize a troupe of entertainers "to tour military bases and entertain soldiers with something they really want to see."

The idea was originally Howard Levy's, says Fred Gardner. Levy agrees. "I saw Jane in New York. She was feeling at loose ends after the Winter Soldier thing and was complaining about what she could do besides make fund raising appearances for the USSF, and I suggested something like a Bob Hope-type show, you know, touring the bases and giving the troops some really first-class radical entertainment—sort of an alternative Bob Hope show."

Jane was excited by the idea and began work on putting it together. Soon she had commitments from a score of performing friends, foremost of whom were Sutherland, Elliott Gould, Peter Boyle and Dick Gregory, the comedian. On February 17, Jane announced their plans at a news conference. "Bob Hope and company seem to have a corner on the market in speaking to soldiers," she declared. "The time has come for entertainers who take a different view on the war to reach our servicemen, too. Antiwar shows are what today's soldiers want." Jane said that the Servicemen's Fund would sponsor the show, which would be called the FTA show, and that they intended to open it at the 35,000-man Fort Bragg Army base at Fayetteville, North Carolina. Like "SNAFU" during World War II, "FTA" was a slang acronym used by GIs to mean "Fuck the Army."

As the show rehearsed throughout February and early March, several star attractions dropped out and other lesser-known performers joined. With scripts by Jules Feiffer, Barbara Garson, Fred Gardner and others, the show consisted of a series of satirical skits, many of them bordering on the sophomoric, lampooning the war, the Army, the government and other American institutions. The production started in a burst of good intentions, goodwill and enthusiasm among the members of the troupe. But after it was organized, according to Levy and Gardner, morale went downhill. The tour extended through the spring and summer, and since the Army would not permit the show to be performed on any of its bases, it was forced to play in high school auditoriums or on makeshift stages in GI coffeehouses.

Gardner was the advance man for the show during the early stages of its tour. Writing later in a radical newsletter called the *Second Page*, he said that the reason Jane became so enthusiastic about doing FTA was that she was an actress. She had realized "that the movement might be using her more than she was using the movement. They had set her up to go on talk shows where she made a fool of herself; they were taking her for enormous sums of money. She figured, correctly, that the only way she could stay in the movement without being ripped off was to function as an actress. As she wrote in the show's publicity kit, 'The most important thing for me is to combine my politics and my profession.'"

Although the show started with the best of intentions, it soon became a hornet's nest of political infighting and career opportunism among many of those associated with it. In Gardner's view, two types were attracted to the show—career radicals and filmland opportunists, both of which felt they could advance their fortunes through their association with Jane.

Gardner, already exasperated by the distortions that had been imposed on the movement he had started, found it difficult to see anything revolutionary, even radical, about Jane's FTA effort. He said that Jane and the sponsors of the show claimed that "it raised consciousness" and gave dissident GIs a sense of their numbers by bringing them together to see anti-Establishment skits. But it was 1971, after all, not 1967. "The fact that most soldiers hated the war and the brass was well known, and they didn't need their consciousness raised by Hollywood missionaries. The real reason the show was being produced was that it served the interests of a number of movement bureaucrats and opportunists—including the cast."

The FTA show was the last straw for Gardner. After it played a few Army towns, he came to the conclusion that most of the performers cared less about GIs than about advancing their own careers. He was ready to quit and turn his advance man responsibilities over to someone else.

Jane's newest cause—feminism—arose directly out of her involvement in the GI movement. She had long been discussing the oppression of women with various women in the movement, but until putting the FTA show together she had not really made any attempts to deal with her feelings. Touring army towns before she organized the FTA show, she had become aware of the constant exploitation of women both in the military and in the movement. One of the reasons she wanted to do the show, she said, was to raise the GIs consciousness not only about the war but about women. Bob Hope-type entertainment, she claimed, was the snidest form of sexism, with its starlets prancing around onstage in front of sex-starved soldiers and Hope making the appropriately leering jokes. "We're not going to do that kind of chauvinist show with topless dancers and a lot of tits flying," she declared. "If that's the only kind of entertainment soldiers can get, that's what they'll watch. But that's also why American men and soldiers feel women are to be used as sex objects. The violence against Vietnamese women is terrible, and these shows contribute to it."

About her own past role in contributing to the fantasy of women as sex objects, she admitted, "I have been as guilty as anybody, because I did it from ignorance. But no more."

Why her role in *Klute*, then, where she appeared in the

nude? "I took *Klute* because in it I expose a great deal of the oppression of women in this country—the system which makes women sell themselves for possessions."

Once Jane adopted feminism, it exploded within her more forcefully than any of her other passions. According to many of her friends in the movement, Gardner included, her guilt over her former collaboration in sexism became the dominating force of her activism. Soon she was defining male sexist chauvinism in terms of political concepts such as "imperialism" and would have little to do with any man who did not meet her ideological standards of masculine liberation, Sutherland included. Although they still worked together, their affair began to wane in intensity.

By late spring, according to Howard Levy, the FTA show had become the *bête noire* of the GI movement and the single greatest cause of dissension "between serious revolutionaries and the adventurists who were vying for control behind the scenes." The first show, which was called "The Fort Bragg Follies" and played for three performances at the GI coffeehouse in Fayetteville in mid-March, was a resounding success. It attracted full and enthusiastic houses of appreciative GIs and a sprinkling of government undercover agents at each performance.

The Fort Bragg experience was hard to top. As the troupe continued its tour, it was welcomed with less and less enthusiasm, especially after Fred Gardner quit as advance man. Gardner knew GI's better than anyone connected with the show, and he knew how to get GI audiences out. Once he left, the audiences dwindled; they were limited almost exclusively to already-committed handfuls of soldiers on each base and the radical staff of the local coffeehouses.

James Skelley was a former Navy officer who had received his commission by way of the Naval ROTC at the University of Minnesota in 1967. Disgusted by the Vietnam War, he became one of the founders of the Concerned Officers Movement, a group of active-duty military officers who banded together in San Diego in 1969 to protest the war. He had managed to receive a conscientious objector's discharge, but he remained in San Diego to help coordinate antiwar activities in the main port of America's Pacific Fleet. A tall, laconic, articulate man with a liberal streak of skepticism about any and all absolutes, he met Fred Gardner and immediately liked him for his combination of radical dedication and discriminating intelligence.

Through Gardner, Skelley met Jane when she went to San Diego State University to speak in April and again in May, when she and Sutherland returned to put on the FTA show—they hopped aboard the aircraft carrier *Constellation*, which was preparing to sail for combat duty in Vietnam. When the FTA troupe was denied permission to perform aboard the carrier, Skelley persuaded Jane to march in a demonstration against the sailing of the ship. Afterward he agreed to succeed the disgruntled Gardner as advance man for the show.

One of his first tasks was "advancing" the troupe's appearance at the Shelter Half coffeehouse outside Fort Lewis in Tacoma. "They were not really interested in the GIs up there," Skelley recalled to me, "and that surprised me because I thought the GIs were what the coffeehouse projects were all about. The place was liberally postered with revolutionary slogans and pictures of revolutionary heroes like Huey Newton and Che Guevara. There was very little attention paid to the question of GI rights. Most of the activity was aimed at converting GIs into active revolutionaries and enlisting them into the radical cadres.

"Well, the show came in and did its performance. The audience was so-so, half GIs and half local radicals. But what pissed me off was afterward. The staff held a party for Jane and the rest of the cast. It was a typical cocktail party, you know, with drinks and canapés. But what was worse was that the GIs were excluded. I mean, the staff locked up the place. It was them getting their kicks rapping with the celebrities, while the GIs were sent on their way. To me, that was the phoniest kind of elitism. Apparently this had occurred before. As far as I could see, the staff ran the Shelter Half mainly for the benefit of the staff, and the GIs were just an afterthought. It was this kind of thing that had Freddie Gardner so pissed."

Skelley said that by the time he joined the FTA show, it was riddled with dissension. Gardner agreed, adding that the GI movement in general and its corresponding fund-raising efforts through the Servicemen's Fund were even more seriously strife-ridden. Howard Levy contended that Jane had lost sight of her original goals in the GI movement and was impatient to make it conform to her own vision of it. Since the Fund still largely represented Gardner's view, and since she had broken off with Gardner, much of the ensuing dispute between Jane and the Servicemen's Fund apparently derived from her disenchantment with Gardner and his more deliberate tactical policies. Jane was still working through the Fund, Levy told me, but a serious rift had developed.

Levy said that it was then that Jane decided to pursue the notion he had put in her mind the year before about organizing the Hollywood entertainment industry. In the spring, after the FTA show was launched, she, Sutherland and others in the FTA troupe organized a group of film celebrities in Hollywood and named the organization Entertainment Industry for Peace and Justice (EIPJ). Their first gathering took place in April 1971 at a hotel on Hollywood's Sunset Strip. It was convened primarily as a strategy meeting to work out ways of expanding fund raising efforts for the FTA show and "continuing the entertainment industry's fight to end the war and bring our servicemen home."

By June EIPJ had, among other sponsors, Burt Lancaster, Sally Kellerman, Richard Basehart, Barbra Streisand, Brenda Vaccaro and Tuesday Weld, plus several well-known producers, writers, directors and musicians. Jane and Donald Sutherland became members of the central steering committee, which coordinated the activities of the several subcommittees representing various occupational specialties in the film industry— actors, directors, writers, technicians, and so on.

At a large EIPJ meeting in June at the Musicians Hall in Los Angeles, Jane stated in a speech that what was needed in Vietnam was "a victory for the Vietcong." This not only created a great deal of controversy within the film community, it caused an explosion of public indignation when it was reported across the country.

Later that summer Jane, Sutherland and several members of the FTA cast went to Santa Rosa, California for location shooting on Jane's new movie, *Steelyard Blues*—described in its prerelease publicity as "a wacky, anti-Establishment comedy about a band of social misfits who outwit the law in the merry and sympathetic tradition of Bonnie and Clyde." *Klute* had recently been released to good reviews—especially for Jane— and she felt that *Steelyard Blues* should be another installment in her crusade to make films of social and political significance. The picture was to be directed by Alan Myerson, the director of the FTA show. It was his first feature film, and Jane again played a prostitute.

In the meantime, relations between Jane and the Servicemen's Fund deteriorated further, and the feud soon led to a complete break. The Servicemen's Fund withdrew its financial support of the FTA show. Jane and Donald Sutherland thereupon took full control of the show, incorporating it under its FTA acronym and calling their corporation "Free Theater Associates." With money from the Servicemen's Fund drying up, they made plans to take the show on a tour of the Pacific with funds raised by themselves through EIPJ.

In October, Jane published an article in the *New York Times Sunday Magazine* in which she declared herself a full-fledged feminist. She said that she had received her final inspiration while filming *Steelyard Blues*. The article was a fervent plea for women's liberation. Jane made a special point of declaring that her feminist passion did not come out of any personal psychological problems but was the result of her recognition that "the oppression of women—both blatant and subtle—was a social problem which all women shared."

Concurrently she appeared on television in a series of skits in which she played the role of six different women—housewife, teacher, Playboy bunny, secretary, nurse and hippie. The program was designed to show "each of these types as they are oppressed by today's society."

About her relationship with Donald Sutherland, she would only say that she could no longer conceive of having a relationship with a man and doing for a man what she had done for Vadim. "It will never happen again. I will never be a wife again." Nevertheless, she said, she still believed in the old-fashioned kind of love she had had with Vadim—"Your heart speeding up when you hear his voice over the telephone, your fit of dizziness when you see him, your feeling of loneliness when he's away. I still believe in that kind of love because it's the most beautiful in the world. . . . Still, I do not have that kind of love right now. But I'm not unhappy about this. I am very serene with the man I'm having a relationship with right now [Sutherland]. We are friends. We think the same things. When we're together, it's delightful; when we are apart, we remain friends. I mean, he is not indispensable to me, I am not indispensable to him. He doesn't feel as if he possesses me, and I certainly don't feel that I possess him. Our attraction involves learning and respect, and we don't expect our relationship to continue forever. . . . We don't even feel the need to be physically faithful, because we know that sleeping with another person does not diminish what we feel for each other."

The public sign of dissension in the FTA show came just before Jane and the rest of the troupe prepared to leave for their Pacific tour. Country Joe McDonald, a popular rock star who had been appearing with the show on its domestic tour, called a press conference and announced that he was quitting because of Jane and her friends. He called Jane "simple-minded," "totalitarian" and "unable to work truly collectively." He said he had been active in the peace movement from its earliest days, whereas Jane and Donald Sutherland had only been involved for the past two years. "The press has catered to them, but the movement has been duped by them," he charged. "Their place in the hierarchy is much lower than they think it is . . . they've assumed a position of authority they don't have, and I'm not going to be any part of their ego trip.

"I want to demystify Jane Fonda and Donald Sutherland," McDonald went on. "They're novices. I think she's had a bad effect on the movement. She has created dissension. People are starting to look at her as a leader of the movement, which she is not. Nor is Sutherland. . . . Jane insists on being the producer and on raising all the money, and her secretary and her press agent are the secretary and press agent for the FTA show. No one else has any say.

"The FTA show should be a true collective," McDonald went on, "and it should be up to the collective to decide what they want to do. I would have stayed with the show if it were possible to work out the conflicts collectively. But it's just one or two people making the decisions, and they wield complete control."

FTA left for the Far East at the beginning of December 1971 with a stop in Hawaii. As an alternative to Bob Hope's annual Christmas tour, it offered plenty of contrasts. Where Hope's show had glossy production numbers, a big band and a succession of scantily clad starlets, FTA had makeshift props and a small combo, and the performers kept their physical charms hidden under jeans and baggy sweaters. Where the Hope show clipped along on brisk, risqué one-liners spiced with patriotic flourishes, FTA loosely mixed satirical readings, songs and skits to underline such assertions as Jane's: "We must oppose with everything we have those blue-eyed murderers—Nixon,

Laird and all the rest of those ethnocentric white American male chauvinists!"

But where Hope and his troupe were whisked from base to base as VIPs, Jane and company encountered official harassment virtually everywhere they traveled. Judging from the mixed success of the performances, the authorities may have overestimated FTA's appeal. At one show in Japan, a group of hecklers rushed the stage and were warded off only at the last moment. At another show, in a large gymnasium in Iwakuni, Japan, roughly one-third of the audience walked out before the show was over. Most of the people who attended the performances, according to cast member Holly Near, were there to see Jane. "That was the big disappointment," she told me. "I thought we'd have a much greater effect than we did. Oh, don't get me wrong, I think the show was a success to a certain degree, but . . . the majority of the audiences came to see Jane. In other words, if she hadn't been connected with it, I'm sure our audiences would have been nonexistent."

Once they saw Jane, many were disappointed. One soldier-fan who had been hoping to see *Barbarella* on stage lamented: "She looked too plain and sounded too shrill."

chapter 29

"HANOI JANE"

Jane returned from the Far East tour to face a renewed barrage of public outcries as she continued to call for a Vietcong and North Vietnamese victory. Howard Levy provided an informed analysis of what drove Jane on. "She's very alert and perceptive. I don't doubt, I've never doubted her sincerity. But sincerity is a funny thing with Jane. For some strange reason her sincerity drives her into obsessive-compulsive behavior. As a revolutionary she has one flaw. She is unable to put things into any larger perspective. She came into the movement late, not only in her life but in its life as well, when it had already been torn apart by tactical quarrels and ideological infighting. She never really learned the nature of the movement, the nature of radicalism for that matter, and she just didn't have the ability, or patience, whatever you want to call it, to work within the rules. Revolution has rules like everything else, rules that have evolved through years and years of trial and error. In effect, she tried to start her own version of the movement, which is what a lot of people did, mostly young and not-too-well-educated people. Now this is something only someone who doesn't really understand the nature of revolution would do.

"She just couldn't work within the logical perspective of the revolutionary idea in America. In a really oppressed country, where ninety-nine percent of the population are serfs and one percent the economically elite, it's possible for a rapid revolution to take place, and when I say rapid I mean even then something that takes time—years and years. But to expect that to happen in the United States is the most immature kind of wishful thinking. To think you can make something like that happen means you are stuck with a bad case of ego-grandiosity. I'm afraid to say it, but I think Jane caught a bad case of ego-grandiosity. From then on, when she started thinking she could do something which, if she looked at it in some kind of historical perspective, couldn't be done, it was all downhill for her. She not only hurt herself with the general public, she hurt herself with the movement, too, or what was left of it. I really hated to see that, because I think Jane could've been a real positive force in things. Basically, she lost the ability to discuss, to negotiate. I'm not sure she ever had it, mind you, but if she did, she lost it to this sense of moral superiority she has. That's why it's so damaging to have personalities in the movement. In the public's mind, they become the movement itself, and Jane certainly wasn't the movement."

Jane flew to Paris in January 1972 to make a long-postponed film for French director Jean-Luc Godard, who was lately devoting his talents to producing long, tedious Maoist pictures like *La Chinoise*. The new picture, which was to costar Yves Montand, was called *Tout Va Bien* (Everything's O.K.) and would prove to be another of Godard's exercises in revolutionary propaganda. At least Jane was being consistent in her desire to restrict herself to making movies of political and social significance.

While in Paris, Jane stayed with Vanessa in a large, plain apartment on the Left Bank which she shared with five other women and which was organized along the lines of a feminist commune. "Godard," she told a reporter, "is the only person I've met who's truly revolutionary." What she meant was that Godard was living a revolutionary life—he produced his films through a film cooperative he had formed with several other film-industry friends and spent every waking moment of his life in pursuit of his own communist dream. Jane added that she was undeterred by the criticisms and downright expressions of hatred she had been the target of. "These days, a lot of people hate me," she said. "They say, 'Where's her sense of humor?' I haven't lost my humor at all. But it's hard to feel any humor when our bombs are killing innocent Vietnamese!"

Tout Va Bien, probably the least known, least seen of Jane

Fonda's films in this country, had the most serious personal
impact on her of any movie she had done up to then. In it she
plays Susan de Witt, a self-satisfied American television reporter in Paris engaged in preparing a filmed report on French
labor. In the company of her French husband, an avant-garde
filmmaker played by Yves Montand (well known in Europe
for his leftist politics), Jane visits a sausage factory to do some
filming. On their arrival they find themselves in the midst of
a wildcat strike. The workers, all of them women, lock Jane
and Montand into an office with the middle-class plant manager, who gives them his self-serving version of the reasons
for the strike and bemoans the plight of the modern managerial
class in the face of uneducated, selfish workers. But Jane gets
a different story from the workers the next day, and this leads
to a violent, albeit ambiguous, breakdown of her marriage and
she realizes that she, in effect, is like the sausage workers while
her husband symbolizes the values of the bourgeois, patronizing
plant manager.

It was not so much the story as the making of the film that
deeply affected Jane. She had gone to Paris happily looking
forward to working under the celebrated Godard's direction for
the first time; since she, Montand and Godard all shared a more
or less common political attitude, she was sure that a major
revolutionary picture could result. After the movie was finished, however, she was not so happy. Godard proved to be
tyrannical and altogether "undemocratic" in his approach to
Jane, rejecting her script suggestions and treating her on the
set—it was not her imagination—just the way the plant manager of his film treated the women in the sausage factory. In
the end, after she saw the completed film, she could not help
feeling that Godard had intentionally made of the character of
Susan de Witt a parody of Jane herself. (Later, Godard would
release a cruel filmed discussion about Jane, in connection with
Tout Va Bien, which would reinforce her suspicions.)

But the experience had a positive effect too. It was the first
time Jane had played the role of a woman who was "politicized"
as a result of undergoing an experience on film. Susan de Witt
was the precursor of many of the roles that would later revitalize
Jane's career. As well, the experience she underwent was one
essentially of arriving at a recognition of the difference between
the way things are and the way they are made to seem. She
underwent the experience on one level through her character,

on another as Jane Fonda working under the direction of Jean-Luc Godard. Thus it was not only Susan de Witt who was politicized, it was Jane too, but in a different fashion than she had been up to then. Now she began to see a way of wedding her acting talents to her political beliefs. There was a profound difference between spouting ideology from a speaker's platform and actually provoking people to change their views. She had learned that her political harangues directed at an indifferent America had made no difference. What was needed, she began to see, was for America to undergo experience itself, the experience of recognizing the difference between reality and illusion of life in America. What better way to achieve this than through movies—the medium of illusion. If the reality of the film industry—cameras, celluloid, projectors and screens—was used to create illusion, then the illusion of film could be used to create reality and make America confront it. Not through preaching, but simply through good storytelling.

She returned to Hollywood in early April to be on hand for the Academy Awards, for which once again she had been nominated, this time for her role in *Klute*. At first she intended to refuse the Oscar, as a protest against the system, if she won. "But a woman who is much wiser than I am said to me, 'You're a frigging subjective individual, an elite individual, it's really typical of the bourgeois middle-class family girl to want to refuse the Oscar.'" She was persuaded that accepting the award would be a political tactic, because "the Oscar is what the working class relates to when it thinks of people in movies. That's what the masses of people in America, who think I'm a freak and who think that people who speak out in support of the Panthers and against the war are all some kind of monsters, relate to. It's important for those of us who speak out for social change to get that kind of acclaim."

Great pressure was put on Jane by many of her radical friends to make an impassioned political speech if she won. But after a long talk with her father, she decided not to. Although he disagreed thoroughly with her politics, Henry Fonda managed to convince Jane that her already well-known sentiments would be infinitely more eloquent if left unspoken. "I said, 'I implore you not to,'" Henry Fonda said afterward.

Win Jane did, and when she followed her father's advice and saw its positive effects, a gradual change came over her. Not in the intensity of her emotions about the war and the

American system, but in the way she expressed them.

Henry Jaglom, an offbeat movie director and friend of Jane's, claimed that her silence at the Oscar ceremonies was a "pure political act in itself. Sure, a lot of people were unhappy that she didn't take advantage of the moment to let loose. But Jane showed what she was made of. Everybody in Hollywood was waiting to come down on her. It was a beautiful piece of political theater, what she did. And the next day she could call up all those slob producers and movie moguls and raise more money than she'd raised in the past two years, just because they'd be so grateful she didn't fuck up their happy little gathering."

After the Oscar ceremonies, Jane remained in California for a while, planning new projects and giving speeches. She spoke at an antiwar rally in San Francisco's Golden Gate Park on May 1 and exclaimed , "All over the world America is regarded as an enemy." She described the fighting in Vietnam as "an uprising of the people of the South." Whether her assessment was an unintentional slip of her real belief, she was taken to task again for her lack of knowledge about the history of the Vietnam conflict.

Jaglom defended her: "So what if she made an occasional error? The woman was talking to the real issue, which was the fact that the United States was clobbering the hell out of the Vietnamese people. I mean how could anyone quibble over minor factual errors when so much more was at stake? What was at stake was that we were destroying Vietnam, and our people weren't being told the truth about what we were doing. Those were the issues that were really important. It makes me laugh when I hear people arguing about whether Jane's figures on the number of tons of bombs being dropped every day were right or Laird's figures were right. The fact is, an awful lot of tons were being dropped, and an awful lot of Vietnamese civilians were being wiped out while we argued the figures. That's what Jane was really saying. She was trying to get attention away from these silly diversionary games and onto the real problem."

Jane had met Tom Hayden a short time before winning her Oscar. Hayden, one of the country's original civil rights and antiwar radicals as a student, had matured into an experienced, hard-nosed revolutionary. Not only did he have a long and distinguished record of organizing, he possessed a sharp, incisive intelligence and a talent for logical theorizing and effective writing. With a battered face that made him look like a cross between a young Jimmy Durante and a worn nickel, Hayden was a cool, forceful activist without any of the martyr's hysteria that many of his colleagues possessed. He was one of the few radical leaders who was taken seriously by Establishment politicians. Most of the optimistic idealism of his early days as a leader of the SDS had been wrung out of him by beatings and cold jail cells in the South, by the misery he saw in Newark's black ghetto, and by the first-hand evidence of the venal quality of American militarism he had picked up during two trips to North Vietnam. He had been sentenced, as a defendant in the Chicago conspiracy trial, to five years in prison and was free on bail pending the outcome of his appeal (which would eventually prove successful). He couldn't leave the country. When Jane told him she wanted to visit North Vietnam, he told her he would see what he could arrange through his contacts with the government in Hanoi.

Jane went to New York at the end of June to attend a press conference for the opening of the film version of the FTA show. Bob Zarem, a longtime friend and well-known New York public relations man, set up the affair. "Shortly afterward, I left for France on my vacation. I picked up a Paris *Herald Tribune* one day and was astonished to learn that Jane was in Hanoi. She hadn't told me, or anyone else, a thing about it."

Jane traveled to Hanoi incognito in mid-July at the invitation of the North Vietnamese. While she was there, the news media at home reported almost daily that she had urged American servicemen to desert during broadcasts over Radio Hanoi and was also making other pro-communist statements. When she returned, it was to face the wrath of an irate nation. The people of the United States could tolerate Jane's previous forays into radicalism, but actually to go to Hanoi and "consort with the enemy"—that was too much!

"Hanoi Jane!" "Red pinko!" "Commie slut!" Such epithets, mixed with a handful of cheers, greeted her when she landed in New York. Branded a traitor by two Republican Congressmen who demanded an investigation, Jane brushed the charges aside. "What is a traitor?" she asked at a news conference hastily put together by Zarem's secretary. "I cried every day I was in Vietnam. I cried for America. The bombs are falling on Vietnam, but it is an American tragedy."

Jane was profoundly affected by her trip. As she related the details of her stay in Hanoi, her anguish was plainly visible. She defended her loyalty by saying that the things she had done were done for the sake of America. "The bombing is all the more awful when you can see the little faces, see the women say, 'Thank you, American people, for speaking out against the war.' I believe that the people in this country who are speaking out are the real patriots."

When asked if she might only be seeing one side of the issue, she responded, "There *are* no both sides in this question." She contended that the United States was completely wrong and North Vietnam was blameless for the war, and she angrily referred to President Nixon as a "cynic, liar, murderer and war criminal."

Asked if she thought she wasn't being used by the North Vietnamese for propaganda purposes, she replied, "Do you think the Vietnamese blow up their own hospitals? Are they bombing their own dikes? Are they mutilating their own women and children in order to impress me? Anyone who speaks out against this war is carrying on propaganda—propaganda for peace, propaganda against death, propaganda for life!"

The news conference was a mobbed, tumultuous affair. Everyone there sensed that they were facing a changed Jane Fonda. She wasn't giving a performance—she was deadly serious and firmly convinced of everything she said. Where once her antiwar stance had seemed to many an exercise in rhetoric, now her sentiments came from the very core of her being. She was distraught and flushed as she talked to the newsmen. Gone were the calculatedly defiant responses of previous news conferences. Her voice trembled with the agony of her emotions and the frustration of trying to talk to people who remained skeptics and preferred to believe in illusions.

Many Americans were won over by Jane's visible anguish— she was like a mother who had just lost a child. Others were not, and what were once mild doubts about her sincerity were transformed into furious challenges to her sanity. With the new wave of criticism, it became clear that the federal government and others no longer thought of Jane Fonda merely as a nettlesome nuisance. Jane was now considered a tool of the Communists.

The government was growing more and more concerned with Jane's activities. The arrest in Cleveland had been the first indication of this. Following that, she became the subject of intense FBI and military surveillance, her movements quickly filling up secret dossiers in Washington. Then she was investigated by the Internal Security Committee of the House of Representatives—successor to the notorious House Un-American Activities Committee—because of her involvement in the FTA show. The Committee alleged that Jane and her cohorts in FTA were out to subvert America's armed forces. Now she was being recommended for prosecution on charges of treason by Congressmen Fletcher Thompson and Richard Ichord.

Jane accused Thompson of trying to make political hay with his Southern conservative constituency in an election year (he was running for the Senate) and announced that she looked forward to an investigation, even a prosecution. "I welcome the opportunity to tell Congress what I have seen in Vietnam," she told the press. "But I have done nothing against the law. Furthermore, the Nuremberg Laws define President Nixon's actions in Vietnam as war crimes and give every American citizen a legal basis and moral right to resist what is being done in our names."

As it turned out, the Justice Department decided that Jane was right—she had not broken the law. But Ichord and Thompson pressed on. They sponsored a bill in the House of Representatives that would have made it a felony in the future for any citizen to visit a country at war with the United States, whether declared or not. The measure, dubbed unofficially the Fonda Amendment to the 1950 Internal Security Act, failed to pass—no doubt because the entire question of whether North Vietnam was really at war with the United States or the United States was at war with North Vietnam had never been resolved by Congress.

The most compelling outcome of Jane's journey to Hanoi was more personal than political, however, for she suddenly found herself involved almost daily with Tom Hayden. Like Jane, Hayden in 1972 was viewed by many within the radical mainstream as a pariah. After the Chicago trial, his influence within the movement had waned, no doubt because he had refused to join some of the other defendants in their regular disruptive courtroom behavior. He had moved to northern California to join a political commune, only to be expelled after a year for "male sexism" and "intellectual elitism." When he met Jane he had recently been abandoned by his longtime radical girlfriend and, according to another friend, was "struggling through a deep despondency and depression."

Says another friend, "Jane was astounded by the fact that Tom, once the shining light of the movement, the man who probably had more achievements to his credit than anyone else from the sixties, was like a Trotsky-in-exile when she met him. She was fascinated to find out what had happened. So she sought him out, and her curiosity very quickly turned to empathy. They had each been to North Vietnam and had millions of things to talk about. Out of that grew their mutual attraction. To Tom, Jane wasn't the shallow movie star he expected her to be. To Jane, Tom projected a power of mind that struck her with a measure of awe. She wanted what he had to give—knowledge and experience and a more penetrating way of looking at things. And he wanted what she had to give, which was respect. Plus the opportunity to make a political comeback.

Jane and Tom Hayden cemented their political and romantic alliance during the early summer of 1972. In August they traveled to the Republican convention in Miami to join radical "counterdelegates" protesting the war and to speak at a rally honoring George Jackson, the black convict killed by guards at San Quentin during the summer.

Jane's trip to Hanoi had put her in a more militant mood than ever. Added to that was her desire to impress Hayden with her revolutionary ardor. But with the Nixon administration promising that "peace was at hand" and with the military draft on its last legs, the antiwar movement had shrunk to a shadow of its former size and passion. To be sure, there were loud and harried demonstrations at both 1972 Presidential conventions. But they lacked the numbers and spontaneous fire of four summers before. What was left at Miami was the hard-core, never-say-die cadre of a movement on the verge of expiring for want of an issue.

Jane was not about to let it die, though. After tearfully describing on the *Dick Cavett Show* the horrors of what she had seen in North Vietnam in the wake of American bombing, she announced that she and Tom Hayden were going to tour the nation "right up until election day to counter the lies of the Nixon administration and tell the truth about what the United States is doing in Vietnam."

Calling themselves the Indochina Peace Campaign, Jane and Hayden set out in September on a nine-week, ninety-city tour of the country while Nixon and McGovern conducted their own more conventional campaigns. Holly Near, the young California singer and pacifist who had been a member of the FTA cast, accompanied them. "It was a grueling trip," she recalled to me, "but we found a lot more people eager to hear what we had to say than we thought. Jane and Tom would speak, I would sing a song or two. Then we'd show slides that Jane took in Vietnam and answer questions. It was all pretty low-key. There was very little harassment and no heckling to speak of. It sort of restored my faith in the American people, and let me tell you, we really hit some isolated places. Jane was fantastic—I've never seen anyone so dedicated. Even if people didn't agree with her politics, they listened to her with respect and consideration. It was an altogether exhilarating experience."

If Fred Gardner had been the Andreas Voutsinas of Jane's beginnings as a radical, Tom Hayden was the Roger Vadim. Where Gardner had given her the impetus, encouragement and tutelage to become an activist in the face of her initial hesitancy, Hayden supplied the refinement, confidence, security and acceptance she had been seeking since Gardner. Ever since Jane had met him, she sensed that Hayden was everything a revolutionary man should be—brilliant, tireless, and largely liberated from the residual male chauvinism other radical leaders had not been able to overcome. Besides that, he was an established star of the movement—the perfect mentor to help her refine her radical ideology and commitment.

Once the election was over—with the McGovern campaign against the war obliterated by the Nixon landslide and the antiwar movement dissipating fast—Jane flew to Norway to begin filming the screen version of *A Doll's House*, Henrik Ibsen's classic play about a turn-of-the-century Norwegian woman who fights to liberate herself from the domination of her husband. Joseph Losey, the director—an American expatriate who had left the United States for political reasons during the McCarthy era and settled in England—had few pleasant things to say about working with Jane on the picture, despite the fact that they shared similar sentiments about the United States. "I have directed the most temperamental stars of all time," a journalist quoted him as saying, "but I have never encountered the likes of Jane Fonda."

Yet Losey had desperately wanted Jane for the movie. He

was sympathetic to the women's liberation movement and believed that *A Doll's House* would be the ideal vehicle with which to make an artistic statement about his position. Knowing how Jane felt, he had concluded that she was the perfect actress to play Nora. He quickly changed his mind, however, once filming began. "After my experiences with her in Roros [Norway], where we shot the picture, I have decided she's terribly confused. She wastes time and energy on too many causes."

According to Losey, Jane was arrogant, imperious, thoughtless and unprofessional. "She was spending most of her time working on her political speeches instead of learning her lines, and making innumerable phone calls about her political activities." Losey finally had to threaten Jane that unless she agreed to work with the rest of the company, he would stop shooting. They finally reached an agreement, he said, but even then things didn't improve much. "Her problem, I think, is her family, her uptight background, and her marriage to Roger Vadim."

Losey added that in his view, Jane had armed herself to avoid being hurt by men. "And for a woman to encase herself like that is not an easy way to live. . . . She shrinks from any man touching her, with the exception of Tom Hayden. . . . The problem with Jane is that she has little sense of humor. Working with her is not an experience I would like to go through again."

Filming of *A Doll's House* lasted through the middle of December, 1972. While in Norway, Jane announced that she and Tom Hayden were in love and were planning to marry "as soon as I am able to."

Michael Maslansky, the film's publicist, said, "There is real feeling and affection between them. They are very much in love and spend as much time together as they can, most of it planning antiwar activities. But it's strange, I have never seen them hold hands or kiss. . . . They spend most of their time trying to convert people to their point of view."

Explained Hayden: "We have agreed not to talk in public about our engagement. What we want to talk about is the peace movement."

Jane agreed. "We are campaigning for peace together. That is what we are interested in. Our relationship is a very private thing, and we don't intend to let it interfere with our activities in the movement."

When President Nixon instituted a massive saturation bombing of the Hanoi area late in December, allegedly to force the North Vietnamese government's hand in the peace negotiations, Jane and Hayden reacted with horror. Jane, in Stockholm after finishing *A Doll's House*, took part in a demonstration against the bombing at the U.S. embassy and was promptly splattered with a can of red paint by a hostile observer. The paint was symbolic of what might happen at any time, for Jane had lived since her visit to Hanoi with almost daily threats on her life.

From Stockholm, she and Hayden flew to Paris to meet with the chief North Vietnamese negotiator at the Paris peace talks. He told them, Jane said, that the renewed bombing "would be futile, that Hanoi would not be bombed into compromise of its fundamental national rights."

Jane and Hayden returned to New York late in December just after her thirty-fifth birthday. Shortly thereafter Jane flew to the Dominican Republic, where she obtained an overnight divorce from Roger Vadim. On January 21, 1973, in her modest, sparsely furnished house off Laurel Canyon Boulevard on the San Fernando Valley side of the Hollywood Hills, she and Tom Hayden were married. The free-form ceremony was conducted by the Reverend Richard York, a progressive Episcopalian priest. The festivities, which included the singing of Vietnamese songs and the dancing of Irish jigs, was attended by more than a hundred well-wishers, including a group of Vietnamese students, Jane's father and brother.

Jane, wearing a pair of scuffed pants and a Vietnamese peasant's blouse over her protruding abdomen (she was by then four months pregnant), introduced everyone to everyone else and made a short speech. She described her travels throughout Vietnam and explained admiringly how the family ties there were the closest she had seen in any country of the world. She told how children were the most important people in Vietnam because they meant home and love and togetherness—qualities that had escaped her throughout her life but which she now felt she was on the verge of finding. She announced that she was expecting Tom Hayden's child and that she had decided to marry Hayden in order to start a truly revolutionary family— one based on home, love and togetherness.

Two days later the Reverend York received a "letter of Godly Admonition" from the Episcopal Bishop of California, suspending him from further priestly duties for marrying a divorced woman without permission from the Bishop.

chapter 30

HOLLYWOOD LIMBO

With her second marriage, Jane's life settled onto a course that seemed destined to bring about an end to her acting career. Before leaving for Norway to make *A Doll's House*, she had agreed to write her autobiography for a large New York publishing house. But after her wedding to Hayden, she dropped the project and rededicated herself to what had become their mutual revolutionary concerns. Hayden convinced Jane that an autobiography containing the story of her radical political transformation, published by a capitalist publisher interested only in profits, would open her up to charges of hypocrisy as well as naiveté. If Jane was interested in the revolutionary change-over of America, she would not achieve it in the pages of a movie star autobiography, no matter how well intentioned it was. Revolution, as Fred Gardner had tried to convince her two years before, was possible only through the long and tedious process of political organizing, of gradually changing the perceptions of society. In the words of Jane's brother, "The thing Tom taught her right off was that you don't achieve revolution overnight. That was Jane's problem all along, trying to change people and getting frustrated when they failed to change purely on her say-so. Lots of others had been telling her this, but because she wasn't in love with them she didn't listen. But she was in love with Tom, and because *he* said it she listened."

276

Soon after their marriage, Jane and Hayden moved from the house in Laurel Canyon to an even more austere abode in the rundown seaside community of Venice, just west of Los Angeles. Jane gave herself over completely to Tom Hayden's political tutoring and the two embarked on a joint effort to expand the scope of their Indochina Peace Campaign. Many who knew them believed that their move to what Henry Fonda later described as "that shack" in Venice was in the nature of a political statement—a conspicuous commitment to live the impoverished life of revolutionaries in fact as well as in spirit.

The truth was more prosaic. Jane, having exhausted most of her money on her antiwar efforts, was now nearly broke, and Hayden had long been without any funds at all to speak of. What little money trickled in during the next year derived from their fund raising efforts for the peace campaign, and most of that they spent on further travels and public appearances, showing films of the destruction and death in Vietnam.

On July 7, 1973, Jane gave birth to her child by Hayden, a son. They named him Troy O'Donovan Garrity, after the alias Hayden often had used during his underground days. Her newborn did little to temper Jane's outspokenness. Indeed, as one devoted friend said at the time, "Troy's birth was a profound event for Jane. It was much more politically symbolic than simply having a baby. In her mind Troy was emblematic of all the things she was fighting for—a new order in America, an order in which young men would grow up accepting and respecting the equality of women and would not have to worry about having their lives wasted fighting other men's wars. If anything, Troy's birth deepened Jane's commitment and gave it a substance that was much more solid than before. Tom she could learn from intellectually, but the baby provided her with her ultimate emotional focus. From being a bit scattergun in her emotional approach to the cause, she became intensely zeroed in on what exactly it was that motivated her and what she wanted to do."

Shortly after the birth of her son, Jane triggered a new wave of public antagonism by disputing the first American prisoners of war who returned from the Far East with stories of systematic, widespread torture in the North Vietnamese prison camps. Her reaction was that of a mother whose child has been accused of wrongdoing—relfexive, angry-hysterical, blindly disbelieving. She accused the POWs of being nothing less than "liars

and hypocrites," insisting that the gentle North Vietnamese
were incapable of such barbaric practices. But as more and
more repatriated prisoners confirmed the initial stories, she
changed her tune. She conceded that there might have been
some isolated instances of torture. "But if so, what do you
expect when these American fliers were the very same men
who rained bombs on you and killed your loved ones for years.
Nobody's perfect, not even the Vietnamese. And if a scattered
few have engaged in less than perfect behavior, who are we
to blame them?" When two of the prisoners she had interviewed
in Hanoi came back and announced that they had been tortured
into talking to her, she was silent.

By mid-1973, Jane Fonda was among the most controversial
and disliked public figures in the United States. She compounded her disfavor by coming out on the side of the Arabs
in the wake of that year's Arab-Israeli War. Undoubtedly influenced by Vanessa Redgrave, a rabid Communist and outspoken supporter of the Palestine-Arab cause, Jane declared
her own support of a Palestinian state. Israel was simply a
lackey of the United States. Justice in the Middle East would
be secured only when the displaced Palestinian people had a
nation of their own. Many American liberals, particularly those
among America's influential Jewish community, had been
merely bemused by Jane's tirades about Vietnam and the POWs.
But her comments about Israel and the Palestinians—well, they
went beyond the pale. She was branded as an anti-Semite and
the movie industry, dominated by Jews, angrily joined in the
boycott of Jane Fonda. Within a short time, she could not even
buy an acting job. Hostility toward her was exacerbated by the
fact that *A Doll's House*, poorly reviewed, had been a financial
disaster.

Jane didn't back down, though. On the contrary, she announced that she was ready to renounce her acting career if
the alternative was to bow and scrape to movie moguls whose
feelings about Israel were "purely of the knee-jerk reflex type."
Hollywood was ready to oblige her. As the head of one large
studio said, "The bitch will never be allowed inside my gates
again."*

But then there occurred a series of events that brought Jane

---

*More recently Jane has demonstrated her sympathy for Jewish causes. During
the summer of 1981 she appeared at several rallies in support of imprisoned
Jews in Russia and Soviet Jewish emigration to Israel.

back into limited, albeit temporary, favor. It was the time when revelations about Watergate and Nixon had begun to tumble down on the American people. In the fall of 1973 and spring of 1974, as the Ervin Committee and the Special Prosecutor's Office peeled back the malignant underside of the Nixon administration, Jane was able to vindicate herself. She pointed out repeatedly, on television talk shows and in newspaper interviews, that everything she had alleged about Nixon and his administration during the previous four years had turned out to be true. Not only had she been among the leading lights on Nixon's notorious "enemies list," but she had been the subject of intensive and illegal FBI surveillance and espionage. When Jane instituted a massive lawsuit against Nixon and other government figures, many people sympathized with her, even applauded her.

But then, as was often the case with Jane, she overplayed her hand. It was one thing to express one's satisfaction at being proved right; it was another to belabor the obvious. Soon the public, wrapped up in the larger implications of Watergate, grew bored by Jane's anger. Then her lawyers advised her to cease and desist, telling her that her continued public perorations could imperil her chances of winning her lawsuit.

By August of 1974, when Nixon resigned from the Presidency, Jane was being invited to appear on fewer and fewer talk shows. Nor were her views any longer sought out by the news media. And with the rapid if inglorious termination of the American presence in Vietnam the following year, she was left essentially without a cause to prosecute—at least a cause of sufficient social concern to engage the interest of the public. Tom Hayden found himself in the same predicament. The Indochina Peace Campaign no longer had a reason for being. Despite the spiritual scars left by Watergate and the war, and despite the combined inflation-recession that had plunged the country into deep economic distress during 1974 and 1975, the American public was not interested in radical socialist reform, not to mention revolution. The public was, nevertheless, disoriented and restless. It was in this condition of social confusion and anomie that the perceptive Tom Hayden saw an opportunity to convert his outsider's revolutionary theories into a political movement of more compelling mainstream attraction.

California was one of the first states to reflect the country's political and economic disorientation by electing the eccentric young ex-seminarian, Jerry Brown, as its governor in 1974. Brown was the son of powerful former governor Pat Brown. Although he campaigned in stiff, three-piece Ivy-League suits, through a combination of Jesuitical oratory and Buddhist-tinged preachings he managed to dispel any image of himself as an heir-apparent or a politics-as-usual candidate. Promising to overthrow the longstanding oligarchy in California that had vested most of the power and money in the state in the hands of the privileged few at the expense of the many, Brown appealed to enough members of the younger working-class generation to get elected. Once in office, he pursued the fulfillment of his campaign promises with religious zeal and enlisted many of those outside the Establishment who had supported him to endorse his new style of state governance. Among those whose support Brown had sought was Tom Hayden, like himself, a bright, rebellious Irish-Catholic with the temperament of an evangelistic martyr. Hayden had not been an important factor in Brown's election, but he had endorsed the new governor to his small California constitutency of aging hippies, radical workers, Vietnam draft evaders and disillusioned, out-of-work veterans. After Brown, not much older than Hayden, was installed in the state capital in Sacramento, he began to consult Hayden for advice on various labor and economic strategies.

Several of Hayden's revolutionary confederates of that period are today bitter at what they view as their former leader's sell-out to the Establishment, even though it was the slightly unorthodox Establishment personified by Jerry Brown. According to them, Hayden allowed himself to be seduced into the reformist but nonrevolutionary new mainstream of California politics. Says one: "Hayden flipped out when he discovered that Jane Fonda was attracted to him, and then he really went bananas when she agreed to marry him. This was a whole new ballgame for him. For a while he tried to pretend to us that it made no difference. But then the subtle changes began. He began to realize what it all meant, the personal potential his being the husband of Jane Fonda provided—the radical glamor, so to speak. It was a chance to make a political comeback after having been down so long. But to seize that chance he would have to shed his image as an extreme left-winger and adopt a more moderate stance—not become a non-radical, mind you, but just work through the system a little more. After the war, the media would have forgotten about

Tom, just as they did all the other leaders. But being married to Jane gave him cache, access. He realized however, that if he was going to be able to keep the media's attention, he'd have to soften his revolutionary rhetoric. Jane's too. He convinced her to shut up for a while. Once he managed that and started getting some attention again, he began to believe it was the right way to go. I mean, once he began to say and do less radical things, he began to think less radical things."

Hayden dismisses such interpretations as the ravings of self-deluded radicals who are unable to function in the real world. According to him, his moderating attitude in 1975 was not a matter of seduction but a pragmatic realization that, with the Vietnam War over, he had to find another issue through which to advance the cause of social and economic justice he still so fervently believed in. With this strategy in mind, Hayden and Jane gradually closed down the Indochina Peace Campaign and replaced it with a new organization and a new idea. The organization they called the Campaign for Economic Democracy [CED]. The idea behind it was to refocus the energies and funds of the political Left in California on the plight of the state's disadvantaged minorities. Since improving the economic and educational status of California's have-nots was not inconsistent with the goals of the Brown administration, Hayden declared that the CED could serve to enhance the new governor's aims. Brown didn't disagree, giving the CED its first legitimacy among the local media.

Out of the tenuous common cause came at first a trickle, then a progressively greater influx of funds into the CED. Hayden, with Jane usually at his side, began to deliver by hand "position papers" outlining the CED's goals and strategies to local newspapers. Hayden is not an accomplished speaker. But he is a penetrating writer, and he used that skill to engage the interest of hard-bitten editors. The basic aim of the new organization, as he put it, was to establish itself quickly as a potent political force within California, representing women, blacks, Mexican-Americans, underpaid factory and farm workers, the elderly, illegal immigrants—anyone living in California who was effectively excluded from participation in the ruling process by virtue of their socio-economic status—and to join in coalition with other such groups. CED was to take on the coloration of an alternative political party of the poor as well as function as the principal lobbyist of California's deprived in Sacramento and in local governmental jurisdictions. Its vital issues, at least to start with, would center on the obligation of the state to ensure a complete English-language education for Mexican children so that they could compete in the state's labor marketplace when they grew up; and to pursue alternate forms of energy, particularly solar energy, so that the lower economic classes would not be forever beholden to the pricing and credit whims of the mammoth, impersonal oil and gas companies.

What distinguished Hayden's position papers from those of other organizations seeking to represent the same diverse constituency was the responsibility he placed upon the people to participate in the solution of their problems. It had long been the practice of most reform organizations to preach that the state alone had the obligation to solve social problems. Hayden decreed that anyone seeking improvement in his or her life and economic circumstances had an equal responsibility. The state could supply all the educational opportunities possible, as it already had done to a limited extent. But unless poor people forced their children to exploit those opportunities, they themselves were to blame for their children growing up with no chance to make a decent living. The state was an ogre, to be sure, but not of the dimension they had often been told. Only if the younger generations took advantage of what was available to them educationally would they be in a position to press the state for even more advantages for succeeding generations.

At first Hayden's theories found little acceptance among large groups of poor people who had been conditioned by their leaders to believe that the government was responsible exclusively both for their welfare and for their plight. But the CED doctrines received the cautious approval of the tax-paying and welfare-supporting middle class of California. For once, the middle class was informed by certain sympathetic newspapers, they had a radical organization in their midst that doesn't put all the onus on them, but tells the poor that they are as responsible for their own uplifting as anyone else. It may not have been a premeditated tactic, but Hayden's doctrines were a stroke of public relations genius. Within a few months he was no longer looked upon by basically straight-and-narrow Californians as the wild-eyed radical fanatic of yore. He came across now as a reasonable and responsible political reformer.

During her first burst of political activism at the beginning of the Seventies, many observers thought that Jane Fonda might end up one day seeking political office. California had become notorious, albeit perversely so in many quarters, for providing aging show-business personalities with second lives as political office holders, some of them lofty in power indeed. Ronald Reagan was the governor of the state at the time, and an ex-movie hoofer, George Murphy, had until recently been one of the state's two senators in Washington. And then there was John Tunney. Tunney was not an entertainer, exactly, but for all the impact he had as a Senator he was often referred to derisively as one. Tunney was coming up for reelection in 1976. No one seriously considered the possibility that Jane would make a bid to run for his seat. But had she tried to become a candidate, no one would have been surprised, either.

It was no surprise, then, when not Jane but her husband announced that he would run for the seat held by Tunney. Yet Hayden's candidacy was at first perceived as somewhat of a joke by most Californians. He had no real constituency and he had no financial power base despite his friendly relations with Jerry Brown. And he still had lots of bitter enemies, either directly or as a result of his association with Jane. But Hayden proved his mettle. He worked tirelessly throughout 1976, with Jane as his chief fund-raiser, to make a serious impression on the voters. And although he didn't come close to winning in November, he did capture a significant enough number of votes to gain a further stamp of respectability as a political spokesman. Tom Hayden suddenly appeared to have a bright future as a politician in California.

It had been Hayden's marriage to Jane that had gradually brought him out of the poverty-paved back alleys of radicaldom. Now the ultimate irony was to be played out. For it was Hayden's growing stature and power, along with the appeal his election campaign turned out to have among southern California's trendy show-business community, that helped to bring about the professional rehabilitation of Jane Fonda. Within the movie industry it became fashionable, suddenly, to admire and even support Tom Hayden, the underdog senatorial candidate, if not actually vote for him. His pluck, intelligence and programs, once given a forum, were deemed worthy of attention.

Just as suddenly, Jane began to be offered movie roles again. Hayden came to be viewed as a potentially powerful future political force in the state. If some day he succeeded in achieving a position of power, it would not be to the movie industry's advantage to be remembered as a one-time enemy of his wife. Besides, Hayden's modest success meant that California, perhaps the entire country, was in the process of moderating in its animosity toward Jane.

chapter 31

FUN WITH DICK AND JANE

With the arrival of Tom Hayden as a potential political force in California in mid-1975, Hollywood proposed its definition of what it was possible, politically, for Jane to do in movies. In response, Jane defined what was politically acceptable to her. Recalling her experience with *Tout Va Bien*, she said, "I will only make films that don't lie. No, I don't insist on 'message' films. But I do insist on films, on roles that tell the truth, or at least try their damnedest to. I'm interested in political films. But I'm not interested in turning audiences off. I want to turn them on. Not convert them, necessarily, but turn them on, make them think. As far as I'm concerned, any movie that tells the truth is a political film, only because most films don't tell the truth, or even try to."

Jane's definition was not incompatible with its own, Hollywood decided, particularly in view of recent demographic studies that showed that the great majority of the post-Vietnam, post-Watergate audience market consisted of people under 40. Presumably they yearned for truth rather than escapism. Jane began to receive scripts again.

One of the first she saw was a bitingly amusing satire on contemporary American life called *Fun with Dick and Jane*. It was a script that appealed to Jane on several levels. It made rollicking good fun of middle-class American pretensions. In

reaction to the events of the plot, it transformed the lead woman
character from a dumb, docile housewife into a strong, schem-
ing and aggressive family leader, while the chief male character, her husband, became a dutiful follower. Finally, it
entertained while burying its trenchant message in the story's
seams.

The plot was simple but neatly inventive. Dick Harper, a
rising young California business executive, is suddenly fired
by his company. His and his wife Jane's smugly affluent,
upwardly mobile world abruptly collapses in an avalanche of
unpayable bills—even the recently installed lawn in front of
their house is repossessed. Totally incapable of coping, Dick
regresses into indecisive self-pity. Jane is forced to take over
the course of their lives. As she does so, she becomes more
daring and aggressive, and their roles are reversed. As a result
of Jane's efforts, which involve ripping off the very system
that ripped them off, they survive. Not only that, but they
survive in a style more opulent than they'd been accustomed
to. Jane beats the system at its own game, something that Dick
was never able to do.

Starring as Jane Harper opposite George Segal as her husband, Dick, Jane made the movie late in 1975 for a mere
$100,000. Its release in 1976 produced a favorable critical
reaction. The movie was both entertaining, wrote the reviewers,
and had something significant to say. It was social comedy of
the type Jane Fonda had done so well earlier in her career, but
social comedy with a much sharper, truer bite. "If this is the
kind of work Jane Fonda proposes to specialize in," wrote one
reviewer, "more power to her. Nobody does it better."

But comedy was not what Jane wanted to specialize in.
Although mildly satisfied with the film, she realized that "it
went too often for the cheap laugh at the expense of a more
riveting insight," as she later put it. Jane did not trust comedy
to carry the burden of what she wanted to impress upon the
world. Yet *Dick and Jane*, in terms of Jane's politics and her
still uncertain career, was a master-stroke of good strategy. It
not only made a lot of money and restored her to respectability,
which is to say "bankability," in the eyes of the Hollywood
establishment, it also allowed her to pay another installment
of her dues to the radical movement. The most political thing
about *Dick and Jane* was the fact that Jane Fonda had proved
that commercial movies could be made which were also critical

of the American system. As far as much of the general mov-
iegoing public was concerned, Jane could now say whatever
she wished to newspapers and talk-show hosts about Vietnam,
Blacks, women, socialism—as long as she continued to make
them laugh in movie houses. Of course, there remained a significant portion of society that would never forgive Jane Fonda
for becoming what she had. But then, Jane was no longer really
out to reach them.

Indeed, by 1976 Jane was no longer proselytizing news
reporters and talk-show hosts with her radical politics. After
the release of *Dick and Jane*, America began to see another
"new" Jane Fonda—a woman who went on the Merv Griffin
and Johnny Carson shows to talk not about Vietnam or the
Black Panthers but about the responsibilities and trials of being
a mother, about day-care centers, about home-heating bills and
the avariciousness of the oil companies, about rent control,
about sexism in the office, and the like. These were subjects
the average American—particularly women—could identify
with, and they did. In a poll taken by *Redbook* magazine in
the fall of 1976, Jane made the list of the ten most admired
women in America.

Jane was once again changing her image, to be sure, but it
was not all a matter of public relations on her part. Some of
the impetus had come from Tom Hayden, who by then was in
the midst of his senatorial election campaign in California. It
was not that Hayden really thought he had any chance to win.
The campaign was meant to establish him as a credible force
on the political scene and pave the way for better things to
come. Jane could not damage his chances by reverting to the
Jane Fonda of a few years before.

Some of the impetus had come from the communist Jean-
Luc Godard, who had relased his cinematic *Letter to Jane*—a
scathingly critical assessment of Jane's radicalization in which
he attacked her naiveté and lack of political intelligence and
urged her to stop talking revolution until she really knew what
she was talking about.

But most of the impetus behind the more moderate Jane
Fonda came from another encounter she had with Vanessa
Redgrave.

In the fall of 1976 Jane traveled to France to make her next
movie: *Julia*, based on a recently published memoir by writer
Lillian Hellman. Set in 1930s Europe during the rise of Nazism,

Julia told the story of Hellman's real-life friendship with a left-wing woman in Vienna who became involved in anti-Nazi activities and was eventually killed. Jane played the role of Hellman—the principal part—and Vanessa Redgrave played Julia. The Hellman role was one that Jane had actively lobbied for from the moment she'd read Lillian Hellman's book, and although director Fred Zinneman, a Hollywood veteran, wasn't convinced she was right for it, she was given it. Once signed, Jane then lobbied for Vanessa Redgrave to play the title role. Producer Richard Roth thought: "Why not? It was perfect symmetry. The two most famous left-wing women of the seventies playing two left-wing women of the thirties. I liked it. Of course, the fact that Jane and Vanessa were both terrific actresses didn't hurt either. Not to mention that they both agreed to work cheap."

By 1976 Vanessa Redgrave was arguably the most brilliant, electrifying actress of her time—perhaps the only woman of genuine genius in her profession. To go up against her was "a gutsy gamble on Jane's part," said a top movie agent. "Redgrave dominates the screen whenever she works, and Jane risked having herself compared unfavorably. These were, after all, heavy roles. Jane had no peer at comedy, but she'd never really made a mark in serious screen drama as a woman."

He may have been right. Vanessa Redgrave would win an Academy Award for her performance in *Julia*, whereas Jane would emerge with only muted tributes for a "respectable" and "competent" acting job. But in the larger context of her career, Jane's gamble succeeded. Although Redgrave did dominate the screen in the relatively few scenes they had together, Jane carried the picture with her virtually nonstop on-screen presence. This was a Jane Fonda no one had experienced before—a quiet, reflective, mature woman without the rebellious abrasiveness or ingenue innocence that she typified in almost every role she had played before.

During the making of *Julia*, Jane became dismayed by Vanessa Redgrave's off-set activities. Redgrave, when Jane had last seen her, was already deeply involved in radical political activities; in fact at the beginning, Jane had modeled her own political involvement on Redgrave's. But at that time in the late 1960s Redgrave had still been capable of rational discussion about her beliefs. Now the British actress had become a whirling dervish of political extremism. Barely a moment went by during the filming of *Julia* when Redgrave was not handing out leaflets, engaging in arguments, endeavoring to convert every passerby she cornered. Jane was at once amazed and frightened. She was amazed that she could no longer talk to Vanessa; in Redgrave's single-minded radical dogmatism she allowed no disagreement, even discussion. Jane was frightened by the obsessive political creature Vanessa had become. The fact that the focus of Redgrave's political obsession—the Palestine Liberation Movement and its offshoots—was narrow and one-dimensional did not trouble Jane as much as her almost manic intensity. Jane began to find her old friend's manner irksome, at times irrational. Vanessa didn't realize, or was incapable of realizing, what a laughing-stock she had become. Jane looked at her as she might gaze at a mirror and shrunk from what she saw. For the first time she understood—experienced!—why others had become so exasperated with her. From that moment on, Jane resolved to change her style of politicking. She could not allow herself to become an American Vanessa Redgrave.

Julia, although it garnered favorable reviews as a human interest story, did not exactly succeed in fulfilling the acting-cum-political goals Jane had spelled out for herself the year before. Under the seamless, traditional Hollywood directorial style of Fred Zinneman, the film failed to make a clear political statement about fascism. It failed even more to say anything significant about the roles of women in the world. Despite the fact that the movie was billed, albeit vaguely, as a sort of feminist manifesto, Jane's acting expressed little that in modern terms could be interpreted as "liberated."

This was due in large measure to the nature of Hellman's original material. In writing about herself in the 1930s, Hellman had rooted her character firmly in her relationship with the writer Dashiell Hammett, with whom she had lived. (Hammett was played by Jason Robards in the film.) In every significant respect their relationship had been the traditional male-female one—he the leader, the boss; she the emotional and intellectual follower. Even her first solo trip to Europe in search of Julia was inspired and financed by Hammett, and when she returned from her travels she resumed the relationship, apparently unchanged by the traumatizing events she had witnessed.

Jane simply could not wring from this base material the woman of fiercely independent substance she had hoped to portray when she first set her sights on the part. Even if she had been able to, it's doubtful that director Fred Zinneman would have permitted much of it to show, since he was interested in telling a good story and not in providing a platform for Jane's politics. *Julia*, for all the feminist hoopla that accompanied its release in the women's magazines, ended up being a "women's picture" of the Hollywood type that was so popular in the thirties and forties. It gave the illusion of female independence. But the illusion bore little relation to the reality.

Realizing this, Jane resolved to use some of her newfound earnings to start her own production company. By so doing, she would not only gain a measure of control over her future films and the roles she played, but she would be in a position to declare her own independence of the traditional Hollywood financing and decision-making process—a political act in itself, as she saw it. In order to play the women she really wanted to portray—women who undergo a significant experience and end up irrevocably changed, independent, self-sufficient, and proud of it—nothing could be more effectively symbolic than for her to become a genuinely independent filmmaker.

Accordingly, in 1977 Jane formed IPC Films, Inc., and began to search for scripts that she could produce under its banner—real as opposed to illusory films, films with a clearcut modern feminist point of view that would appeal to men as well.

As a partner in her venture she chose Bruce Gilbert, a moviemaking and producing friend from the Vietnam-protest days. Gilbert, a relative novice in Hollywood, was also committed to the idea. Jane had been trying to articulate since her experience in making *Tout Va Bien*. In fact it was Gilbert who finally articulated it for her, which was the primary reason she invited him to join her in IPC Films. Gilbert, simplifying the idea, had said: start with an ordinary individual solidly wedded to society's traditional values and beliefs. Place that character in a story whereby he, or she, as a result of the logical flow of appropriate events, undergoes a deep emotional experience and become politicized by it, i.e., awakened to the reality he or she never realized existed before. Have that awakening reality struggle against the old, safe illusions and beliefs. In that way, the character will gain the audience's sympathy. Then, when the character's new reality triumphs over his or her old illusions, and when the character is transported into a greater political awareness, the audience will have no choice but to follow. It too will become politicized.

Gilbert's explanation was a graphic illustration of the formula Jane had been seeking since 1972 but had not been able to put her finger on. The way Gilbert expressed it, it made eminent sense. It summed up exactly what Jane wanted to do, and it was a major turning point in Jane's artistic-political life. From then on, she ardently sought to put the formula into practice.

Nancy Dowd was a young feminist screenwriter who had worked on the FTA shows in 1971 and had been befriended by Jane. They had since drifted apart, but when Dowd heard that Jane was looking for feminist material for her new company, she contacted her and asked her to read a script outline she had written. It was the story of a young American housewife, her Marine officer husband, and the impact the husband's obsession with Vietnam has on his wife.

Jane was excited by the story idea: it was a natural metaphor for the effects of the Vietnam War on America, it possessed a solid feminist perspective, and it had a potentially juicy part for her. She and Bruce Gilbert commissioned Dowd to develop it.

During this time Tom Hayden, having won only a moral victory in the 1976 election (S. I. Hayakawa, an elderly, conservative educator, won the Senate seat), returned to his Campaign for Economic Democracy expecting to broaden his political base for another run at high office four or six years hence. At the time, Hayden viewed his performance in the election as boding well for his political future, as did Jane. Between her extended trips to movie locations, Jane continued to promote Hayden and work on their CED projects. Their marriage seemed to grow stronger. Yet there was an important element in it that struck friends as the antithesis of the feminist, liberationist principles Jane espoused. When she was away from Hayden, on her own, acting, or working with Bruce Gilbert on movie projects, she remained independent, self-assured and intellectually demanding. But when she was with Hayden, she seemed to revert to being a more-or-less conventional wife—still radical in her attitudes, to be sure, but also the obeisant follower to his leader. There seemed to be no role reversals in their relationship. Yes, Hayden took care of Vanessa and Troy when Jane was away, even performed other domestic chores when she was home. But these were merely surface symbols of a "democratic" marriage. In truth, Jane remained deeply dependent on Hayden for her self-image.

Her renewed success as an actress was not enough to provide her with a complete sense of satisfaction—her success had never been enough. Her identity and sense of self-worth, as always, had to come through the man with whom she was involved.

chapter 32

COMING HOME

So Jane would strive to make the changes she hadn't yet made in life through her film roles, and through the political-cinema formula she and Bruce Gilbert had devised for IPC Films. The first important chapter in the process came through her performance as Sally Hyde, the wife of the Marine Corps captain, in the film version of Nancy Dowd's story, which was called *Coming Home*.

But it was not Dowd's screenplay that was used to make the movie. Early on, after Jane and Gilbert had committed themselves to the film, and after they had obtained part of their production money, they came to loggerheads with Dowd over certain details of the story. Dowd had written a tale that focused primarily on the evolving, changing relationship between Sally Hyde and another serviceman's wife—a genuinely feminist story about women from different backgrounds who discover a mutual attraction to each other through their work at a hospital for disabled veterans. It was a daring premise for a commercial feature film, but one that even Jane knew would not succeed. When she and Gilbert tried to get Dowd to recast the story and make it into a bittersweet male-female romance, Dowd balked. As a consequence, Jane and Gilbert took the project away from her and commissioned a new screenplay from veteran writers Waldo Salt and Robert Jones.

The new version of Dowd's story was certainly more com-merical—indeed, it took on the dimensions of genuine tragedy. In it, Sally Hyde's macho Marine husband Bob compulsively puts in for another tour of duty in Vietnam. After he ships out, Sally, the quintessentially "proper" young American wife, left with nothing to do but endlessly rearrange the furniture in their quarters, volunteers to work a few hours a day at the nearby veterans' hospital. There she meets Luke, a handsome but bitter paraplegic whose body had been shattered in Vietnam. Naively at first, but then with increasing concern and compassion, Sally sets out to get to the bottom of Luke's anger and soothe him. Soon she falls in love with him and, as he begins to reveal himself to her, is stunned by what she learns of the Vietnam war. Luke has been unable to have sex since having been shot up in Vietnam. Sally rearouses his sexual self-awareness and then leads him through a tender sexual consummation of their relationship. Then her husband returns and discovers what Sally has been up to. Sally must choose between Luke and her in-sensitive husband. It is never clear whether Captain Bob Hyde's fury is due more to his wife's infidelity as such or to the fact that she had been sleeping with a paraplegic enlisted man. The latter, however, is made to seem the greater blow to Hyde's pride. In any event, Hyde abandons Sally with Luke, and in a concluding scene that in its incredibility robs the movie of much of its tragic unity, commits suicide. Sally Hyde is left alone, but is much the wiser about men, about Vietnam, about herself. The audience is made to feel that she has indeed been politi-cized, has left the Sally Hyde of old to the past and is ready to embark on a yet greater journey of self-discovery.

Except for the Hyde suicide scene, *Coming Home* in the Salt-Jones version was a well thought-out cinematic realization of the formula Jane and Gilbert had established. Sally under-goes a logical radical transformation that, thanks to Jane's skillful, sympathetic portrayal, carries the audience along with her. The film, directed by Hal Ashby, received enthusiastic acclaim in most quarters when it was released in 1978, and it established a glowing new reputation for Jane in Hollywood as an independent filmmaker.

Only after its release did news about the difficulties and squabbles surrounding its production surface. Jon Voight, who played Luke and later won an Oscar for his performance, made a publicity tour in conjunction with the film's release and hinted repeatedly at furious fights between himself and Jane over matters of interpretation. Nancy Dowd disowned the movie, telling a reporter, "The original of *Coming Home* was probably the best writing I've ever done. But I'm ashamed of the movie. . . . It is a male supremacist film: men choose between ideas, and women choose between men."

Jane turned forty during the filming of *Coming Home*. Her birthday had little emotional effect on her, she later told me: "No, there was none of the trepidation you often hear associated with people who turn forty. I hardly thought about it. I didn't feel forty, whatever forty is supposed to feel like. The only thing it did to me was make me resolve to begin taking better care of myself."

As usual whenever Jane resolved to do something, she attacked it with all guns firing. She had been a regular smoker and consumer of an erratic, on-the-road diet for more years than she cared to remember. Suddenly she became a complete health and fitness addict, changing her diet and patronizing every exercise class she could find time for. And, as usual whenever she became captivated by a cause that benefited her, she became convinced that others could benefit too. Accordingly, after *Coming Home* was released, she opened an exercise salon for women in Beverly Hills called "Jane Fonda's Workout." She located the salon in a low-rent neighborhood, charged low prices, and offered a rigorous dance-and-exercise program modeled on the one that she followed. Her implied promise to her potential customers was: Look at my body at forty years of age—you too can have such a body. More explicit was her admonition: "Every woman owes it to herself to keep fit. You can't be liberated when you remain a slave to bad physical and nutritional habits. Getting fit is a political act—you are taking charge of your life." Many of the women who heard Jane's words took a look at her body and said: "Why not?" The salon was an instant success, and it soon evolved into a profitable franchise operation.

Jane followed *Coming Home* with the role of Ella Connors in a crypto-Western social drama, set in the waning days of World War II, called *Comes a Horseman*. Ella Connors was a female turn on the traditional Hollywood saga of the ruggedly individualistic loner fighting the forces of evil—in this case a greedy, predatory oil company seeking to acquire the land of a small group of ranchers in a hardscrabble Montana valley.

The movie, directed by Alan Pakula of *Klute* fame, was promoted as a political vehicle with a bittersweet love interest (James Caan as Jane's fellow rancher). It turned out to be a case of Hollywood once again preying on the gullibility of American audiences. By trying to recreate the myth of the old Western hero in modern women's terms, and by using Jane Fonda in the process (hadn't her equally celebrated father personified the myth in his heyday?), everyone associated with the film made it clear that lucre, not art, was the main concern.

Jane nevertheless did not fail to find a political justification for making the picture. What she liked about it, she said, was that although her character was doomed to lose the fight against the oil company, the fight itself "we represent the spirit of struggle. . . . What should have happened is that all the small ranchers in the valley should have organized and banded together. Then, maybe, we would have won."

So *Comes a Horseman* was a political-message film. But few people got the message. Few saw it after it opened to lackluster reviews.

California Suite, which Jane made next, was another story. Based on the Broadway comedy hit by Neil Simon, it earned splended notices for Jane but received only lukewarm reviews as a whole. An interwoven series of minimovies covering slices of the lives of four couples staying at the Beverly Hills Hotel, the film was a curiously flat and tedious version of the stage show except for that portion of it which covered the story of Jane, again playing a woman journalist, and her former husband played by Alan Alda, a New York screenwriter-gone-Hollywood. Jane told reporters that she enjoyed portraying the hard-bitten, hyperintense, "liberated" Hannah Warren because "it proved the challenge of playing a woman I didn't like, who was very different from me."

Audiences and critics saw it another way. They perceived in Jane's Hannah Warren the woman they were sure Jane had actually become since her political conversion: insufferably aggressive, overbearing, preachy, intolerant of others; in the end, a pitiable and semitragic figure. It was a gentle irony as well as a neat bit of casting—Jane decrying the character to the press, playing to a public convinced by her past that the character was in fact she.

Other than Jane's ring-true performance, however, *California Suite* offered little in the way of "politicizing" entertainment. It was just another Hollywood version of meaningful social comedy, and for most viewers the meaning was lost in the facile, often simpleminded burlesque. Indeed, many critics were repelled by the movie's overall slickness and cheap stereotyped gags about blacks and homosexuals. Fonda-watchers wondered aloud about how Jane had permitted herself to be associated with it.

The answer was money. *California Suite* was a high-budget, big-studio Hollywood production and Jane was able to walk away from it with $500,000 for her few weeks of work. This dedicated socialist had no qualms about earning so much. "I didn't create the system," she said, answering a reporter's accusatory query. "If they want to pay movie actors such outrageous sums while schoolteachers and farm laborers are forced to work for peanuts, I can't change that, at least not now. It's better that I get the money, don't you think, rather than someone else who'll blow it on Rolls Royces and million dollar Bel Air estates? At least I know that a lot of it goes to help other people, not just myself."

Which was true. A large portion of everything Jane had earned since *Fun with Dick and Jane*—well over a million dollars by 1978—had gone to finance Tom Hayden's political aspirations and to promoting social and education projects related to CED. Now, there was a new endeavor for Jane to plow her money into.

Jane and Tom bought an old ranch-camp in the hills above Santa Barbara. It was not to be a rustic personal weekend retreat *à la* Ronald Reagan's nearby and now famous Rancho Cielo, however. Instead, Jane and Tom set out to establish the camp as an educational center for underprivileged children from minority families in California. As Jane told me in 1979, it was a "place to teach these kids how to lift themselves up from their bootstraps and lead the social revolution that's so long overdue in this state." When I asked her to respond to remarks by some of her local critics to the effect that her and Tom's purpose was really to train the next generation of minorities to vote for Tom Hayden in some down-the-line election, she said, "That's just plain B.S. We are teaching these young people how to organize their communities for themselves, not for Tom. The things people will invent!"

Jane and Tom had set up a home for themselves and their own children on the property, and they recruited a staff of CED workers to run the educational side of things. The only real self-indulgence they permitted themselves was Hayden's. He had always loved to fish, and he began to spend much of his time at the Santa Barbara ranch trekking about with rod and reel, catching and cooking dinner for himself, four-year-old Troy, ten-year-old Vanessa, and whomever was visiting. Jane, often away on a succession of movie locations, was seldom in attendance in 1978.

Besides, she had other fish to fry. Jane's last two films had been major studio productions. Since *Coming Home*, she and Gilbert had been seeking another movie project. When they were unable to find anything suitable, they took the next logical step: they developed a project of their own.

The inspiration came originally from Hayden. As part of his CED efforts in 1975, he had lobbied against California's rapidly expanding nuclear power industry, condemning it not only as perilous to human life but as another government-sanctioned chapter in enslavement of the average wage earner by the big-business establishment.

In 1976 Jane had tried to buy the rights to the story of Karen Silkwood, a young technician at a nuclear fuel manufacturing plant in Oklahoma. Silkwood had died in a mysterious auto-mobile crash, and many believed that her death had been en-gineered to prevent her from telling what she knew about safety violations at the plant. Jane had announced at the time that she would portray Silkwood and that the movie she intended to make "would point the finger at the people responsible for her death." Jane was never able to acquire the rights, however, and the film went unmade.

In 1978 Tom Hayden, Jane with him, was once again deep in the dispute over the building of nuclear power stations in California, demanding as an alternative that the state and federal governments finance the development of solar power. With her purpose originally to help Hayden disseminate his views, Jane decided to try to develop a movie project on the issue of the dangers of nuclear power. When she and Gilbert put out the word, they received a flood of crude, hastily written scripts. Almost all were worthless. But one caught Gilbert's eye. Al-though it had no part for Jane, it was powerful in story values, taut with suspense, and written with professional sophistication. Put together by a little known director-screenwriter named James Bridges, it was a Woodward-Bernstein type tale about a reporter who inadvertently discovers the offical cover-up of a serious radiation leak at a nuclear plant.

When Jane first read the script she was impressed but rejected it because it didn't contain a role for her. What if we could get the writer to change the journalist into a woman? Gilbert suggested. With that, Jane's enthusiasm blossomed. They called in James Bridges for a meeting.

Bridges, a shy, unassuming man, agreed to rewrite his script according to Jane's wishes. Once finished, he was pleasantly stunned by Jane's reception of it. He was stunned further by her and Gilbert's insistence that he direct the picture, which Bridges called *The China Syndrome*. The title came from the jargon of the nuclear engineering industry and referred to a reactor "meltdown" burning a hole through the earth that would reach all the way to China.

When I interviewed Jane Fonda a few weeks before *The China Syndrome* was released in the early spring of 1979, she described it as "a hard-hitting suspense thriller the likes of which hasn't been made in Hollywood in years." Did it have political overtones, I asked? "You could say so," she replied. "But it's not a message film. It's just about life and death, everybody's life, everybody's death." Jane had no idea, nor did anyone else, that events were already underway that would turn an ordinary Hollywood "suspense thriller" into a national *cause célèbre* and, by extension, make her both a prophet and a huge profit.

When *The China Syndrome* first appeared in March, reviewers greeted it much in the spirit that Jane had described it—it was adjudged a "superior thriller" with a "rather simplistic message." Although most of the early commentators liked the story-telling aspects of the picture and gave the actors—especially Jack Lemmon as the plant manager torn between company loyalty and personal ethics—high marks, they were less happy with the story's premise. Wrote Richard Schickel, the chief reviewer for *Time* magazine: "The film depicts the utility company that owns the plant and the contractor that built it resorting to lies, corruption and violence to prevent the public from discovering how narrowly a disaster was averted, how large is the potential for similar incidents in the future—and never mind the sizeable body of scientific opinion about the improbability of a chain of accidents anything like that posited in the film."

Similar critical scoffing emanated from many other quarters. "The entire conceit is bizarre," exclaimed another reviewer. "As science fiction it works; as realism it's obvious claptrap."

Nor was the nuclear industry itself silent. One spokesman complained that the movie rendered "an unconscionable public disservice by using phony theatrics to frighten Americans away from desperately needed energy sources."

Less than two weeks after *The China Syndrome* opened, newspapers and television screens throughout the country headlined the explosion and meltdown at the Three Mile Island nuclear plant near Harrisburg, Pennsylvania. So much for "sizeable body of scientific opinion." So much for "bizarre premises." So much for "phony theatrics." Not only did the "improbable chain of accidents" depicted in the film occur for real in Pennsylvania, but local and federal authorities, as well as the company that ran Three Mile Island, proved as evasive as their film counterparts when it came to explaining the causes and possible consequences of the real-life event.

Three Mile Island transformed *The China Syndrome* from a slick job of moviemaking into a cinematic manifesto of the antinuclear movement in America. It galvanized even those hundreds of thousands if not millions who had previously been indifferent to the nuclear power issue. The public suddenly saw Jane in terms of her prophetic vision, particularly when they learned that she had been instrumental in initiating and producing the movie.

With "antinuke" sentiment spreading rapidly across the country in the wake of Three Mile Island and *The China Syndrome*, Jane and Tom Hayden decided to seize upon it as a springboard for the national launching of Hayden's drive for important political office. Consequently, in the fall of 1979, they commenced a cross-country speaking and fund-raising tour, centered on the issue of nuclear power, with a speech by Hayden at the National Press Club in Washington and a joint appearance a few days later on the nationally televised program *Face the Nation*.

Hayden, wearing a suit instead of his usual blue jeans and work shirt, delivered a rousing prepared address within the relatively private confines of the press club. But when he and Jane went on *Face the Nation* to answer questions from a panel of relentlessly skeptical journalists, both came across as nervous, ill-prepared and naive. Indeed, in the period of a half-hour Tom Hayden's big-time political ambitions seemed to go down the drain. Stammering, shifty-eyed in the manner of his and Jane's greatest *bête noir* Richard Nixon, and unable to give coherent off-the-cuff answers to several of the reporters' questions, Hayden was almost an embarrassment to watch. Jane tried gamely to come to his rescue with her own answers and remarks, but she too grew tongue-tied and uncertain as she took refuge in the usual debater's ploy of statistics and emotional irrelevancies. Her quavering voice rose and grew panicky as she repeatedly painted herself into rhetorical corners.

The image-shattering appearance on *Face the Nation* did not deter Jane and Tom's cross-country trip, however. When confronted by ideological opposites, or even by dispassionate journalists, Tom Hayden seldom performed well unless he was reciting a prepared speech. But when surrounded by supporters or by those who shared his latest political posture, he came alive with spontaneous oratorical persuasion and sincerity. On their tour, Hayden and Jane were usually among friends and he got plenty of positive feedback. But at the end of the tour he returned to Los Angeles deeply dispirited. His dream of capturing a national constituency had clearly foundered on the rocks of the political big time in Washington. He was a realist, though. Abandoning his aspirations for the Senate in 1982, he returned to what he did best—organizing local political and social constituencies and presenting the latest tenets of economic democracy.

chapter 33

THE FONDA
SYNDROME

Jane shared her husband's distress. Her own hope of one day being known not just as Jane Fonda, but as the wife of the equally celebrated politician Tom Hayden, seemed forever lost. With it went the balance of her public arrogance. Perhaps because she was by then well past forty, her fierce need to fight the establishment, to tilt at windmills, had begun to abate. And Jane had made another movie just prior to the release of *The China Syndrome*. Called *The Electric Horseman*, its release late in 1979 to indifferent reviews provoked a further sense of dismay in her. In the picture she played another woman reporter who teams up with a handsome but has-been rodeo performer (Robert Redford) to expose hypocrisy and corruption in the marketplace.

One reviewer, in criticizing the film, wrote: "Somebody ought to talk to Jane Fonda. While we are grateful to have her back on the film scene after those years in limbo, she's beginning to grate, not only as a political creature but as an actress. She seems to have settled into playing the same part over and over. Enough awreddy, Jane! We've gotten the message—it's okay to be a woman. If we get any more of these pictures, we'll have to call what Jane does 'The Fonda Syndrome.'"

Jane might have been willing to take the advice to heart except for the fact that she had already announced a new film to be produced by her IPC company. Called *Nine to Five*, it was a comedy about three harried secretaries in a business office. Jane had made it clear that it was to be a political picture designed to espouse the cause of the nation's female working force, especially office workers "who get screwed royally in a dozen different ways." To ensure box-office interest, Jane announced also that her costars would be Lily Tomlin and—Dolly Parton.

Nine to Five, when it was released late in 1980, served only to further dilute the seriousness with which Jane had been taken after *The China Syndrome*. A weak, inconsistent script, Dolly Parton's well-meaning but parodied performance, the usual obvious role-reversal symbols, and Jane's seeming reluctance to assert her character in traditional Fonda fashion, all resulted in a movie that politicized no one, only bored them.

Could it be that Jane had finally acknowledged that she was over-exposing herself in a series of one-dimensional "political" parts? According to a friend, yes. "After *Nine to Five*, Jane felt she'd blown it, blown the credibility she had struggled so hard to achieve. 'I think I'll just make simple movies for a while,' she said when it was over. After the incredible high of *China Syndrome*, she felt she had lost her way. She was still very focused on what she wanted to do politically on screen, but she believed she had lost her sense of judgment about what would work, what wouldn't."

But Jane would not pause in her drive to make more movies. To critics who claimed that she was overexposing herself solely to earn as much money as she could, she answered: "No, that's not it at all. I want to prove to the public that I can flourish in spite of all the controversy." Making one film after another was for her a political act in itself. "There's a stereotype in people's minds that if you're politically active for social change then you're going to suffer as an artist because you can't do both. I keep going to avoid any chance of a subliminal message getting out that 'they did her in.' People root for a survivor who sticks her neck out. Maybe I represent someone who fights back and doesn't stop and still survives."

This will probably serve as Jane Fonda's credo for the future. She will continue to fight her political battles, but now exclusively on the screen. We can expect the Fonda Syndrome—the cultural phenomenon that is Jane Fonda—to be in the forefront of our awareness for years to come. That is where, beyond anyplace else, she aches to live. It is her ultimate political act. And with her gift for surviving, and for changing—we can expect many further manifestations of Jane Fonda.

Filmography

Tall Story *(1960)*
Director/Producer: Joshua Logan
Screenplay: J. J. Epstein
Adapted from: the play by Howard Lindsay and Russel
                 Crouse, in itself adapted from the novel, *The*
                 Homecoming Game by Howard Nemerov
Costarring: Anthony Perkins
Jane's character: June Ryder

Walk On The Wild Side *(1962)*
Director: Edward Dmytryk
Producer: Charles K. Feldman
Screenplay: John Fante and Edmund Morris
Adapted from: the novel by Nelson Algren
Costarring: Anne Baxter, Capucine, Laurence Harvey,
                 Barbara Stanwyck
Jane's character: Kitty Twist

The Chapman Report *(1962)*
Director: George Cukor

Producer: Richard D. Zanuck
Screenplay: Wyatt Cooper and Don M. Mankiewicz
Adapted from: Irving Wallace's novel by Grant Stuart and
Gene Allen
Costarring: Claire Bloom, Glynis Johns, Shelley Winters
Jane's character: Kathleen Barclay

Period Of Adjustment *(1962)*
Director: George Roy Hill
Producer: Laurence Weingarten
Screenplay: Isobel Lennart
Adapted from: the play by Tennessee Williams
Costarring: Tony Franciosa, Jim Hutton
Jane's character: Isobel Haverstick

In The Cool Of The Day *(1963)*
Director: Robert Stephens
Producer: John Houseman
Screenplay: Meade Roberts
Adapted from: the novel by Susan Ertz
Costarring: Peter Finch, Angela Lansbury
Jane's character: Christine Bonner

Sunday In New York *(1964)*
Director: Peter Tewkesbury
Producer: Everett Freeman
Screenplay: Norman Krasna
Adapted from: the play by Norman Krasna
Costarring: Robert Culp, Cliff Robertson, Rod Taylor
Jane's character: Eileen Tyler

Les Félins (Joy House) *(1964)*
Director: René Clément
Producer: Jacques Bar
Screenplay: René Clément, Pascal Jardin, Charles Williams

Adapted from: the novel by Day Keene
Costarring: Lola Albright, Alain Delon
Jane's character: Melinda

La Ronde (Circle Of Love) *(1965)*
Director: Roger Vadim
Producers: Robert and Raymond Hakim
Screenplay: Jean Anouilh
Adapted from: the play by Arthur Schnitzler
Costarring: Marie Dubois, Claude Giraud, Anna Karina
Jane's character: "The Married Woman"

Cat Ballou *(1965)*
Director: Elliott Silverstein
Producer: Harold Hecht
Screenplay: Walter Newman and Frank R. Pierson
Adapted from: the novel by Roy Chanslor
Costarring: Lee Marvin, Michael Callan
Jane's character: Cat Ballou

The Chase *(1966)*
Director: Arthur Penn
Producer: Sam Spiegel
Screenplay: Lillian Hellman
Adapted from: the play and novel by Horton Foote
Costarring: Marlon Brando, Angie Dickinson, James Fox,
          E. G. Marshall, Robert Redford
Jane's character: Anna Reeves

Le Curée (The Game Is Over) *(1966)*
Director/Producer: Roger Vadim
Screenplay: Roger Vadim, Jean Cau, Bernard Frechtman
Adapted from: the novel by Emile Zola
Costarring: Peter McEnery
Jane's character: Renée Saccard

Any Wednesday (Bachelor Girl Apartment) *(1966)*
Director: Robert Ellis Miller
Producer: Julius J. Epstein
Screenplay: Julius J. Epstein
Adapted from: the play by Muriel Resnick
Costarring: Dean Jones, Rosemary Murphy, Jason Robards
Jane's character: Ellen Gordon

Hurry Sundown *(1966)*
Director/Producer: Otto Preminger
Screenplay: Thomas C. Ryan and Horton Foote
Adapted from: the novel by K. B. Gilden
Costarring: Michael Caine, Diahann Carroll, Faye
Dunaway, Robert Hooks, Phillip Law, Burgess
Meredith
Jane's character: Julie Ann Warren

Barefoot In The Park *(1967)*
Director: Gene Saks
Producer: Hal Wallis
Screenplay: Neil Simon
Costarring: Charles Boyer, Mildred Natwick, Robert
Redford
Jane's character: Corie Bratter

Barbarella *(1967)*
Director: Roger Vadim
Producer: Dino De Laurentiis
Screenplay: Terry Southern, in collaboration with Roger
Vadim, Claude Brule, Vittorio Bonicelli,
Clement Biddle Wood, Brian Degas, Tudor
Gates, Jean-Claude Forest
Adapted from: the novel by Jean-Claude Forest

Costarring: John Phillip Law, Milo O'Shea, Anita
                Pallenberg
Jane's Character: Barbarella

They Shoot Horses, Don't They? *(1969)*
Director: Sydney Pollack
Producers: Irwin Winkler and Robert Chartoff
Screenplay: Robert E. Thompson
Adapted from: the novel by Horace McCoy and the earlier
                screenplay by James Poe
Costarring: Michael Sarrazin, Susannah York
Jane's character: Gloria

Klute *(1971)*
Director/Producer: Alan Pakula
Screenplay: Andy K. Lewis
Costarring: Donald Sutherland
Jane's character: Bree Daniels

Steelyard Blues *(1972)*
Director: Alan Myerson
Producer: Donald Sutherland
Screenplay: David S. Ward
Costarring: Donald Sutherland, Peter Boyle
Jane's character: Iris

F.T.A. *(1972)*
Director: Francine Parker
Producers: Jane Fonda, Donald Sutherland, Francine Parker
Assistant Production Supervisor: Nancy Dowd
Screenplay: the cast with Robin Menken and Dalton Trumbo
Costarring: Michael Alaimo, Len Chandler, Pamela
                Donegan, Rita Martinson, Paul Mooney, Holly
                Near, Donald Sutherland, Yale Zimmerman

Tout Va Bien *(1972)*
Directors: Jean-Luc Godard and Jean-Pierre Gorin
Producer: J. P. Rassan
Screenplay: Jean-Luc Godard and Jean-Pierre Gorin
Costarring: Vittorio Capprioli, Yves Montand
Jane's character: Susan De Witt

A Doll's House *(1973)*
Director/Producer: Joseph Losey
Screenplay: David Mercer
Costarring: Edward Fox, Trevor Howard, Delphine Seyrig, David Warner, Anna Wing
Jane's character: Nora

The Blue Bird *(1976)*
Director: George Cukor
Producer: Paul Maslansky
Screenplay: Hugh Whitemore and Alezei Yakevlevich
Adapted from: the play by Maurice Maeterlinck
Costarring: Ava Gardner, Will Geer, Patsy Kensit, Todd Lookinland, Nadezhda Pavlova, Elizabeth Taylor, Margarita Terekhova, Cicely Tyson, Georgy Vitsin
Jane's character: "Night"

Fun With Dick And Jane *(1976)*
Director: Ted Kotcheff
Producers: Peter Bart and Max Palevsky
Screenplay: David Giler, Jerry Belson, Mordechai Richler
Costarring: George Segal
Jane's character: Jane Harper

Julia *(1977)*
Director: Fred Zinneman
Producer: Richard Roth

Screenplay: Alvin Sargent
Adapted from: the story by Lillian Hellman
Costarring: Vanessa Redgrave, Jason Robards
Jane's character: Lillian Hellman

Coming Home *(1978)*
Director: Hal Ashby
Producer: Jerome Hellman
Screenplay: Waldo Salt and Robert C. Jones
Adapted from: the story by Nancy Dowd
Costarring: Bruce Dern, Jon Voight
Jane's character: Sally Hyde

Comes A Horseman *(1978)*
Director: Alan Pakula
Producers: Gene Kirkwood and Dan Paulson
Executive Producers: Irwin Winkler and Robert Chartoff
Screenplay: Dennis Lynton Clark
Costarring: James Caan, Jason Robards
Jane's character: Ella Connors

California Suite *(1978)*
Director: Herbert Ross
Producer: Ray Stark
Screenplay: Neil Simon
Costarring: Alan Alda, Michael Caine, Bill Cosby, Walter
               Matthau, Elaine May, Richard Pryor, Maggie
               Smith
Jane's character: Hannah Warren

The China Syndrome *(1979)*
Director: James Bridges
Producer: Michael Douglas
Screenplay: James Bridges
Costarring: Michael Douglas, Jack Lemmon
Jane's character: Kimberly Wells

The Electric Horseman *(1979)*
Director: Sydney Pollack
Producer: Ray Stark
Screenplay: Paul Gaer and Robert Garland
Adapted from: the story by Shelly Burton
Costarring: Willie Nelson, Robert Redford
Jane's character: Hallie Martin

Nine To Five *(1980)*
Director: Colin Higgins
Producer: Bruce Gilbert
Screenplay: Colin Higgins and Patricia Resnick
Adapted from: a story by Patricia Resnick
Costarring: Dolly Parton, Lily Tomlin, Dabney Coleman
Jane's character: Judy Bernley

On Golden Pond *(1981)*
Director: Mark Rydell
Producer: Bruce Gilbert
Screenplay: Ernest Thompson
Adapted from: the play by Ernest Thompson
Costarring: Henry Fonda, Katharine Hepburn, Dabney
              Coleman, Doug McKeon
Jane's character: Chelsea Thayer Wayne

Rollover *(1981)*
Director: Alan Pakula
Producer: Bruce Gilbert
Screenplay: David Shaber
Adapted from: the story by David Shaber, Howard Kohn and
               David Weir
Costarring: Kris Kristofferson, Hume Cronyn
Jane's character: Lee Winters

ABOUT THE AUTHOR

*THOMAS KIERNAN is the author of twenty
books, including biographies of John
Steinbeck, Sir Laurence Olivier, Roman
Polanski, Yasir Arafat, and an earlier study of
the life of Jane Fonda. His* The Arabs *won the
1976 Saturday Review Prize as the best book
of that year on international affairs.* The Miracle
of Coogan's Bluff, The Secretariat Factor, *and*
Shrinks, Etc., *are among his other widely
selling works. Kiernan was educated at the
University of Notre Dame and Columbia
University. Married and the father of three
children, he lives in the New York area.*

Glittering lives of famous people!
Bestsellers from Berkley

✱✱✱✱✱✱✱✱✱✱✱✱✱✱✱✱✱✱✱✱✱✱✱✱

___ **JANE FONDA: HEROINE FOR OUR TIME**   06164-7—$3.50
Thomas Kiernan

___ **BRANDO FOR BREAKFAST**   04698-2—$2.75
Anna Kashfi Brando and E.P. Stein

___ **CONVERSATIONS WITH JOAN CRAWFORD**   05046-7—$2.50
Roy Newquist

___ **THE JEAN SEBERG STORY: PLAYED OUT**   06314-3—$3.95
David Richards

___ **LADD: A HOLLYWOOD TRAGEDY** Beverly Linet   05731-3—$2.95

___ **MISS TALLULAH BANKHEAD** Lee Israel   04574-9—$2.75

___ **MOMMIE DEAREST** Christina Crawford   06302-X—$3.95

___ **MOTHER GODDAM** Whitney Stine with Bette Davis   06454-9—$3.50

___ **MY WICKED, WICKED WAYS** Errol Flynn   06479-4—$2.95

___ **NO BED OF ROSES** Joan Fontaine   05028-9—$2.75

___ **RICHARD BURTON** Paul Ferris   05711-9—$2.95

___ **RITA HAYWORTH: THE TIME, THE PLACE AND THE WOMAN**   06751-3—$3.50
John Kobal

___ **SELF-PORTRAIT**   04485-8—$2.75
Gene Tierney, with Mickey Herskowitz

___ **SHADOWLAND: FRANCES FARMER** William Arnold   05481-0—$2.75

___ **SUSAN HAYWARD: PORTRAIT OF A SURVIVOR**   06425-5—$3.50
Beverly Linet

___ **TYRONE POWER: THE LAST IDOL**   04619-2—$2.75
Fred Lawrence Guiles

___ **EDDIE MY LIFE, MY LOVES** Eddie Fisher   06755-6—$3.50